Leisure and Recreation:
Introduction and Overview

Leisure and Recreation:

Introduction and Overview

Clayne R. Jensen

Dean, College of Health, Physical Education,
Recreation and Athletics
Brigham Young University
Provo, Utah

Lea & Febiger

Philadelphia, 1977

Library of Congress Cataloging in Publication Data

Jensen, Clayne R.
  Leisure and Recreation.

  Bibliography: p.
  Includes index.
  1. Leisure — United States. 2. Recreation — United States. 3. Recreation leadership. I. Title. GV174.J46   790'.0135'0973   77-22992   ISBN 0-8121-0595-8

Published in Great Britain by Henry Kimpton Publishers, London

PRINTED IN THE UNITED STATES OF AMERICA

Print Number: 4   3   2   1

Preface

This book emphasizes facts and insights into leisure time and leisure time activities and what these mean and will mean to Americans. Further, attention is given to the recreation and park field as a profession, and particularly to professional preparation and professional opportunities. The text was prepared with the following main purposes in mind:

> To provide an overview of present conditions and trends relating to leisure time and to the recreation and park movement.
>
> To dwell on the opportunities that have resulted and will result from leisure trends, and to describe the conditions under which these opportunities can be more fully realized.
>
> To identify specific problems relating to leisure time and to discuss the potential solutions.
>
> To help those entering the recreation and park profession see more clearly its scope and magnitude, and to better know the job opportunities and conditions of employment.
>
> To cause all those who read the book to understand more thoroughly the social and economic forces that influence work and leisure, and to be aware of trends and potential results, both positive and negative.

It is intended that the book will be especially interesting and useful as an introductory text for those entering college preparation programs in recreation and related fields, and as a text for collegiate general education courses in recreation and leisure studies.

The book contains the most current and pertinent information available on the various topics that would logically appear in a book of this kind, and a dedicated effort was made to present the information in an interesting and highly readable style. It is sincerely hoped that everyone who reads the book will be stimulated, and will gain insight into how to use his or her own leisure more wholesomely and how to influence desirable uses of leisure by others, through either professional or nonprofessional channels.

The author expresses special appreciation to Drs. Clark Thorstensen and Richard Heaps for their contributions in the areas of sociology and psychology.

Provo, Utah   CLAYNE R. JENSEN

Contents

Leisure and Recreation:
Introduction and Overview

1

Interpretations, Meanings and Concepts

At the time our nation was born a little more than 200 years ago, many aspects of people's living patterns were essentially as they were at the beginning of the Christian era. The nation's population was predominately rural, and the life style had strong agrarian characteristics. Technological advances were few, and the industrial revolution had not yet begun. Transportation was by non-mechanized methods, communication techniques were still primitive and the many conveniences afforded by electricity and power-driven machines were unheard of. Even as recently as 100 years ago the living patterns had not changed very much. In the last century, however, and particularly in the last half century, the life styles of Americans have changed markedly in almost every respect. Change has been our most consistent and dominant characteristic. Compared to standards of early times, change is still occurring with bewildering rapidity, and apparently this trend is going to continue during the foreseeable future.

Our present circumstances would certainly have to be viewed as an overall improvement over the conditions of earlier times, but still the rate and magnitude of change have caused some difficult social and personal problems. Our new style of living has created an environment where people live in parts. Most members of the work force seldom see the whole of their efforts in the final product. Thus work has lost much of its satisfaction, and many workers have less interest and less pride in their jobs. Tailors, lacemakers, pottery makers and cobblers of previous times would see their items of craftmanship begin with raw materials and end in finished products, with pride to be gained from the quality of the end-result. Such pride never comes to a factory worker who runs a machine that only sews labels in shirts, or one who turns bolt #32 on new automobiles as they move along the assembly line. Factory work and assembly line production have had a deteriorating effect on workers' satisfaction and sense of achievement. As a result

3

more people are seeking achievement and personal reward in off-the-job activities.

With the giant gains that we have made in economic productivity combined with the search for satisfaction and accomplishment during leisure time, a tendency has developed among the population to think that everything that is needed can be purchased. People try to buy status, acceptance, fuel for the ego, this and that, even happiness. The theme of the third century of this country may well be "they thought they could buy it, but it wasn't for sale."

It is true that in some respects increased purchasing power, when used wisely, can contribute positively to life. It can contribute only in certain respects and only up to a certain point, however, and beyond this more purchasing power has little meaning. Several important ingredients of success and happiness—accomplishment, service to others, and self-development—simply cannot be bought. It is important for us to recognize this and conduct our lives accordingly.

Actually the most meaningful and useful commodity that any of us has is time. If time is effectively applied to the more important aspects of life, it can make a greater contribution to success and happiness than any of the other conditions we are able to control. That portion of our time known as *leisure* has increased significantly, and this means more time for travel, additional education, meaningful entertainment, cultural activities, community service, and neighborliness. Arnold Toynbee stated, "Time must and should occupy the center of man's intellectual and emotional interests. The essence of time, like that of man's existence itself, is only a permission to partake creatively in a world whose contents and properties offer a great variety of worthy experiences."[1]

There are some who believe that the use of leisure time is the final test of a civilization—the most accurate measure of society's values. It is true that when people have a reasonable amount of security combined with sufficient leisure they can seek social, cultural, and spiritual rewards that are not available in a toil-dominated environment. The choices that people make under these circumstances determine the kind and quality of their leisure activities, and this has a large influence on the tone of society and in effect it measures the level of civilization.

Certainly the present concern over the impact of increased leisure upon the stability of society and the progress of civilization is no idle matter. The scores of published articles and books dealing with this and related topics emphasize the important implications of leisure time. The elements of the American culture that function to create more and more leisure—lengthening life expectancy, earlier retirement, increased mechanization and automation, shorter work weeks, rising standard of living and improved communication and transportation—

continue at an accelerated pace. Fortunately we now stand at a point in history when the potential and opportunity for "the good life" through increased leisure are unparalleled. How we reached this point, which factors have contributed toward it, what are its unique characteristics, and what we should be doing about it form the basic content of this book.

Since one of our principal users of leisure time is recreation, it is only natural that the terms *leisure time* and *recreation* are often used together and are considered closely related. It follows then that the content of the book has to do primarily with leisure time and recreation.

LEISURE AND LEISURE TIME

The word *leisure* is derived from the Latin word *licere* which means to be free. It is also related closely to the long-existing French word *loisir*, to be permitted. The essence of leisure seems to be freedom—freedom of time and attitude. In terms of time, leisure is that period of life not spent in making a living or in self-maintenance. As an attitude it is related to free will, lack of compulsion and freedom of choice.

Certain specialists in recreation, sociology and economics have made some rather fine-line distinctions among the terms *free time*, *leisure time* and *leisure*. Even though the distinctions are too fuzzy to be meaningful to many people, it seems worthwhile to present some of the statements made by noted authorities. However, it should be recognized that, despite the close distinctions made by those who study the subject, most of the population consider free time, leisure time and leisure as essentially the same—and in a general sense they are the same, because these terms represent uncommitted or off-the-job hours, and the things that people choose to do during those hours. They indicate the portion of life separate from biological and economic requirements, that which is left over after the requirements of existence and subsistence have been met.

Miller states that *free time* is the time available to the individual to be spent at his discretion after the necessary work and other survival duties are accomplished. He says that *leisure time* is that portion of available free time devoted to the pursuit of leisure values. He goes on to say that *leisure* is different from free time or leisure time in that it is the complex of self-fulfilling and self-enriching values achieved by the individual as he uses leisure time in self-chosen activities that recreate him.[2]

de Grazia believes that *free time* is thought of as the opposite of work and therefore as unproductive. He believes that *leisure* and free time are entirely different, stating ". . . today's time is considered free when not at grips with work. Work is the antonym of free time, but not of leisure. Leisure and free time live in two different worlds."[3]

Nash claims, "It is possible to be free from the pressures of daily life and still not have leisure. This occurs when one has no interest in leisure and no ability to make worthy use of his free time, is subject to conditions that are not propitious, or lacks the facilities that enable him to express his interests, make use of his abilities, and take advantage of his conditions."[4]

If the distinctions made in these statements are accepted, then the term *leisure* is synonymous with the meaning of recreation, and is different and yet closely related to the meaning of leisure time and free time. However, there are other well-known authorities who choose to group free time, leisure time and leisure into one generalized category with only minor distinctions in their meanings. This is illustrated by the following statements.

> Leisure is commonly thought of as surplus time remaining after the formal duties and necessities of life have been attended to. It is the free time, enabling a person to do as he chooses.[5]
> Leisure: For purposes of social analysis the concept is usually narrowed and widened to mean simply freedom from activities centering around the making of a livelihood.[6]
> Leisure—discretionary time, time to be used according to our own judgment or choice.[7]
> Leisure, then, is essentially a block of time. The fact that the word "leisure" conjures up many things in the minds of men should not blind us to the fact that when we are concerned with leisure we are primarily concerned with a period of time in which the feeling of compulsion is minimized. This is in contrast to those hours when we are compelled to work or prepare for work.[8]

True leisure is not the opposite of work in the sense of being opposed to work. In work there is a narrowing, a focusing, a concentration of faculties. During true leisure there is a widening of consciousness, an unfocusing, a broadening and expanding, and a greater diffusion of attitudes, interests and pursuits. Because of our dedication to work schedules and other highly structured aspects of life, we tend to bind ourselves to the clock and feel that leisure time is something to be occupied, an hour's worth of fulfillment for every hour spent, and everywhere there are diligent efforts to do just that. The good in leisure time is possible only for those who can free themselves from the time machine. Conversely, leisure time cannot be equated with idleness. Leisure is a positive attitude while idleness is a negative one.

Significance of Leisure Time

Aristotle described leisure as "the first principle of all action." Leisure has also been described as the main content of a free life and the nurse of civilization. Like virtue and unlike labor, leisure is its own chief reward. The amount and quality of any society's leisure activities set its tone, define its version of the good life, and measure the level of its civilization.

Bertrand Russell said, "To be able to fill leisure time intelligently is the last product of civilization," and a century earlier Disraeli had stated, "Increased means and increased leisure are the two civilizers of man." Long before that, Socrates said, "Leisure is the best of all possessions." Time to do as he pleases—to create, to play, to seek enrichment and satisfaction—has long been a dream of the common man. The dream has become at least partly true, with the promise of still more to come, but with such freedom of time must come an understanding of its potential for quality or lack of quality, for good or for bad.

Sebastian de Grazia has warned us that, if the trend toward automation continues, one of our great challenges will be to construct a worthwhile society largely on the concept of leisure rather than totally on the concept of work.[9] He indicates that America stands on the threshold of an era when the opportunity for a good life through increased leisure time is unequaled. Dr. Alexander Reid Martin of the American Psychiatric Association calls this time "the latest and greatest freedom of all."

The basic problem associated with increased leisure time is that it is not inherently good or bad, but has tremendous potential for either. It simply presents a new opportunity to succeed to greater heights or to fall lower. It does not guarantee better individuals or an improved society, but requires the making of choices; to assure wise choices we must provide adequate education and good leadership.

RECREATION

For centuries recreational activities were regarded as significant only because they were thought to restore an individual's energy and enable him to take part again in work. It was the restoration of the power to work that made it valuable, not any significance of its own.

In the first professional textbooks on the theory of recreation and play that appeared in the United States during the 1930s and 1940s, recreation was emphasized as a form of human activity that needs no other purpose, and is engaged in primarily for its own sake. The idea was fostered that recreation and play were activities carried on during free time, voluntarily chosen, pleasurable, and not concerned with meeting economic or social goals. However, this view of recreation did not last long. As more and more public and volunteer agencies began to sponsor leisure programs, the conviction grew that recreation should be designed to make a significant contribution to the individual and society. It should be goal oriented and conform to acceptable standards of social morality.

Recreation Defined

Recreation is a term which probably cannot be defined in a manner acceptable to all. Some view it as a *process of involvement* in activities of a great variety through which people achieve their recreational objectives. Others view recreation as a *result* or *outcome* and not a process, and claim that whether recreation actually occurs depends on what happens to the individual, physically, mentally, and emotionally, in

Figure 1. Tranquility can be one of the treasured benefits of leisure. (National Park Service photo.)

other words whether he reaches a recreated state. A basic question then is whether recreation should be defined as a *process* or a *state of condition*.

To the typical man on the street, recreation simply means what we do for fun—our hobbies, amusements, pastimes—the activities that provide pleasure, relaxation, and entertainment during our free time. However, it is important for professionals in recreation and education to be more exact. What we are talking about and what we are dealing with must be clearly understood. We must have some agreement as to what is and what is not included.

Following are some definitions that view recreation as a *process or involvement*.

Recreation consists of activities or experiences which are carried on voluntarily in leisure time. They are chosen by the participants either for pleasure or to satisfy certain personal needs. When provided as part of organized community programs, recreation must be designed to achieve constructive goals.[10]

Any activity pursued during leisure, either individual or collective, that is free and pleasurable, having its own immediate appeal, not impelled by any immediate necessity.[11]

Any activity which is not consciously performed for the sake of any reward beyond itself, which is usually engaged in during leisure, which offers man an outlet for his physical, mental, or creative powers, and in which he engages because of inner desire and not because of outer compulsion . . . recreation is any form of leisure time experience or activity in which an individual engages from choice because of the enjoyment and satisfaction which it brings directly to him.[12]

The tendency of some people to describe recreation as a *result* or a *state of condition* is illustrated in the following quote from *Parks and Recreation Magazine:* "We are beginning to rethink what recreation is. In the emerging view, the traditional emphasis of leisure and activities is not central; it is the effect on people that is the core of the definition."[13] Following are some definitions along this line:

Recreation is an emotional condition within an individual human being that flows from a feeling of well being and self-satisfaction. It is characterized by feelings of mastery, achievement, exhilaration, acceptance, success, personal worth, and pleasure. It reinforces a positive self-image. Recreation is a response to aesthetic experience, achievement of personal goals, or positive feedback from others. It is dependent on activity, leisure or social acceptance.[13]

Recreation is a feeling of well-being and results from experiences in which the individual receives the pleasurable and gratifying response to the use of his physical, mental or creative powers. In short recreation is the essence of any experience in which the individual directly gains personal enjoyment and satisfaction.[14]

There is no need to debate which of the definitions is correct because none of them is incorrect. Certainly recreation can be logically viewed from either of these vantage points. It seems that we most frequently think of recreation as a form of involvement or participation, but certainly we can also correctly think of it in terms of a result or state of condition of the participant.

David Gray offers a suggestion which somewhat unites the two lines of thinking: "Recreation is the process of engaging in activities during leisure time, with a set of attitudes that makes possible the obtainment of leisure values." [15]

Regardless of the viewpoint from which recreation is defined, people generally agree that it has the following specific characteristics:

1. It directly involves the individual for the purpose of achieving individual values.
2. It is entered into voluntarily, usually if not always during leisure time.
3. The motivating force is enjoyment or satisfaction as opposed to material or social gain.
4. It is wholesome to the individual and society.

A Characteristic of Quality

The deeper meaning of the term recreation goes beyond the amusement and hobby concept to include those activities of the highest order of creativity, cultural, and civic values which enrich the lives of human beings and elevate the tone of society. Clear definition and effective perpetuation of this enlarged concept of recreation among recreation professionals and community leaders are critical, because it is a concept of fundamental importance which is already lagging well behind.

The term *recreation* implies that the participant is recreated in some manner, physically, psychologically, spiritually, or mentally; that he becomes refreshed and enriched; that he is revitalized and more ready to cope with the routines and trials of life. Recreation should be clearly distinguished from simple amusement, time fillers and low-quality activities. To qualify as recreation, an experience must do something of a quality nature to the participant.

If we accept the idea that recreation actually recreates the person, then many of the so-called recreational pursuits are not recreation at all, but only time fillers and time wasters, which in many cases are actually detrimental rather than constructive, which fatigue rather than rejuvenate, decrease rather than recreate and actually deprive participants of the enrichment opportunities vital to them.

Experiences that frequently provide recreation take many forms. People enjoy fishing, skiing, singing, photography, dancing, playing a guitar, swimming or going to a good play; nevertheless one person's recreation may be another person's drudgery. Building a boat, for example, can be an ideal form of recreation to one person, whereas to another it would be work. Even with the same individual an activity that is recreational at one time or under certain conditions does not always yield satisfaction which makes it recreation. Sometimes a person feels like playing golf or participating in a square dance group; at other times he prefers a much different form of involvement. When a person is physically fatigued he usually has little need for vigorous physical recreation. When he is mentally or emotionally fatigued, activities that require heavy concentration are not usually appealing. Recreation can be experienced by a person alone, with a few others or in a large group. In some forms it consists of enthusiastic participation; in others, a quiet relaxation, listening or watching. Recreation often takes the form of diversion and helps to bring one's life into balance.

The appeal of certain forms of involvement varies with age, physical ability, intellectual development, and individual change. With maturity a person's recreation tends to change from simple to more complex, and from frivolous to more serious in terms of defined personal and social objectives. As one's economic status improves his recreation involvement usually changes toward activities which are more sophisticated and socially prestigious. With advanced age the trend is from more active to less active participation, and with increased education people tend toward structured or group-oriented activities.

Dr. James S. Plant, a noted psychiatrist, has pointed out that it is in the doing of a thing rather than in the results it produces that we have the real elements of recreation.[15] In other words an essential characteristic of recreation is that it is an end in itself and has value per se. Dr. Plant further emphasized the fact that "recreation is an integrating experience for the individual because it catches, strengthens and projects his own rhythm." In illustrating this he points to the difference between the tool and the machine. The tool is an expansion of the individual, is subject to his control, and moves at his pace. The machine on the other hand imposes its rhythm on the individual, who must adjust himself to its commands. This is a fundamental difference between the machine age and earlier times of individual craftsmanship.

A recreational experience is truly recreative and valuable on a continuing basis when:

It is interesting, and artificial motivation is not necessary to arouse interest

It is fun, and can remain so over a good portion of one's life

It is refreshing to the body, mind and spirit

It is engaged in for its own sake and not for some extraneous reward

It releases energy, tension and emotion

It provides for human association, recognition, response and understanding

It leads to other worthwhile interests

It does not exploit or harm anyone else

It maintains the participant's dignity and status as a person

It leads to social sensitivity and cooperation

It makes life meaningful and well rounded

It gives one opportunity to spend some time being idle without concern, walking with nowhere to go, thinking without problems to solve, and making things that sometimes have no practical use

It is its own great reward

A HIERARCHY OF LEISURE TIME USES

Figure 2 is a diagram of a hierarchy of leisure time uses. Notice that the top category involves service to others. This can be one of the most satisfying and certainly one of the most beneficial uses of leisure time. It unfortunately has lost some of its popularity, and is receiving too little emphasis these days by those in leadership positions.

Also high on the scale is direct involvement in creative participation. Even though practically all people are capable of service, many have limited potential for creativity; nevertheless, practically everyone has more creativity potential than he ever uses.

The next category, active participation in activities that have been designed or modeled by others, is one of the major uses of leisure time, and for the most part is considered a desirable use.

The next category, having to do with emotional involvement based on observation of others in performance or as the result of someone else's creative work, is also considered desirable, if kept in proper balance with the higher forms.

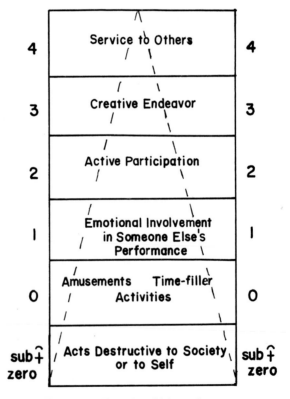

Figure 2. Hierarchy of leisure time uses.

The category labeled zero involves amusement and time-filler kinds of entertainment. Such involvement actually makes no worthwhile contribution to the person or society. The best that can be said is that it is a guard against doing something worse. Many movies, much of television and radio, and an overabundance of professional spectator sports fall into this category.

In the bottom category are the activities with subzero value. These are detrimental to self or society—crime, delinquency, drug abuse, alcoholism and gambling. Unfortunately the rate of crime and delinquency in the United States has somewhat paralleled the increase in leisure time.

PLAY

It has been common practice to differentiate between activities of children and those of adults by labeling the former play and the latter recreation. Joseph Lee, who is often referred to as the father of the recreation movement in America, defined play for children as creation or the gaining of life, and play for adults as recreation or the renewal of life.

In the minds of many people, recreation can be included under the broad definition of play, and in the minds of other people the opposite is true, that is, play can be included under the broad definition of

Figure 3. A child playing on low-cost playing equipment constructed by an innovative recreation leader.

recreation. Some consider the two terms generally interchangeable, but with play applying primarily to children's activities and recreation applying to adults'. Psychologists and child development specialists believe that play has great significance in the normal growth and development patterns of children, and they strongly advocate that children have opportunities to express themselves extensively through normal play outlets. Play among children is part of the serious business of life.

Most recreation authorities agree that play of children provides for an essential group of developmental needs during the formative years. Recreation for adults functions to recreate physically, psychologically, emotionally and mentally, after the wear and tear of other activities, and it serves to put one's life in proper balance and perspective. The concept of recreation includes more of the idea of leisure values and self-fulfillment goals—the recreative, relaxing, creative, renewing and restoring function—than does the concept of play. Play carries the meaning of free, happy, joyous, full-of-fun and natural expression; it is made up of activities and attitudes which have developmental significance for children.

The natural drive among children to play and the particular play patterns that they tend to follow have been long-time topics of discussion and research. Several theories have been set forth in an attempt to explain this form of human activity. Among the better accepted are:

> *The Surplus Energy Theory*—which in short means that the energy that remains after necessary work has been accomplished is naturally used up in "blowing off steam" through play activities.
>
> *The Catharsis Theory*—which is closely related to the above theory in the sense that it relates play to the release of emotions and stress.
>
> *The Recreation Theory*—which is based on the premise that recreational participation is, at least to a point, more effective in recovering from fatigue than idleness or rest.
>
> *The Instinct Theory*—which expresses the idea that there is a natural sequence of play patterns which are essential to normal maturity and necessary for the development of all aspects of the individual.
>
> *The Recapitulation Theory*—which holds that children tend to instinctively relive the past history of their culture through play, e.g. cowboys and Indians and other role-playing experiences.

These, along with selected less standard and less prominent theories, are treated in interesting style in an appendix to this text.

COMMON MISCONCEPTIONS

With the large number of books and articles that have been written during recent years on leisure and recreation, and with other forms of increased attention, a number of misconceptions have arisen. It is important to identify these misconceptions and try to correct them.

1. The concept is often accepted that recreation is strictly the antithesis of work. It is true that for many people the hours of employment are repetitive, boring and exhausting. Today relatively few people find recreation in their work, but there are some individuals whose vocations are so absorbing and satisfying as to make them a form of recreation. Thomas Edison, for example, gave himself so completely to creative work in his laboratory that he felt no need for recreative diversion. It is not uncommon to find scholars engaged in research or businessmen involved in a new enterprise whose work yields the kind of excitement and satisfaction that is commonly associated with recreation. Thus, when recreation is viewed as a result or a state of condition, it can be said that recreation truly is possible while on the job. In general, however, recreation takes place during off-the-job hours, and it usually involves a form of diversion from work.

2. Leisure time and recreation are frequently treated as though they are essentially the same or inseparable. It is true that in most instances opportunities for recreation are confined to leisure hours. Therefore, recreation is primarily a leisure time activity. However, not all leisure time is spent in recreational pursuits. Much of it is wasted or occupied with activities which do not have recreative results. Leisure time can be filled either with true recreation or with simple amusers, time fillers, time wasters, or decreative activities. Leisure time is represented on a time chart and does not necessarily indicate either participation or outcome. Conversely, recreation is dependent upon individual involvement and individual results; it is not a block of time.

3. Some people stress the concept that recreation must be earned by doing useful work. This would imply that recreation is not essential of itself and is not viewed as an end; instead, it is a sort of recuperative interlude between periods of work. This concept echoes the eye-for-eye and tooth-for-tooth philosophy which leads to the work-play-work-play cycle. It fails to recognize the significant nature and vital purpose of recreation itself—a desirable state of being whether in preparation for work or not.

4. Some see recreation as a means of solving or alleviating personal and community problems. True, it has been demonstrated repeatedly that recreation can be a means of achieving these and other useful individual and social objectives. Everyone knows from his own experience, however, that these are not the primary reasons people enter recreational pursuits and gain satisfaction from them. Fortunately the concept of recreation as having value per se and the concept that it produces valuable results are by no means incompatible. In fact, a recreational experience is likely to bring greater satisfaction to an individual if it also contributes to his personal development and betterment of his community.

5. A distinction is often made between recreation and cultural arts. This implies that recreation includes sports, outings, socials, and similar kinds of activities, but that the graphic and performing arts belong in a different field. This concept is not compatible with accepted definitions of recreation, and certainly it is true that many of the satisfactions associated with recreation result from participation in cultural arts activities. The increasing importance which these activities hold in community recreation programs affords evidence that they make a worthwhile contribution to the recreational life of countless numbers. Any interpretation of recreation that excludes the cultural arts is inadequate.

6. The tendency to define recreation in terms of specific activities is difficult to justify. Even though certain activities frequently yield pleasurable experiences to a large number of people, they are merely means of achieving recreation and are not recreation themselves. In fact some people may find participation in certain "recreation type" activities unsatisfying or even distasteful.

7. Another misconception is that recreation, unlike education, is essentially without purpose or discipline. This is because recreation is identified with relaxation or pleasurable involvement. In many forms of recreation there is a high

degree of concentration, physical exertion and mental application. Some forms are keenly challenging and press the participants almost to their limits. These forms of recreation certainly result in individual development. In fact, recreation has been called a functioning laboratory for the practice and implementation of leisure skills and much of the content of the school curriculum.

THE THREAT OF THE EASY LIFE

When we think of the various trends that are contributing toward easier living, we ought to be immediately struck by one of the bitter lessons taught by history: that as civilizations rise they tend to create the conditions that contribute to their own destruction. Usually a nation's decline slowly and insidiously begins when it is at the peak of its strength and prosperity, when the life of action becomes displaced by the life of ease, when overemphasis upon the intellect eats away at the virility of the nation, when its citizens in their complacency no longer possess the vigorous and ambitious qualities of their forefathers who led the nation to greatness, when the termites of corruption gnaw away at the moral foundation, and when leisure, increasing in quantity, becomes synonymous with boredom, emptiness, unrest, apathy, and a desperate search for relief through cheap entertainment designed only to stimulate the emotions and excite the senses.

As educated and free people, we possess the ability to shape our own destinies at least to some extent. As Socrates observed, "Whom then do I call educated? First those who control circumstances instead of being mastered by them, those who meet all occasions naturally and act in accordance with intelligent thinking." We must think intelligently and make wise decisions relative to our increased leisure and how it will be used. Too many wrong choices by too many people will have a cumulative destructive effect.

As our leisure continues to increase, will we be able to resist the temptation of the soft and easy life? More and more our economy is involved in the production of things that make life easier and more comfortable—electric carts to make our golf easier, all kinds of gadgets to eliminate muscular effort from our work, numerous contraptions to make our drinks cooler, our domestic duties lighter and our chairs and beds softer. Historically it has been proved that people cannot be trusted with too many easy alternatives. Pericles, speaking of conditions in Athens in 431 B.C., described one of the few occasions in history when they could be trusted: "When our work is over, we are in a position to enjoy all kinds of recreation for our spirits . . . our love of the beautiful does not lead to extravagance; our love for the things of the mind does not make us softer."[16]

In Athens the national ideal was the man of wisdom and the man of action, and what is honored in a country is cultivated there. But even

Athens was unable to maintain indefinitely a society which believed in the wholeness of man and which created a place where people lived well together. Eventually even this nation of "athletes" succumbed to the temptation of easy options and became a nation of spectators.

THE DANGER OF CHOICE

Freedom of choice persists as one of man's prized possessions. In a sense it is ironic to think that, given a choice, people do not know how to choose. In order to be able to choose correctly a person must be equipped with information about appropriate alternatives, and must be disciplined about choices pertinent not only to the good of himself but to the good of all. If a person's experiences provide him with only a narrow range of choices, and if the range includes only low-quality alternatives, then what chance does he have to make choices that would be beneficial to his own development and that of society?

The essence of making good choices about use of leisure time is the ability to determine that which is good and valuable. This leads to the complex involvement of sense of values, a matter with which people have struggled for centuries. Fortunately there are some near absolutes as to what is accepted as good and valuable, but there are also some aspects of this question which are not agreed upon even within a single society, to say nothing about the differences that exist among societies.

Developing a sound sense of values on which to base right choices is an extremely complex and ongoing endeavor. It begins with the educational process in the broadest sense, not only with the formal educational system. Some would say simply that what is good and valuable should be determined by the group or by those in control. The folly of this procedure is illustrated by the fact that in a head-hunting society the most efficient headhunter would be considered the best citizen. The ardent and staunch communist, following the code of that controlling group, would represent the highest standard of conduct. There must always exist a more basic set of criteria by which even those in control are critically measured.

The ideal of what is good and valuable lies somewhere between the two concepts of absolutism and local practice. Certain basic concepts such as the inherent right of every individual to be educated and develop his personality to its fullest, or the right to "life, liberty and the pursuit of happiness," tend toward absolutes. The proper steps in acquiring these rights, and the extent to which they can actually be attained, are uncertainties. Fortunately, it is those values which are interpreted equally for all men and which work out for the best for all people over the long period which gradually gain the stamp *of good* and *valuable*. This is true because people seem to have certain built-in ideals: they want good things for themselves, their neighbors and community, and particularly their posterity. We have become civilized because we want to be civilized, not because we have been compelled to be so. Out of the conscience of men has grown a strain of universal ethics, an accepted basic code of conduct. Unfortunately, the fringe areas around the basic code are far from universally accepted, and it is with these aspects of conduct that much controversy and need for adjustment occur.

The amount of leisure that people should have and what they should do with it are fringe area questions. There are no pat answers and no universal agreements. Therefore, we must continue to struggle with these questions and experiment with alternative solutions relating to them.

As language developed, man was able to label his choices. He tasted something he pronounced good, later tasted something more to his fancy and described it better, and finally ate something which he called best. In similar fashion he learned to judge distances. A way from home was far, but someone went beyond and that was farther, and then one day someone travelled still beyond and that was farthest. Similarly we have developed a scale of thought where we rate experiences and practices as poor, fair, average, good, and excellent. In some situations what is good is a real enemy of the best. In terms of leisure time pursuits, how many people choose the average or the mediocre? The mediocre is not evil or bad, it just is not good and certainly is not the best.

The important problem of choosing among leisure time alternatives ranging along a scale from poor to excellent is currently a difficult problem faced by the masses of our population. Leaders in the recreation and park field must help to provide people with the right alternatives and with the background to make the right choices.

Often when people choose the poor or the mediocre we explain it by saying "that's human nature." But it is also human nature to exhibit genius and creativity and to aspire to worthy service. Does one refer to the lower or the higher order of human nature?

One of the fallacies of leisure time choices is the idea that people are faced with only two alternatives, a good choice and a bad choice. Usually there is a multitude of alternatives between the extremes from which to choose. Further, different individuals have different ranges of choices, depending upon their resources and abilities. There is the one-talent man and the ten-talent man, and those with talents in between. In the most common man there is a tremendous reservoir of potential creativity, but in order to capitalize on it each one must choose to put himself into a position of challenge. He must try new things, seek new experiences and strive for the excitement of higher achievements.

THE EXCITEMENT OF CHALLENGE

The tendency to listen to it, to watch it, and to read about it has detrimental effects on people's development and takes some of the edge from living. The person who places himself in life's arena of active involvement is the one who stands to gain. He experiences the adventure of challenge and faces the risk of achievement or failure.

Each year thousands of people seem to fall into the course of least resistance, which is usually the one with the least potential for achievement and satisfaction. The spectator takes no chances; he is always right, and he needs no fortitude and develops no courage. Even though real satisfaction comes predominately from the acts of doing, making and achieving, the soft cushions of the playhouse or even the concrete benches of the stadium become attractive to more and more people each year.

Nowhere in the realm of life's activities are there so many acceptable and socially approved struggles as in childhood play and adult recreation. These activities frequently place people in contests with opponents or against predetermined standards of success. The forces of challenge carry young and old to indoor contests and to athletic fields. They take people into the tropical forests, the deserts, and the Arctic, into the air and under the sea. Men endure hardships during long travel and in lonely places devoid of modern accommodations and comforts. They fight heat, cold, insects and poisonous snakes in order to find

Figure 4. People satisfy their needs for challenge and excitement in different ways.

adventure and challenge. Rob people of these adventurous opportunities and you take away much of the drama of life, and partially destroy the urge to live.

In children's games the concept of challenge has been expressed by the risk associated with "it." If you get caught you are *it*. In tag games the chaser is it. The last one there is it. In baseball the runner is it. In football the ball carrier is it. To the hunter or the fisherman the pursued is it. Even though the it concept is not essential in all play and recreational activities, there is a certain need for it in every person's life. Mature adults are usually able to transpose the it challenge into more significant activities, but the concept is still present.

In earlier times children (and adults) had adventures and challenges placed before them in everyday life. They had trees to fell, horses to ride, streams to swim, mountains to climb, wilderness to explore and fish to catch. Out of everyday adventure and challenge they achieved some alliance and dependence. Today life is different but the challenges can still be equal. Let us teach children to ski, swim, play football, achieve marksmanship, climb high mountains, learn outdoor living skills and practice survival techniques. Too many of our programs have substituted milk-toast activities for challenging participation that involves a reasonable amount of risk. Also let us teach lifelong hobbies such as photography, art and music appreciation and participation, and craftsmanship.

Above the entrance of an old Greek palaestra was the phrase "strip or retire," which translated means "get into action or leave"—enter the race or step aside and let someone else run. We should not be advocates of unnecessary or unreasonable danger or risk, but we should recognize that absolute safety and absolute security have never been man's greatest needs. Adventure and challenge with a reasonable degree of risk have always ranked before these.

One contributor to happiness is the facing of meaningful challenges where there is a fair chance for success. We crave struggles where the outcome is in doubt. Traditional forms of work more nearly conformed to the struggle pattern than many leisure pursuits, but leisure pursuits if chosen intelligently can suffice in place of the lack of such challenges in the work life of many people today. It is firmly believed that people are truly happier when achievement and anticipation of adventure lead them from one thing to another in an endless series. It is also believed that adventure comes in a variety of forms, including physical, social, emotional and mental involvement.

THE LEARNING OF SKILLS AND INTERESTS

The motivation for individuals to participate in leisure time activities which are beneficial and satisfying may come from several sources.

Rich and varied childhood experiences in the early years in the home and school assume primary importance.

What useful things do people in America do with their leisure? They do good turns for their neighbors and build strength in their communities through service; they read books, write poetry, build cabins, make pottery, sing songs, play music, paint pictures, sail boats, play tennis, practice photography, call square dances, knit and crochet, garden, refinish old furniture, participate in plays, fish, hunt, hike, experiment in science and collect everything and anything. Further, they go to the ends of the earth to see canyons, climb mountains, chase caribou, catch sailfish, visit cathedrals, study art, follow migratory birds and dig for dinosaur eggs. They go to the coldest part of the Arctic and the hottest part of the desert. They climb glaciers and search the bottom of the sea. On and on they go. Why do people do these things? Through curiosity, conquest, achievement, mastery, adventure and challenge, the activity drive forces them to press on to horizons which they have heretofore not experienced.

Where do we learn our recreational skills and develop our interests? According to information gathered by Nash[17] and supported generally by psychologists and sociologists, the majority (about 70%) of people's interests start in the immediate environment of the home. The school ranks second, contributing between 10 to 20%, and the remainder of the interests and skills come from involvement in recreation programs and a variety of experiences in other settings.

Who are the teachers of new recreational skills and interests? Since most skills and interests are initiated in and around the home, it follows

Figure 5. Many people in America enjoy learning ethnic dances of other countries. In addition to the skill and enjoyment that result, they contribute to education and insight relative to peoples and cultures of other lands.

that parents and other family members contribute the most. School teachers, particularly at the elementary level, close relatives, youth organization leaders, and friends all contribute their share.

How old are people when they develop interests and begin participating in their different recreational pursuits? The answer is both interesting and enlightening. Well over half begin before age 10 and approximately 70% start before age 12. Many interests are initiated in the first few years of life. Only about 20% are acquired between the ages of 12 and 21, and only 10% after age 21. The significance of this information is obvious with respect to young people's exposure to wholesome skills and appreciations. This by no means implies that people over age 21 cannot learn new skills and develop new interests, but this does not happen routinely.

In summary, youth is the prime time to lay down basic behavior patterns, to learn skills and develop appreciations that will last a lifetime; the home is the prime contributor, and those who live in and close to the home do most of the teaching of these recreational interests and skills.

The following important conclusions can be drawn:

1. The learning of new recreational activities can take place at any age, but the formative years during childhood and youth are by far the most likely times for this to happen.
2. It has been learned that to a large extent those activities which a person performs well at age 25 will hold his interest through a major part of life, whereas those activities that he does poorly at age 25 will tend to lose his interest from that point on.
3. Adults learn new activities less frequently and with greater difficulty because they are less educable in this respect and are unwilling to spend the time and energy necessary for practice.
4. Adults tend to be overly self-conscious about their lack of skill and are therefore reluctant to enter new activities. This seems to channel them into becoming watchers and listeners.
5. A high percentage of adult interests are started during the years of youth in the environment of the home.
6. Parents and other family members are the most responsible for stimulating recreational interests.
7. Everybody has a reservoir of skill and creative potential which has never been realized—and in many cases never will be realized.
8. The available research supports the claim that the happiest people enjoy active involvement. They have intense interests in people and things.
9. There is little relationship between economic condition and enjoyment of life, except in the case of the very poor, whereas there is a much higher relationship between enjoyment and active involvement.
10. The happiest people are those who enjoy life day by day while travelling hopefully toward some definite end.
11. Spectator activities beyond a minimal level make a limited contribution to enjoyment and satisfaction. Too much spectator involvement is simply a time filler or time waster.

Can the eagerness for participation and achievement with which every person is born be perpetuated further into adult life? Can we capture and maintain the childhood qualities of wanting to be actively involved as opposed to being passive bystanders? Can we hold on longer to curiosity, inquiry, the desire for challenge and the need for achievement? Is it and will it be possible to fill the leisure hours of both childhood and adulthood with truly satisfying pursuits? Do we have the ability to make the retirement years really the golden era of life?

At best, the present answer to all of these questions is *maybe*. *Maybe* we will be able to perpetuate the importance of using a portion of leisure time in performing service for others. *Maybe* we will motivate people toward involvement in challenging and creative activities, and furnish them with opportunities for creative outlets. *Maybe* we will succeed in teaching people on a mass scale the importance of avoiding large amounts of time fillers, simple amusers and time wasters. One of the great challenges of the future for recreation professionals,

Figure 6. Tennis is an excellent recreational skill, and the fastest growing sport in America.

educators and community leaders is to change this answer from *maybe* to *yes*.

REFERENCES

1. Toynbee, A.: Conditions of survival. Saturday Review, August 29, 1964.
2. Miller, N. P. and Robinson, D. M.: *The Age of Leisure*. Wadsworth Publishing Co., Belmont (Calif.), 1963, p. 5.
3. de Grazia, S.: *Of Time and Leisure*. Doubleday and Co., Garden City (N. J.), 1962, p. 233.
4. Nash, J. B.: *Philosophy of Recreation and Leisure*. Tom C. Brown Co., Dubuque, 1964, p. 161.
5. Neumeyer, M. H. and Neumeyer, E. S.: *Leisure and Recreation*, 3rd ed. Ronald Press Co., New York, 1958, p. 1.
6. Danforth, H. G. (revised by Shirley, M.): *Creative Leadership in Recreation,* 2nd ed. Allyn and Bacon Inc., Boston, 1973.
7. Meyer, H. D., et al.: *Community Recreation*, 4th ed. Prentice-Hall, Englewood Cliffs, 1969, p. 29.
8. Brightbill, C. K.: *Man and Leisure*. Prentice-Hall, Englewood Cliffs, 1961, p. 21.
9. de Grazia, S.: *Op. cit.,* p. 221.
10. Kraus, R. G. and Bates, B. J.: *Recreation Leadership and Supervision*. W. B. Saunders, Philadelphia, 1975, p. 5.
11. Neumeyer, M. H. and Neumeyer, E. S.: *Op. cit.,* p. 19.
12. Butler, G. D.: *Introduction to Community Recreation,* 5th ed. McGraw-Hill, New York, 1976.
13. Leisure–society–politics. Parks and Recreation, May 1972, p. 52.
14. Gray, D. E.: Exploring inner space. Parks and Recreation, December 1972, p. 19.
15. Gray, D. E. and Greben, S.: Future perspectives. Parks and Recreation, July 1974, p. 25.
16. Nash, J. B.: *Op. cit.,* p. 231.
17. Nash, J. B.: *Op. cit.,* p. 15.

2

Historical Overview of the Recreation and Park Movement

This chapter contains an overview of the development of recreation and parks in the United States with some mention of forerunner concepts in earlier history which have had some influence on the movement in America. The historical information in this chapter is not all inclusive, because certain important historical data are included in other chapters where the information relates directly to the subject matter there. For example, the chapter entitled "Trends in the Development of the Profession" includes a section on the origin and growth of professional preparation programs, and a section on the growth of professional and service organizations. The chapter on federal government involvement includes selected historical information which explains how the different branches of government became involved in recreation. The same kind of selected historical information is included in the chapters relating to state government and municipal recreation. The historical overview presented here will give the information in the subsequent chapters additional meaning.

The need for recreation and park programs in each country and civilization has developed at its own time and pace, but the movement is not of recent origin. Play and recreation activities are as old as the recorded history of man. The idea of parks has been traced to the Sumerians, a people even more ancient than the Egyptians. In a book entitled *A History of Garden Art* by Marie Luise Gothein, reference is made to the cedar woods of Humbaba with their straight cared-for paths and their neatness as "the starting point for art history,"[1] This author traced the western Asiatic parks from the vineyards and fish ponds of the Sumerian King Gudea (about 2340 B.C.) to the hanging gardens of Babylonia (about 1000 B.C.) and the introduction of flowers in parks in the seventh century B.C. She relates that the Greeks wrote about the parks and gardens of Persia.

Doell and Twardzik reported that "the need for practice of the Greek games established the outdoor gymnasium, and one form of the gymnasium became the academy, and the academy became the seat of learning, actually the home of Greek philosophers. Hippodromes, gymnasiums and academies became portions of Greek parks."[2]

The affluent Romans perpetuated parks with their numerous villas and hunting grounds. Although the villas were initially located on the outskirts of towns or in the countryside, they were later constructed in the city of Rome. This move to "bring the country to the city" was paralleled centuries later by Fredrick Olmstead in his planning of Central Park in New York City, and subsequently by other park planners and government officials who arranged for large tracts of park land inside city limits.

Land holdings for recreational purposes in earlier civilizations were principally kept by provincial rulers for their own pleasure. By the later part of the thirteenth century, however, public grounds were established in Italy for the leisure of all people. Gothein wrote, "Not only for shooting but for other sport, places were provided, and especially for ballgames which developed in the 15th century, chiefly in England; later they spread all over the continent in the form of football, croquet, and lawn tennis, and when people had more room these games were introduced in private gardens with properly laid-out squares and courts."[1]

Figure 7. Ice skating in Central Park in the early 1800s. (Library of Congress photo.)

During the late part of the eighteenth century, England's parks and gardens were developed in an informal manner with natural landscapes and native shrubs. Thus true "people's parks" came into existence.

The earliest city parks in the United States were in the form of community commons. There were town squares that were used for public meetings and socials. When William Penn laid out Philadelphia, in 1682, the plan included numerous squares and corner plots. During the 1820s and 1830s a new trend emerged when several outdoor gymnasiums were built in Massachusetts and New York. In 1853 one of the milestones of park development occurred when New York City acquired the land for Central Park. During the second half of the nineteenth century numerous other cities followed New York's example and acquired large tracts of land for park development.

The recreation and park movement in the United States has developed along two main themes: *natural-resource-oriented* recreation and *municipal* recreation, often called *community* recreation. The former is frequently referred to as *outdoor* recreation, while the latter is sometimes called *activity-oriented* recreation. However, in this chapter the latter category is broader than "activity." It includes urban park systems and related facilities—zoos, gardens, museums, etc.

The *resource-oriented recreation* movement has included those forms of outdoor recreation that depend largely upon the utilization of natural resources: camping, hunting, fishing, exploring, boating, mountain climbing, and skiing. *Municipal recreation* includes the areas, facilities and programs developed within a community for the citizens of that locality. Municipal recreation often involves performing or the witnessing of performances: athletics, dramatic arts, music, crafts, playground activities, etc. Obviously there is no sharp line of division between the categories. For example, both water and snow skiing utilize natural resources to a large extent, and they require skilled performances. The same could be said of scuba diving, cycling, and mountain climbing, and to a lesser degree of fishing, hunting, and camping. It is nonetheless true that throughout the development of the recreation and park movement there has been a generalized distinction between the two broad categories of *resource-oriented recreation* and *municipal recreation*. Further, within the framework of municipal recreation park designers and activity programmers have been separated.

Fortunately in recent years some melting together of these categories has occurred. Coordination and cooperation are more pronounced now than in the past. This melting effect can be partially attributed to the fact that during the past two decades national leaders in all walks of life have given increased attention to the importance of recreation to both the individual and society. This has resulted in greater attention to the total field, with limited regard for categorization. Emphasis has been placed on the idea that the leadership needed now and even more in the future can be furnished best by those having a substantial base of information, a sound philosophy and a broad scope of the total field of leisure time pursuits.

One of the most significant events in the melting of the categories was the merger in 1965 of six national organizations serving the park and recreation field: the American Association of Zoological Parks and Aquariums, the American Institute of Park Executives, the American Recreation Society, the National Association of State Park Directors, the National Conference on State Parks and the National Recreation Association. The merger resulted in what is now known as the National Recreation and Park Association.

RESOURCE-ORIENTED RECREATION

The conservation movement, which has had a significant impact on resource-oriented recreation, was prompted by the romantic and artistic efforts of poets, writers, artists, photographers, explorers and mountain men. Certainly the writings of George Catlin, William Cullen Bryant, James Fenimore Cooper, and John Muir were influential in initiating a feeling for protecting areas of pristine beauty. Emerson and Thoreau provided a philosophy toward nature which enhanced the saving of aesthetic resources.

Natural resources conservation started in the United States as early as 1626 when the colony of Plymouth passed an ordinance that prohibited cutting timber on the colony land without official consent. In 1710 the town of Newington, New Hampshire, acquired a 110-acre community forest to be used by the townspeople for lumber for public buildings. In 1799 the United States Congress appropriated $200,000 to purchase timberlands. These early beginnings of forest management were based primarily upon economic supply and demand—the need for ready access to lumber to build public buildings and ships—but these actions unknowingly set the stage for a large number of other acts of conservation and preservation which have had a tremendous affect on the availability and use of natural resources for recreational purposes.

By the time of the Revolutionary War the American colonies were beginning to realize the need to control the shooting of game, and prior to 1775 twelve of the thirteen colonies had enacted closed seasons on certain game. In 1844 the first association for the protection of game was formed in the state of New York. In 1871 Congress passed a much-needed bill for the protection of bison. The next year New York named a seven-member commission to study the advisability of reserving wild lands for watershed preservation. By 1873 the state of New York had purchased 40,000 acres of forest land. This is accepted as the first substantial purchase of state forest reserves, which now total more than 2½ million acres in that state, mostly in the Adirondack and Catskill Mountains.

On April 10, 1872, in Nebraska, Arbor Day was declared, to create an awareness of the need for trees in metropolitan areas. In that same year Yellowstone National Park was reserved as a "pleasuring ground," and this marked the beginning of the national park system in the United States (and in the world). In 1874, Dr. Franklin D. Hough presented a paper at a meeting of the American Association for the Advancement of Science on "The Duty of Government in the Preservation of Parks." In 1875 the American Forestry Association was established to help unify a movement to save forests.

The emphasis on resource management and conservation resulted in demands for more knowledgeable personnel. As a result universities began to offer instruction in forestry. Colleges of forestry were established at Yale University in 1873 and at Cornell University in 1874. The decade from 1875 to 1885 brought increased emphasis on conservation, which was highlighted by the writings and efforts of Theodore Roosevelt. Much of his conservation philosophy was expressed in his book *The Wilderness Hunter*, and he along with Gifford Pinchot gave significant national leadership during the late 1800s. In 1881 a Division

Figure 8. Hunting and fishing have long been favored outdoor recreational activities. (Library of Congress photo.)

of Forest Management was established within the U.S. Department of Agriculture.

During the late 1800s increased attention also began to be generated for wildlife management. California and New Hampshire established state game commissions in 1878, and in 1883 the American Ornithologists' Union was organized.

President Harrison created the first national forest reserve in 1891—the Yellowstone Timberland Reserve, now part of the Shoshone National Forest. Before his term expired he had set aside other forest reserves totaling 13 million acres.

On March 31, 1891, the Park Protection Act was passed, which provided protection for wildlife in the national parks. The following year the Sierra Club was founded. In 1898 Gifford Pinchot was named head of the Forest Division of the federal government, and the forest conservation movement began to expand greatly under his leadership. He brought the word "conservation" into popular usage in application to natural resources. In 1899 Congress passed a law that allowed the recreational use of forest reserves. This was the first law to recognize the recreation value of forests.

The states began to take a more active role as Niagara Falls, New York, was set aside as a public reservation in 1885. The same year Fort Mackinac was given to Michigan and marked the beginning of that state's system of recreation areas. In 1885 New York instituted the first comprehensive administrative forestry act in America, and that same year California, Colorado, and Ohio created state boards of forestry.

The conservation movement progressed significantly in the first decade of the twentieth century. The passage of the Reclamation Act in 1902 provided for government aid to help develop water resources, and the Morris Act of 1902 established the Great Minnesota Forest. The first national wildlife refuge was established in 1902 on Pelican Island off the coast of Florida. In 1905 the Bureau of Biological Survey, the predecessor of the U.S. Fish and Wildlife Service, was established. The Division of Forestry was changed to the U.S. Forest Service, and the forest reserves previously administered by the General Land Office of the Department of the Interior were turned over to the Forest Service.

The Antiquities Act of 1906 paved the way for setting aside national monuments by Presidential proclamation. Also in 1906, President Theodore Roosevelt signed 33 proclamations that added more than 15.6 million acres to the forest reserve. In 1908 Roosevelt appointed a national conservation commission with Gifford Pinchot as chairman, to study ways to save the country's natural resources, and in 1909 the commission published an inventory of natural resources in the United States.

By 1916 several national parks and monuments had been declared and set aside under the preservation concept, and during that year the National Park Service was established to administer these areas. The purpose of the NPS was "to promote and regulate the usual federal areas known as national parks, monuments, and reservations, to conserve the scenery and natural and historic objects and the wildlife, and to provide for the enjoyment of the same in such manner and by such means as will leave them unimpaired for their enjoyment for future generations."

In 1919 the American School of Wildlife Protection was established at McGregor, Iowa; it initially consisted of a five-day session which later developed into two sessions. Other noteworthy developments of that era were: (1) the commencement in 1915 of a series of annual American game conferences held under the auspices of the American Game Protective and Propagation Association, which was organized in 1911; (2) the passage by Congress of the Term-Lease Law of 1915 which authorized issuance of long-term permits for summer homes, lodges, and other structures needed for recreation and for public convenience on national forest lands; (3) the establishment of the Rocky Mountain National Park in Colorado; and (4) the first publication of *Park and Recreation*, a journal of the American Institute of Park Executives.

Increased emphasis on state parks brought about the establishment of the National Conference on State Parks in 1921. The Izaak Walton League was founded in 1922. In 1924 the first national conference on outdoor recreation was held in Washington, D. C., with 309 delegates representing 128 organizations. Also during the 1920s the U. S. Forest Service and the National Park Service gave increased emphasis to outdoor recreation. Stephen Mather, the first director of the National Park Service, claimed that recreation at the federal level was a function of the National Park Service. Forester William Greely wrote in *Outlook* (1925), "outdoor recreation ranks today as one of the major resources of the national forests."

A special area now known as the Gila Wilderness in New Mexico was set aside in 1924 to protect wilderness values of the national forests. Aldo Leopold, who was a noted conservationist and an enthusiast of wilderness, was largely responsible for this action.

The depression years of the 1930s were boom years for outdoor recreation. The emergency conservation work programs of the federal government, debatable as they were, fulfilled certain definite needs. They created a demand for trained personnel through the work projects of the PWA, WPA, and CCC. Needed outdoor recreation facilities were constructed, and federally funded positions for 26,500 recreation leaders were made available through work programs. In addition to the

direct effects of these programs on outdoor recreation, the after-
effects, as the men returned to thier home towns, brought recreation to
communities that previously had not experienced organized programs
under leadership. The principle of recreation as a community responsibility was greatly advanced.

Also in the 1930s wildlife management began to gain recognition as a
science. Aldo Leopold's book *Game Management* was published during that decade, and it has continued to serve as an important guide to
wildlife management personnel. The American Wildlife Institute and the
American Wildlife Society were founded, the National Wildlife Federation was formed, and the first North American Wildlife Conference
was held during that decade. Many students of the cooperative wildlife
unit schools were employed in the federally aided wildlife restoration
program, which became effective in 1938.

At the federal level there were a number of other important developments. The Migratory Bird Hunting Stamp Act of 1934 provided
for acquiring lands for national wildlife refuges. Congress established
an advisory board on national parks, historic sites, and monuments.
The Soil Conservation Service was established. The Forest Service
continued to establish identified wilderness areas within the national
forest reserve. The Natural Resources Committee was appointed in
1935 to investigate the country's natural resources, and to plan for their
development and use. Also in that year, Congress passed the Fullmer
Act which established federal aid to the states to acquire state forest
lands.

In 1940 the Bureau of Biological Survey and the Bureau of Fisheries
merged and became the U. S. Fish and Wildlife Service, located within
the Department of the Interior. In 1941 several states passed enabling
legislation for the establishment of state, city, town and school forests.
A few states already had state forests. In 1943 comprehensive interagency river basin planning began with the establishment of the Federal
Interagency River Committee. Further developments along the lines of
conservation included the establishment of the Conservation Foundation and the Inter-American Conference on the Conservation of Renewable Resources in 1948. The United Nations sponsored a conference on the conservation and utilization of natural resources in 1949.

During the 1950s conservation education in the schools and colleges
became more prominent, and local clubs of various kinds became more
active in the conservation movement. The Dingle-Johnson Act of 1951
provided federal aid to state fisheries, and the Watershed Protection
and Flood Prevention Act of 1954 authorized the Department of Agriculture to cooperate with state and local agencies in planning and
carrying out improvements on small watersheds. The Recreation and
Public Purposes Act of 1954 authorized state and local governments

and qualified nonprofit organizations to acquire certain federal lands for recreation use and other public purposes. Congress amended the Coordination Act of 1958 to specify that wildlife and fishery conservation should be coordinated with other features of water resource development, with equal consideration. About that same time the Association of Interpretative Naturalists was formed. Also of major significance was the initiation in 1956 of the ten-year Mission 66 Facility Improvement Program of the National Park Service. In 1957 the U. S. Forest Service launched a five-year special improvement program called Operation Outdoors.

During the 1950s the growing public demand for resource-oriented recreation and sharpening competition for the various uses of natural resources became matters of increasing national concern. Recognizing the need for a nationwide study of these problems, Congress in 1958 established the Outdoor Recreation Resources Review Commission (ORRRC), under the chairmanship of Lawrence Rockefeller, to survey outdoor recreation needs for the next 40 years, and to recommend actions to meet those needs. The report of the Commission consisted of 27 informative volumes. Several significant legislative acts and nationwide programs have resulted from the Commission's report.

The Multiple-Use Sustained Yield Act of 1960 made outdoor recreation an official function of the National Forest Service on the same basis as its other four specified functions. This was really more a formality than a significant official action, because the national forests had been managed under the multiple-use concept for many years.

The establishment of the Bureau of Outdoor Recreation within the Department of the Interior was a major development in the year 1962. In 1964 the Land and Water Conservation Fund Act was passed, with the provisions of the act to be administered by the Bureau of Outdoor Recreation. This act provides matching grant-in-aid funds to the states and their political subdivisions for planning, acquiring, and developing outdoor recreational areas. It has added much by way of leadership and financial support to the federal effort in outdoor recreation.

The Economic Opportunity Act of 1966, more commonly known as the Anti-Poverty Act, includes provisions for a job corps of young people who work in public natural resource areas to develop skills and to train themselves for careers. Much of the work done by these young people is in parks, forests, reservoirs, refuges, and other natural resource areas. Also during the 1960s the Water Resources Planning Act provided for optimum development of the nation's natural water resources, including recreation use. The passage of Public Law 89-174 established the Department of Housing and Urban Development (HUD), and one of its original responsibilities was the management of the Open Space Program to provide "room for living" in and around cities. A large amount of federal money was appropriated for 50% matching grants to states and local governments for acquiring and developing both improved and unimproved open space for parks, recreation, conservation, scenic and historic purposes.

The Appalachian Development Act of 1965 had a significant influence on the recreational use of natural resources in eleven eastern and southern states. The Federal Water Projects Act of 1968 gave full consideration to outdoor recreation opportunities, and to the enhancement of fish and wildlife in planning, constructing, operating and maintaining federal water projects. The Highway Beautification Act of 1965 dealt with controlling outdoor advertising and junkyards along certain federal highways, and with landscaping and the scenic enhancement of highways under the federal aid program.

The Water Quality Act of 1965 established the Federal Water Pollution Control Administration, and charged that agency with assuring an adequate supply of water suitable in quality for all legitimate uses—public, industrial, agricultural, recreational, and the propagation of fish, aquatic life and wildlife. It was officially recognized that, without water of suitable quality, many outdoor recreation activities would not be possible. The water pollution control program is deeply involved in the provision of water of adequate quality for water-oriented recreation activities. The Natural Historic Preservation Act of 1966 authorized matching grants to states and to the National Trust for Historic Preservation in the United States. The Act also authorized 50% matching grants to states for the preparation of comprehensive statewide historic preservation plans.

The Greenspan Program under Public Law 89-321, offered state and local government agencies financial assistance to acquire crop lands for preserving open space and natural beauty, and developing wildlife or recreation areas.

The Air Quality Act of 1967 was passed in recognition that air pollution is a problem of national significance. Its numerous provisions are all pointed toward improving the quality of air throughout the nation, with particular emphasis on metropolitan areas.

In 1968 the Wild and Scenic Rivers Program was started for the purpose of establishing within the United States certain rivers of national significance which possess outstanding scenic, recreational, geographic, fish and wildlife, historic, cultural, or other similar values. It is the intent that these rivers be preserved in their free-flowing condition for the benefit and enjoyment of present and future generations.

The National Trails System was initiated in 1968 in order to accommodate a rapidly increasing population that is becoming ever more enthusiastic about trailing and backpacking. It started the preservation of scenic, historic, and otherwise interesting trail routes throughout various parts of the nation, with the provision that other trails can be added as justified.

The Environmental Education Act of 1970 was passed for the purpose of encouraging and supporting the development of improved curricula designed to enhance environmental quality and maintain ecological balance. 2000103

The Water Quality Improvement Act of 1970 was a revision and expansion of the Water Quality Act of 1965, and it further guaranteed the maintenance of a suitable quality of water for various uses. The Environmental Quality Improvement Act of 1970 charged federal government agencies having influences on the environment with additional responsibilities for protection of the natural environment. The National Environmental Policy Act of 1970 was passed to promote efforts which will prevent or eliminate damage to the environment and stimulate the health and welfare of man, to enrich the understanding of the ecological systems and of natural resources.

In 1971 a federal Boating Safety Program was started to improve boat safety and to foster greater development, use and enjoyment of all the waters of the United States by encouraging and assisting participation by the several states, the boating industry, and the boating public in the development of more comprehensive boating safety programs.

In 1973 the Bureau of Outdoor Recreation completed the national outdoor recreation comprehensive plan entitled Outdoor Recreation—The Legacy of America. The plan was coordinated with and built upon comprehensive recreation plans that had been prepared by all of the fifty states. These plans have had and will continue to have significant influence on the assessment and development of outdoor recreation opportunities.

The Endangered Species Act of 1973 directed the Secretary of the Interior to establish and implement a program to conserve fish and wildlife and certain plants which are identified as endangered.

The Water Resources Development Act of 1974 authorizes the Secretary of the Army, acting through the Army Corps of Engineers, to undertake the initial phase of the engineering and design plan of 17 multipurpose water resource projects at various locations in the nation. The projects have significant outdoor recreation potential.

The enactment of legislation and the launching of significant programs at the national and state levels during the 1960s and the first half of 1970 showed unprecedented interest in the provision of adequate resource-oriented recreation opportunities. These needs were voiced by the country's leaders, which indicated that the recreation movement had come of age. More than ever it became apparent that recreation and park professionals have a challenge and a responsibility to demonstrate their maturity and ability to provide adequate leadership.

MUNICIPAL RECREATION AND PARK DEVELOPMENT

According to the chronicles of history, the earliest city park in the United States was the Boston Commons, established in 1634. When in 1682 William Penn laid out Philadelphia he included in his plan numerous small parks and ornamental plots. In his 1791 plan for Washington, D. C., Pierre Charles L'Enfant provided spacious public parks, squares, fountains, walks and broad tree-lined avenues. The federal government acquired many of the areas included in the plan under an agreement of private land owners signed on March 31, 1791. This agreement empowered President Washington to "retain any number of squares he may think proper for any public improvements or other public uses."

In 1821 outdoor physical education was instituted at Salem Latin School in Massachusetts. During the next ten years college gymnasiums were constructed at Harvard, Yale, and several other New England colleges. Squares, commons and village greens had become numerous in the New England States by the early nineteenth century.

In 1839 Chicago established a park at the old Fort Dearborn site. In 1851 President Fillmore appointed Andrew Jackson Downing, rural architect, to landscape several public parks in Washington, D. C. However, Downing's premature death prevented completion of the plan.

As mentioned earlier, one of the milestones in municipal park development occurred in 1853 when the land for Central Park in New York City was acquired and development of the park was authorized.

Figure 9.   Golfing in New England in 1887. (Library of Congress photo.)

Central Park is particularly significant because of the influence it has had on the development of other large parks in cities of the nation and the world. Central Park designers Olmstead and Vaux had as their theme the idea that Manhattan would be laid out in rows of streets and buildings, and the inhabitants would only occasionally encounter other surroundings. They believed that "the park should not only be an immunity from urban conditions, but in the laying out of its landscape the features should provide the anti-thesis of urban conditions." Olmstead envisioned that, with the growth of New York City, Central Park would be only one of a series of parks which would be dispersed throughout the metropolitan area and connected by parkways. Actually, Olmstead's philosophy has been better developed in some other large cities than in New York itself.[2]

The underlying philosophy of metropolitan parks in America can probably be summed up best by a quote taken from a letter written by Olmstead to the Park Commissioners of the City of Minneapolis in 1886: "The kind of recreation that these large parks supply, and nothing but these large parks supply in every city, is that which a man sensibly obtains when he puts the city behind him and out of his sight, and goes where he will under the understood influence of pleasing natural scenery." Olmstead, an architect by profession, is said to have been the first man to call himself a *landscape architect*.[2]

Quite separate from the city park movement, municipal recreation programming was born with a social conscience. It grew up with the settlement house, kindergarten, and youth movements that fostered the great youth agencies of the nation. Its earliest practitioners were motivated by human welfare; the social ends of human development, suppression of juvenile delinquency, informal education, cultural enrichment, health improvement, and other similar objectives were central. Gradually the social welfare mission weakened and a philosophy which sees recreation as an end in itself has become popular; this is the common view in public recreation agencies throughout the country today.

In the earliest days of the recreation program movement, playgrounds were located in what were then called "underprivileged" neighborhoods. Gradually, as the movement matured and public acceptance increased, the idea grew that any neighborhood which lacked public recreation services was, in a sense, underprivileged, and that centers ought to be provided throughout the community. In some cities where the residents of more affluent neighborhoods employed their power to articulate needs and influence political processes, a preponderance of new facilities often went into the developing suburbs, and what inequalities existed in distribution of facilities favored the more affluent population.

The first record of anyone being employed in a leisure time occupation (other than the park planners themselves) was in 1887, when several women were hired as supervisors for children's playgrounds in Boston. In 1898 New York City opened 31 supervised playgrounds under the direction of the State Board of Education, and soon after that the city moved quickly to develop a large network of playgrounds paid for and administered by the city government. Further, all schools in New York City were required to have open-air playgrounds. By the end of the nineteenth century at least 14 American cities had made provisions for supervised public recreation.

At about the same time the settlement house movement was under way and spreading rapidly in densely populated areas. These social settlements had many of the same characteristics as today's community recreation centers.

The first metropolitan park department was established in Boston in 1892; however this was preceded by the first county department, which was organized in Essex County, New Jersey, in 1885. The New England Association of Park Superintendents (later known as the American Institute of Park Executives) was organized in 1898. By the turn of the century the pattern for municipal park and recreation programs was well established.

In Washington, D. C., it was becoming ever more apparent that L'Enfant, Washington, and Jefferson had shown considerable foresight, because the nation's new capital city took shape much as they had envisioned. By 1898, nearly a century after the government had moved to Washington, the park system was fairly well developed in accordance with L'Enfant's plan of 1791.

The basis for the upsurge in the municipal recreation and park movement was essentially social. Its advocates pointed to such evils as dangerous streets, delinquency, unsanitary living conditions, child labor, congestion of rapidly growing cities and lack of space for play and rest. They declared that the individual should be the center of the educational effort and that activities during leisure were important to a person's overall development.

Public support grew markedly throughout the country. Voters of south-side Chicago approved a 5-million-dollar bond in 1903 to acquire and develop neighborhood parks, and two years later ten neighborhood parks had been opened. The parks, which included carefully planned fieldhouses and spacious outdoor areas, had significant influence on America's recreation movement. The concept demonstrated in these parks represented a milestone in the public's responsibility for provision of facilities and paid leadership. The concept spread quickly into Rochester, Boston and Los Angeles, and in 1904 the first playground commission was established in Los Angeles City.

By 1906 the recreation and park movement had gained such momentum that, at a meeting in Washington of park and playground promoters, a new organization known as the Playground Association of America was founded; this later became the National Recreation Association (1917), and still later it merged with other organizations to form the National Recreation and Park Association (1965). Joseph Lee, a Harvard law graduate and wealthy philanthropist, was president of the NRA for 27 years. Lee argued that play was serious activity in children's social adjustment, and he felt that recreation had vital significance for everyone who wanted a meaningful life. Lee emphasized quality experiences and advocated the need for fixed goals, efficient organization and expert leadership. He recommended education for the wise use of leisure as a means of helping people achieve happy and creative lives.

The founding of the Camp Fire Girls and the Boy Scouts of America in 1910, and then of the Girl Scouts in 1912, started movements that have had great impact on recreation for youth. Additional emphasis was given with the establishment of the Camp Directors Association of America, predecessor of the American Camping Association.

Although destructive to the development of recreation in some respects, World War I (and also World War II) actually contributed impetus to the movement. Men in the services, while being exposed to highly organized and vigorous training, were also exposed to well-organized recreation programs. Further, many civilians clustered in the industrial centers where they also were exposed to organized recreation. Following each war, soldiers and civilians carried back to their own communities the desire to provide better facilities and leadership.

During the period between the two wars the country became increasingly industrialized and highly mobile. These two characteristics had dramatic influences on the amount and kinds of leisure time activities engaged in by Americans.

In Washington, D. C., a major step in the continuing development of the parks of the nation's capital occurred when Congress authorized the National Capital Park Commission in 1924:

> to preserve the flow of the water in Rock Creek, to prevent the pollution of Rock Creek and the Potomac and Anacostia Rivers, to preserve forest and natural scenery in and about Washington, and to provide for the comprehensive, systematic and continuous development of the parkway and playground system of the national capital.

Between 1915 and 1925 more than 20 states passed enabling legislation that permitted their political subdivisions (towns, cities, counties, and school districts) to establish and operate broad recreational programs. Also during this period the 40-hour work week came into sight and public officials, educators and recreation professionals began to think more seriously about expanding local recreation opportunities.

The concept of parks and playgrounds had changed by the quarter century mark. As municipal recreation programs became more accepted, there was a greater demand for facilities such as golf courses, athletic fields and tennis courts. As a result some distinct differences began to appear between the philosophy of the activity leaders (mostly with physical education backgrounds) and the park designers who had not adjusted very well to this kind of park use. As a result facilities, especially for active recreation, were built in many localities, and they were often barren and unattractive. The problem involving playfields and parks was summed up rather well as follows:

> At the end of nearly three-quarters of a century of park development in the United States, the term "park" had come to mean any area of land or water set aside for outdoor recreation purposes, whether it be recreation or a passive or active nature or any of the degrees between these two extremes, and that the recreation is expected to come in part, at least, from beauty of experience.[3]

During the depression of the 1930s several federal public works programs (CCC, PWA, WPA, and others) made important contributions of certain kinds to the development of facilities and organized programs in cities throughout the nation.

In 1934 the Athletic Institute was founded. Since that time the Institute has done an outstanding job of coordinating the efforts of certain professional organizations in the field of recreation.

In 1937 the American Association for Health, Physical Education, and Recreation (AAHPER) was founded as a branch of the National Education Association. Its recreation division has had great impact on the recreation movement, particularly on school-related recreation.

Another sign of professional growth and development was the establishment of numerous state recreation associations in the late 1930s. Even more significant was the organization of the American Recreation Society in 1938.

During World War II manpower and material shortages curtailed the development of facilities, and travel restrictions imposed by gas and tire shortages drastically limited recreation travel. Partly because of this, municipal and neighborhood parks and recreation facilities were in increased demand. Recreation activities were emphasized by the armed forces, as was the need for professionally trained recreation leaders to conduct military and industrial recreation programs and administer USO centers.

Following World War II the Athletic Institute financed a meeting of the American Institute of Park Executives and the American Recreation Society to study the feasibility of unifying the profession. However, this early attempt to merge the organizations was to no avail.

During the early postwar years, with the American economy at its highest level in history, and with the return of large numbers of soldiers and defense workers to their home towns, practically every community of any size initiated some sort of community recreation program. In most cases the programs were sponsored through the local government and supported by tax funds. It was during this period that the municipal recreation and park movement erupted into a truly nationwide trend.

Concurrently and subsequently other agencies gave additional attention to the leisure time needs of people. Voluntary youth-serving agencies became more concerned about the recreational needs of their members, and at industrial plants employee recreation associations developed. The armed forces also continued to provide recreation for their members, and uses of the "great outdoors" for recreation purposes skyrocketed. During the postwar years commercial recreation enjoyed its greatest boom, and more recently specialized programs of recreation therapy for the ill and handicapped have become popular.

Section 701 of the Housing Act of 1954 included provisions for federal grants up to two thirds of the cost for all aspects of comprehensive urban planning, including recreation and park planning. Under Section 704 of the 1965 Housing and Urban Development Act, grants could be made to local public agencies to acquire sites needed for future construction of public facilities, including parks and recreation centers. Under the Older Americans Act of 1965 provisions were made for federal assistance to local agencies for the improvement of centers and programs for the aging, including recreation facilities and activities. In 1974 the Housing and Community Development Act was passed; it enables communities to make applications to the Department of Housing and Urban Development for grants in support of various kinds of community improvements, among which are: (1) preservation or restoration of historic sites, (2) urban beautification, (3) conservation of open space, (4) preservation of natural resource areas or scenic areas, and (5) provision of park and recreation facilities.

Modern technology has revolutionized certain leisure time pursuits. For example, motor boating, water skiing, snow skiing, scuba diving, driving for pleasure, tourist travel, photography, camping, and numerous other forms of recreation have been influenced greatly by technological advances. Further, television has had a significant influence through presentation of activities that would otherwise remain relatively unexposed. A recent example of this is tennis, currently America's fasting growing sport. Television coverage of world class players has probably been the main factor in the upsurge of tennis popularity. Golf, snow skiing and soccer have experienced similar effects.

Because of the steady escalation of leisure time, and of recreation participation, there are now leisure time job opportunities at every level of government (especially the local level), in voluntary non-government organizations, and with private and commercial enterprises. For the most part the jobs are specialized, requiring people with certain personality characteristics and specific competencies. However, along with specialization it is important for today's leaders to have a broad concept of the field as a whole, and to understand the interwoven relationships that exist. Further, today's recreation leaders must have keen insights into sociological needs, and a sincere interest in providing wholesome recreational opportunities.

REFERENCES

1. Gothein, M. L.: *A History of Garden Art*, 2 vols. (Wright, W. P., Ed.). J. M. Dent & Sons, London, 1913.
2. Doell, C. E. and Twardzik, L. F.: *Elements of Park and Recreation Administration*, 3rd ed. Burgess Publishing Co., Minneapolis, 1973.
3. Weir, L. H.: *A Manual of Municipal and County Parks*, Vol. 1. A. S. Barnes, New York, 1928.

3

Trends in the Development of the Profession

The professionals in the field of recreation and parks are those serving in administrative, supervisory, planning and other leadership capacities. They are employed primarily by public and voluntary agencies, although some of those who are professionally prepared choose to pursue private or commercial recreation careers. The proficient professional equips himself for leadership through carefully planned education and high-quality experience.

Generally speaking the professional in this field must be a promoter, a planner, an organizer, a teacher, and a motivator. If he is to serve a worthwhile purpose, his efforts must be based on a sound sense of values that will cause his leadership to benefit both individuals and society.

Since leisure time activities are numerous and diverse, the occupation specialties associated with them are also numerous and diverse. To illustrate, a partial list of such occupations appears below. Recognize that this is a list of *selected leisure time occupations*, and it is not restricted to professional recreation positions, although most of the positions could best be filled by persons who are professionally prepared.

Therapeutic recreation specialists in hospitals
Supervisors of industrial recreation programs
College teachers of recreation or outdoor education
Golf pros at municipal and private courses
Tennis pros and tennis club managers
Swimming pool managers and instructors
Ski instructors and ski school directors
Bowling alley and game room managers
Park naturalists and rangers
Guides for river or wilderness trips
Vacation travel agents and tour guides

43

Museum directors and guides

Directors of zoological and botanical gardens

Park designers and landscape architects

Professional square dance callers and dance teachers

Members of city recreation departments—recreation and park directors, aquatics directors, athletic directors, supervisors of nature activities, directors of arts and crafts, recreation center directors, park maintenance supervisors

Federal government employees in the Bureau of Outdoor Recreation, U.S. Fish and Wildlife Service and other such government agencies

State government employees such as those in state park departments and fish and game departments

Many of the aforementioned are natural occupations for people who are highly skilled, especially if they have reputations which will atttract a clientele. Such persons might become golf pros, tennis pros or ski instructors. The particular curricula that such leaders pursue in college are sometimes of limited importance. Reputation, personality, and expertise often are more important in attracting a clientele. However, for most professionals in this field, the best avenue is through a college program in some aspect of recreation and park management, which prepares the student to assume a professional position and to advance as opportunities come along.

EDUCATIONAL PROGRAMS

In the recent past there has been a shortage of well-prepared professional recreation and park personnel, and as a result there has been a dramatic increase during the past 20 years in the number of colleges and universities offering preparation programs in this field. This has greatly increased the number of college graduates in the field—a trend which will probably continue in the foreseeable future. For example, in 1967 2,070 students graduated from recreation and park curricula. Three years later (1970) there were 4,458, and in 1976 over 13,000. It is projected that by 1980 the number of graduates from these curricula will exceed 20,000 and by 1985 the number might reach 30,000. (These numbers include associate, bachelor and graduate degrees.)

The National Recreation and Park Association reported that in 1960 only 63 institutions offered major programs in recreation. Ten years later (1970) that number had increased to more than 200 and today about 340 institutions offer curricula in some aspect of recreation. Almost half of these are two-year colleges which offer associate degrees only. About 180 four-year colleges and universities offer bachelor's degrees, and of these about 110 offer master's degrees and about 35 offer doctorates. Since this field is comprised of several specialties, the curricula vary at different institutions with each one emphasizing certain specialized areas.

It is interesting to know that a portion of the leaders in leisure time occupations have degrees in liberal arts, physical education, forestry, sociology, business, landscape architecture, industrial arts, fine arts, and other fields different from recreation and park leadership.

Resource-oriented recreation curricula generally are housed in schools of forestry or natural resources, while recreation education and administration curricula are predominantly in schools of health, physical education and recreation. However, in a few institutions the recreation curricula are located in departments such as sociology, humanities, and landscape architecture.

Field work is an important part of the professional preparation of college students enrolled in recreation, and a majority of the institutions include on-the-job experience for credit. A variety of field work opportunities are available in municipal recreation, therapeutic recreation, volunteer agencies, organized camps, etc.

The rapid increase in the two-year associate degree programs can be attributed to two factors: (1) expansion of the number of two-year colleges, and (2) the demand for direct leaders and program technicians who need less than a four-year college degree. The role of an associate degree program is to prepare students for face-to-face leadership positions or for technician jobs. With a two-year associate degree, a student can gain early entry into the field and/or transfer to a four-year program to continue education toward a bachelor's degree. Often students wish to obtain an associate degree and aquire one or more years of full-time on-the-job experience before transferring to a four-year institution for additional study. This on-the-job experience can be valuable in furnishing additional insight into job opportunities. Further, it can make additional study at a later date more meaningful.

Examples of the kinds of jobs often available to associate degree holders are: swimming pool managers or swimming instructors, leaders of athletic activities, park maintenance supervisors, aquatic maintenance specialists, playground activity leaders, and certain park-ranger positions.

Most of the bachelor's degree programs include two or more options or specialized areas, allowing a student to be somewhat of a specialist while obtaining a broad educational background and a solid foundation on which to build a career. Also, valuable information is learned through elective courses in humanities, fine arts, physical education, communications, sociology, business management, English and writing techniques. Most of those who major in this field accept employment in the field after receiving a bachelor's degree; a few stay on for a master's degree, but most students who want to pursue graduate study feel a need for full-time employment experience before going on.

At the graduate level the areas which ordinarily receive emphasis include philosophy related to recreation and leisure, administrative philosophy and procedures, research and evaluation techniques, advanced approaches to personnel management, public relations, and program and facility planning. Sometimes specialized areas are pursued, e.g. therapeutic recreation, industrial recreation or management of outdoor recreation resources. As a rule most of those who earn doctorate degrees in this field are members of college faculties, or aspire to become so, although there are a few exceptions to this. Master's degree holders pursue a variety of lines of employment, usually in the areas of administration and supervision.

George Wilson added meaning to the classification of job opportunities in the overall park and recreation field by stating:

> The umbrella of leisure services covers three broad areas. The *first* is natural resources, including local, state, regional, and national parks as well as other resources and programs utilized for outdoor recreation. The *second* includes education for and about leisure, and encompasses programs indoors as well as outdoors in towns, villages, cities, schools, colleges, universities, institutions, and private and voluntary agencies providing a wide spectrum of community services for the main stream and special populations. The *third* area delivers leisure services, including commercial recreation, tourism, amusement parks and attractions, and a host of related services such as food, lodging, and transportaion.[1]

In coming decades this umbrella of human services will rank high in career potential, along with the energy and computer industries. Since it is a comparatively young field, there need be no hang-ups about equal opportunity in relation to sex, creed, race or ethnic backgrounds. The career ladder provides a framework for satisfying work experiences ranging from face-to-face leadership through top-level management. The ladder will require educational preparation for careers on many and varied levels.

Along with expanding opportunities in the more traditional areas of the field, other careers will be developed to establish cooperative processes in the vast network of leisure services which will become interrelated. Two exciting and emerging processes on the horizon are *community education* and *leisure counselling*. The former, community education, relates to delivery of community and human services, not only utilizing the schools as a resource but involving the community itself—causing the community to become a school without walls. The latter, leisure counselling, will match the interest and needs of individuals and groups with what could otherwise be a bewildering array of leisure activities and opportunities. Both processes will require greatly intensified and specialized career training.

A WORD OF CAUTION

Even though the future of the recreation and park profession appears generally bright, it is important that the impression not be given that this field will present a plethora of employment opportunities in the future. It will undoubtedly experience consistent growth and the profession will gain increased stability and improved status, but the growth and improvement will not be as dramatic as earlier predictions from seemingly reliable sources would indicate.

During the 1960s a number of factors were responsible for excessive predictions relative to this field, and some of the predictions have not materialized. Among these are:

1. The increase in leisure has not been as rapid as predicted, and in particular the work week has not been affected as much as vacations, holidays and retirement.
2. While a tremendous amount of money continues to be spent on leisure, the bulk of it goes to commercial or private programs and these programs employ a low proportion of professionally qualified personnel.
3. The rate of increase in population has lessened dramatically since the 1960s, and some of the earlier predictions about work patterns and the economy have not proved accurate.
4. Budgetary problems in many cities and nongovernment organizations have resulted in fiscal cuts, job freezes or cutbacks, and this has limited the number of new recreation and park jobs.
5. While billions of dollars are spent by the federal and state governments to support recreation, most of this goes into land acquisition and resource development rather than the support of recreation programs under professional leadership.
6. The development of standards and procedures which would cause professionally prepared leaders to be hired instead of unqualified persons has not progressed at a satisfactory rate.

For all of these reasons the market for college trained recreation and park personnel has not expanded in the 1970s as rapidly as predicted. However, it has expanded at a steady and healthy rate, and there is no reason to expect that this trend will not remain intact. The points to be made are: (1) Those who want to make a career of this field need to prepare themselves expertly so they can be competitive in the job market, and (2) the leaders of the profession need to strive for more effectiveness in developing and enforcing standards and procedures that will enhance the employment of those who have prepared themselves well for leadership positions.

GROWTH OF PROFESSIONAL PREPARATION PROGRAMS

Professional preparation is said to have actually started in 1909, when a normal course in play was assembled and published by a committee of 23 pioneers of the recreation movement. This came about because one of the first concerns of the Playground Association of America, after its organization in 1906, was the preparation of professional leaders. Chairman of the committee was Dr. Clark W. Hetherington, and several other prominent leaders of the time were members. Hetherington visited a large number of normal schools and colleges to advise faculty members about courses in play.

After careful investigation of the work being done throughout the country, and in order to meet the demands for playground directors, the committee established three courses, as follows:

1. A normal course in play for professional directors to be taught at normal schools and colleges
2. A course for elementary school teachers designed to be included in the teacher preparation curricula of normal schools and colleges
3. An institute course in play designed for those entering playground service for only a short period and for those already employed without previous training

By 1910, 19 colleges and universities had established schools of forestry, and more than 25 institutions were preparing teachers in the field of physical education. Yet no curricula had the primary purpose of preparing people to manage recreation resources and recreation programs. At that time park superintendents were for the most part people with experience in planning and design or horticulture, while the program leaders were usually those prepared in social work, physical education, or elementary education. Many became established in leadership positions through apprenticeships.

In 1911 the West Chicago Park Commissioners became convinced that recreation leaders should have professional training, and that recreation centers should have programs that were broader than physical recreation. This led to the development of the Chicago Training School for Playground Workers, which later became associated with the Department of Sociology at Northwestern University. At about this same time the People's Institute of New York established a one-year training course for professional workers in community centers, social settlements and child welfare centers. This same year, staff members of the National Recreation Association were successful in instituting in-service training courses at several colleges and universities in the east, midwest and west. Also in 1911 the New York State College of Forestry at Syracuse University became the first college in the United States to offer a program to prepare professionals in park administration and city forestry.

Other noteworthy developments during that decade were: (1) the commencement in 1915 of a series of 21 annual American Game Conferences held under the auspices of the American Game Protective and Propagation Association, (2) the inception of *Park and Recreation* as the journal of the American Institute of Park Executives, and (3) the establishment in 1918 by the National Recreation Association of "Local Social Recreation and Game Institutes." Later the same organization promoted specialized training in music, drama, nature, and crafts.

An increased emphasis on state parks brought about the establishment of the National Conference on State Parks in 1921, attended by 309 delegates representing 128 national organizations. The Izaak Walton League was founded in 1922, and the American Association of Zoological Parks and Aquariums was organized in 1924. During this same era the National Recreation Association organized community recreation training schools, each lasting six weeks. The first was held in 1920, and they continued through 1926, with an average of 35 students attending each of the 26 schools.

In 1926 the National Recreation Association established an advanced (graduate) training program. As in the community recreation schools sponsored earlier by the NRA, the enrollment was limited to approximately 35 students per course. After nine years of operation, the school closed when the depression made it increasingly difficult for graduates to find the kinds of administrative and supervisory positions for which they had been prepared. A total of 300 students were graduated from the course.

In 1935 the NRA started a new kind of training institute. With the worst of the depression over, and as a result of the positive recreational effects of federal government work projects, hundreds of new workers who had little previous training or experience served in recreation positions. These, and experienced workers alike, crowded into the four-week training institutes sponsored by the local agencies and conducted by NRA personnel. The institutes offered courses in music, drama, nature study, crafts, social recreation and games, and organization and administration techniques.

In 1937 the American Association for Health, Physical Education, and Recreation (AAHPER) was founded. This organization, a division of the National Education Association, had an immediate and significant impact on professional preparation. Also in 1937 the first college conference for training leaders in recreation was held under the joint sponsorship of the University of Maryland and the WPA Recreation Division. At this time it was reported that 15 colleges were offering recreation as a major subject. However, the offerings were meager, and they came nowhere near the more substantial recreation curricula of today.

During the 1930s several institutions began educating people in the management of natural resources for recreational use. The Landscape Architecture Department of the University of Massachusetts played a leading role in this regard, and by the mid-1930s the Forest Management Department of Utah State University offered three classes in recreation. A course in national park management was introduced in the College of Forestry at Colorado State University. Courses having to do with wildlife management were also added in colleges of forestry.

In 1935 a recreation major was started in the Department of Forestry at Michigan State University, and in 1936 a four-year undergraduate curriculum in wildlife management was established in the Department of Forestry and Wildlife Management at the University of Massachusetts.

A rather complete program of recreation education at both the undergraduate and graduate levels was instituted at New York University in 1936, and in 1940 Purdue University started a curriculum in industrial recreation. Another milestone was the establishment of the American Recreation Society in 1938.

Immediately after World War II a number of colleges and universities established recreation curricula. North Carolina State University established an option in park administration; Colorado State University organized a Department of Forest Recreation and Wildlife Conservation, and the Great Lakes Park and Recreation Training Institute was established. The demand for recreation services and the resulting need for professionally trained leaders increased rapidly. The National Recreation Association reported that the number of cities with paid recreation leadership increased from 1,740 in 1946 to more than 2,500 in 1948.

In 1946 the Athletic Institute, with the co-sponsorship of other organizations, financed a national facilities workshop that brought together experts from all sections of the country. The workshop resulted in an important publication titled *A Guide for Planning Facilities for Athletics, Recreation, Physical Education and Health Education.* (In 1967 a similar workshop was held from which an updated publication resulted.)

Some significant developments in curricula and professional preparation occurred in the early 1950s, but the gap still widened between the demand for professionally prepared leaders and the supply of such leaders. The Southeastern Park and Recreation Training Institute, and the Southwest Park and Recreation Training Institute were added. Subsequently numerous other regional institutes were established.

In the mid-1950s a park management and municipal forestry curriculum was organized in the Department of Land and Water Conservation at Michigan State University, replacing a similar program established at that university in the Department of Forestry in 1935. A curriculum in park management was started in the Department of Horticulture and Park Management at Texas Tech University, and a park management curriculum was started at Sacramento State College in 1959.

During the 1950s the American Association for Health, Physical Education, and Recreation started an outdoor education project, and the Association also sponsored national conferences on professional preparation in 1954, 1956, and 1958. Additional AAHPER-sponsored national recreation conferences included one on education for leisure in 1957 and one on leadership for leisure in 1963.

Also in the 1950s noticeable changes took place in the underlying philosophy of recreation curricula. During this time it became increasingly apparent that those managing natural resources had to be better informed and more oriented toward public use of resources, while those who were prepared in municipal recreation had to become more knowledgeable and concerned about planning for the use of resources. As a result the base of many of the curricula began to broaden and the preparation of those enrolled was intensified.

By 1960 the increase in leisure and recreation was being more clearly recognized by educators, government officials and the general public. In 1962 approximately 60 institutions of higher education were offering degrees in some aspect of recreation leadership. In 1964 the American Association for Health, Physical Education and Recreation published a booklet entitled *Goals for American Recreation*, which has given much more direction to the field than ever before.

In 1965 the American Institute of Park Executives completed research which indicated that at least 99 curricula in recreation and/or park administration existed. Of these 5 were primarily in park management or park administration, while the majority of the curricula were oriented more toward activity programming and leadership. There were also 28 accredited and 18 nonaccredited schools of forestry, of which eight reported curricula or options in forest recreation. There were 29 colleges or universities with curricula in soil conservation, 33 with curricula in wildlife management, and several other colleges with curricula in other recreation-related fields.

In 1967 the American Association for Health, Physical Education and Recreation sponsored a national workshop on graduate curricula. It resulted in a publication (curriculum guide) which has been widely used. In 1968 this Association co-sponsored with the National Recreation and Park Association a national conference in Washington, D. C., on outdoor recreation in America. It was attended by 250 invited educators, government officials and recreation professionals. Also in 1968 the NRPA sponsored a national forum on "Educating Tomorrow's Leaders," and proceedings were published.

In 1973 the AAHPER and the NRPA jointly published a booklet listing all of the colleges and universities that offer recreation and park curricula, and the options available in the curriculum of each institution.

State, regional and national conferences and conventions relating to education and community service are giving recreation leadership more attention today than ever before. The college curricula relating to this field are improving and becoming more standardized, and the professional leaders in the field are steadily gaining in status and professional prestige.

PRESENT STATUS OF PROFESSIONAL PREPARATION

In 1976, the National Recreation and Park Association reported that recreation and park curricula existed in 158 two-year colleges and 183 four-year colleges. There has been a phenomenal increase in the number of curricula since the end of World War II, when there were approximately a dozen. By 1950, there were 38 college curricula. In 1960, there were 63. In 1970, 227 institutions reported curricula in this field, and in 1976 the number totaled 341. The NRPA predicted that the number would exceed 400 by 1980.

Of the 183 four-year curricula, 35% were housed in divisions of health, physical education, and recreation. Twenty-six percent were allied with colleges or divisions of education, 15% were with arts and sciences, and 15% were with forestry and natural resources. Of the two-year curricula, 46% were allied with health, physical education and recreation. Thirteen percent were with forestry and natural resources, 9% with arts and sciences, 9% with businesses or public services, and 23% with a variety of other divisions within the two-year colleges.

From 1970 to 1976, doctorate programs in this field decreased from 29 to 25 while master's degree programs increased from 79 to 84; baccalaureate programs increased from 138 to 183, and two-year programs increased from 70 to 158.

During this same period (1970 to 1976) the number of doctoral students decreased from 251 to 207 while candidates for master's degrees increased from 1,486 to 2,556. Baccalaureate students increased from 11,577 to 23,266 and students enrolled in two-year programs increased from 3,275 to 8,020.

In 1976, in the baccalaureate and graduate programs, about 40% of the students were females and 60% were males. In the two-year programs, about 45% were females and 55% were males.

Faculty members in the professional programs numbered 1,223, with 841 of these teaching in the four-year institutions and 382 in the two-year colleges. About 75% of the teachers were males and 25% were females.

EXPANSION OF PROFESSIONAL AND SERVICE ORGANIZATIONS

Some of the organizations related to this field have had fleeting but significant importance, while others have maintained an enduring influence through a professional or service function. The history began in England in 1844 when 12 men under the leadership of George Williams gathered for a Bible discussion. The Young Men's Christian Association (YMCA) is said to have had its start in that meeting. It was introduced into the United States in 1851, but did not become a truly national organization until the end of the 1800s. The YMCA became strongly oriented toward recreation soon after its establishment, and since then the provision of recreational opportunities has been one of its important functions.

The Boys Club of America was started in Hartford, Connecticut, in the mid-1850s, and about that same time (1856) the Young Women's Christian Association (YWCA) was started in New York under the original name of the Ladies Christian Union. The name was changed in 1866, and by 1900 it was an organization of national scope.

The American Association for the Advancement of Physical Education was founded in 1885 at Adelphi Academy, Brooklyn, by William Gilbert Anderson. It underwent a reorganization in 1903, and in 1937 it was named the American Association for Health, Physical Education and Recreation, at which time it became affiliated with the National Education Association. Throughout the life of this association it has encouraged the dual development of recreation and physical education as an integral part of our total educational system.

The first association representing the natural resource interests of the recreation was the American Forestry Association, organized in Chicago in 1875. This association has exerted a strong influence in forest land management during the last century. A second influential group in the conservation of resources that has developed strong interests in recreation is the Sierra Club, founded in 1892 by John Muir, its director for two decades. The club was most influential in having Yosemite established as a national park. The dedicated members of this group frequently join forces with other associations, magazines and newspapers to further their cause. For example, Mt. Rainier became a national park in 1899 through the combined efforts of the Sierra Club, the National Geographic Society, the American Association for the Advancement of Science, the Geographical Society of America and the Appalachian Club. Other organizations which have provided significant support to the park movement, especially national parks, are the American Museum of Natural History, established in New York in 1869, the National Audubon Society, established in 1905, and the Wilderness Society, established in 1935.

The first professional organization for persons directly involved in the park movement was formed by a group of municipal park superintendents in New England. The New England Association of Park Superintendents first convened in Boston in 1898 upon the invitation of George A. Parker, then the superintendent of Kenney Park, Boston. By 1904 this group had become a national association, changing its name to the American Association of Park Superintendents. Park superintendents revitalized the association in 1921 with a broader constitution, and recognized that parks were not only places to be viewed but also places where people should have the opportunity to participate in various recreational pursuits. The reorganization also included a change of title to the American Institute of Park Executives.

In 1906 another important association in the recreation and park movement was organized. The National Recreation Association was originally the Playground Association of America, and in 1911 it became the Playground and Recreation Association. The purpose of this association was to assist communities in establishing playgrounds and to generate public support for them. Dr. Luther Gulick was the first president and Henry Curtis was secretary. Joseph Lee, often referred to as the father of the American playground movement, became president in 1910. In 1908 Howard Braucher became executive director, a position which he held for 40 years. The National Recreation Association, as a service institution, was highly influential in promoting playgrounds and in training professionals in recreation throughout its lifetime. In 1938 many of the members of NRA formed a professional society, the Society of Recreation Workers of America, which in 1946 became the American Recreation Society.

Other organizations which have left their mark on the recreation and park movement are the Boy Scouts of America and the Camp Fire Girls, organized in 1910, the Girl Scouts, 1911, the American Society of Landscape Architects, 1916, and the American Camping Association, 1924.

The National Parks Association was formed in 1919 to promote the system of federal parks. This association became the National Park and Conservation Association in 1968.

The National Conference on State Parks was formally organized in 1928, and it has served traditionally as the professional association for both state park professionals and federal park employees. Park and recreation professionals at the local and regional levels with a natural resource orientation were also attracted to this association.

The Izaak Walton League was established in 1922 as a national citizen-conservation organization working for the wise use and conservation of natural resources. The league has consistently spoken out for the preservation of resources for recreational use. In the late 1940s Joseph Penfold, the western representative of the league, recognized the need for a nationwide inventory of outdoor recreation resources. Through his efforts and with the help of the Sierra Club, the groundwork was laid for congressional support of the Outdoor Recreation Resources Review Commission, established in 1958.

The National Industrial Recreation Association was incorporated in 1941 in the state of Illinois. It serves as a national clearing house for the dissemination of information and ideas on employee recreation for about 800 member companies in the United States and Canada.

Several nonprofit organizations have consistently spoken out for improved recreation opportunities. Among these have been the Conservation Foundation established in 1949 and Resources for the Future organized in 1952 under a grant from the Ford Foundation.

The International Recreation Association was established in 1956. During its early existence the association was given financial support from the National Recreation Association, but in recent years it has relied on contributions and memberships. In 1973 it changed its name to the World Leisure and Recreation Association.

In 1965 the National Recreation and Park Association (NRPA) was created by the merger of five national professional and service organizations: the American Association of Zoological Parks and Aquariums,

Figure 10. The preservation of natural resources for use by all ages has been greatly enhanced by professional and service organizations. (National Park Service photo.)

the American Institute of Park Executives, the American Recreation Society, the National Association of State Park Directors, the National Conference on State Parks, and the National Recreation Association. This was a milestone in the history of the movement, and part of its significance was explained in the following statement by LaGasse and Cook:

> The broad park and recreation field has moved through three phases: (1) the state of unity, when recreation was pursued on the estates of large land holders without thoughts of whether it dealt with parks; planning and design; recreation; or forestry, wildlife, and related national resources; (2) the stage of separation when those in organized recreation, parks, and forestry, pursued their individual fields of endeavor with little thought for the others; and (3) the stage of moving the three streams of development toward unity.[2]

As shown in the list of related organizations in Chapter 15 of this book, it is apparent that a large number of other organizations exist which have some interest and influence relative to the recreation and park movement. A review of that chapter will give additional insight into some of the organizations mentioned in this section, and it will enlarge our view of the total organizational involvement in the recreational and park field.

GOALS OF THE PROFESSION

In one sense a profession may be defined as an occupational field which requires a high level of educational preparation, depends primarily upon the effective use of the mental and communicative processes as opposed to manual skills, is based on a substantial and carefully organized body of knowledge, and is perpetuated by unified objectives and professional commitments by its members.

One of the distinct characteristics of a profession is a broad commitment by its members to certain fundamental values or objectives. While it is not necessary or even desirable for everyone to think alike at all times, the members of a profession are certainly obligated to agree upon central purposes. Such agreement gives direction and meaning and provides the unity which is essential to the growth and development of the profession and the purposes that it serves.

Socrates stated, "If a man does not know to what port he is sailing, no wind is favorable." The challenge of having clear direction has obvious pertinence to the individual leader because his worth will be no greater than the values he seeks. Further, leaders with unsound values not only tend to be worthless but are potentially dangerous. If a professional field is to avert floundering by its members and organizations, and avoid serious conflicts relative to purpose and direction, it must have some clearly yet broadly stated guidelines along which to progress.

Fortunately a Commission on Goals for American Recreation was established in 1964 by the American Association for Health, Physical Education and Recreation. The commission consisted of outstanding leaders from throughout the nation, and they prepared six stated goals which have had significant impact. It is important for students preparing for this professional field and for those already in the field to know of these goals, and condensed descriptions of them follow.

Personal Fulfillment

It is natural for people to be motivated by the basic need for adequacy and self-enrichment. Nobody wants to be a nobody; each individual wants to see himself as accepted, able and successful. The extent to which this need is met is a measure of personal fulfillment, and the lack of fulfillment often contributes toward frustration and maladjustment.

Since the American democratic ideal emphasizes the importance of the individual, it follows that the welfare of the individual and his personal development should be of primary concern to public and private agencies that serve people. In accordance with this concept, the paramount purpose of recreational activities is to enrich the lives of people by contributing to their fulfillment as individuals, while at the same time helping them to fit more comfortably into the social structure.

One of the foremost challenges to leaders in the recreation profession is to provide experiences through which the individual may enjoy success in search of self-esteem. It is the task of a leader to assist participants in the development of skills and interests which enrich their lives and result in true satisfaction.

Democratic Human Relations

There are at least three important reasons why recreational activities should contribute to the characteristics of citizenship in a democratic society such as ours.

1. Exclusive emphasis on goals focused primarily on the individual may result in the creation of selfishness and noncooperation. Recreation agencies, along with other institutions in society, have the responsibility of helping to develop those characteristics of good citizenship that are essential in the existence and perpetuation of democracy.

2. In the United States a recreation agency is a social institution. Therefore, the leaders are under obligation to seek and foster social, moral, and ethical values that will preserve and strengthen our democratic ideals.

3. Recreation leaders are unavoidably involved in the conduct of activities the outcomes of which go far beyond fun, relaxation, and immediate fulfillment. As do other experiences in life, recreation influences the personality and behavior in a variety of ways.

Leisure Skills and Interests

Several research studies support the claim that people use their leisure time in skills and interests developed early in life. There is also evidence that what people like at age 25 they will like better with increased age, and what they dislike at age 25 they will dislike more as they grow older. Of course there are exceptions to this rule, but it does define quite a strong trend. Recreation leaders have a definite obligation to be motivators and teachers of desirable interests and skills, cultivating in people tastes for beauty and art, music, dance and literature, helping them to achieve excellence in sports and games and to enjoy the beauty of nature.

It is no coincidence that the words "skill" and "interest" appear together often. Skill is the foundation on which interest is built, and interest leads to the further development of skill. In their leisure time people do, if opportunities are available, what they like to do, and they often like to do what they do well. A high degree of skill in a wholesome activity is the best single guarantee of interest. Not many people, for example, are clamoring to demonstrate their ineptness in tennis, golf, art, music, ballroom dance, or swimming. Plenty of evidence supports the claim that people repeat those experiences which are satisfying and avoid those which are dissatisfying. Therefore, the development of skills, interests and appreciations in wholesome activities is fundamental to the well-rounded development of individuals and to the perpetuation of "the good life."

Health and Fitness

Prior to our mass motorized transportation system people walked most places. Today we ride automobiles with power brakes, power steering, power windows and power seats. Even on the golf course motorized carts have become a substitute for human energy. Elevators carry us upstairs, electric eyes open doors for us, we sit before the television screen an average of 16 hours per week. Too often we are involved in sports merely as spectators, and our most popular outdoor recreation is automobile riding for pleasure. Several degenerative diseases and general lack of efficiency have increased significantly with our modern sedentary living patterns.

In early history most people had no choice between the sedentary and active life. The necessities of survival forced them to be active. Modern man, however, does have a choice, because automation and technology have drastically reduced opportunities for vigorous exercise. Today 98% of the work done in the United States is by machines, 1% by animals and 1% by people. Automation is the handyman of the sedentary life.

An interesting aspect of active living is the contribution it can make toward mental health and emotional stability. Participation in pleasurable pursuits is important to the release of tension and mental stress. The challenge and the opportunity for the field of recreation are apparent. If our work does not supply us with the activity we need for good health and fitness, then this must be accomplished during leisure hours.

Figure 11. Bicycle routes enhance active participation in this wholesome activity. (Bicycle Manufacturers Association in America photo.)

Creative Expression and Aesthetic Appreciation

One of the important purposes of recreation is to stimulate and guide creativity that might otherwise never be tapped. Pursuits which relate to aesthetic values have great potential for giving zest to life. We need well-qualified leaders who are creative themselves, and who have the ability to stimulate others and to draw out of them their innate creative expression. With additional industrial and technological advances and with the dramatic effects of television, there needs to be greater emphasis on serenity, a condition which fosters thought and talent.

Environment for Living in a Leisure Society

The environment in which each of us recreates either alone or in association with others has a great influence on the quality of the recreation experience and its results. Today about three of every four Americans live in urban or suburban areas, and the trend toward urban living, both in numbers and percentages, is still rising. It has been predicted by the Bureau of Census that in the near future 80% of Americans will live in nonrural areas.

Among the tragedies of our time are the degradation and destruction of many of our natural resources, which heretofore sustained both body and soul. We have become too free in the use of tools and machines for converting resources into products for utilitarian ends serving only today's needs. This shortsighted approach has made its contribution to an artifical and culturally sterile environment, which serves less well the long-term needs of people. In the future we will have to guard with increased vigor against this destructive trend.

The recreational environment in the cities and suburbs is as important as that of the out-of-doors, and the problem of maintaining a highly livable level in the cities is even more difficult. In the future superior planning and leadership with respect to our physical environment will be even more important than in the past.

In a book entitled *Outdoor Recreation in America—Problems, Trends and Opportunities*, the present author stated five objectives for resource-oriented recreation.[3] These objectives were stated because of the lack of formulation of any such objectives by any recognized group or agency even though outdoor recreation had received a tremendous amount of emphasis during the years prior to the writing of the book. They pertain to only a portion of the total recreation and park field, yet it seems worthwhile to repeat them in this source. As a preface to the objectives the author pointed out that most resource management agencies involved in outdoor recreation have yielded to the pressures of public demand, sometimes with strong reservations and little long-term planning. Until recently very few agencies have taken aggressive and positive approaches to planning in advance of public demand, although each agency has its own objectives relative to its total program, of which recreation is only one part. The five objectives have been widely exposed, and hopefully they have given some direction to the agencies and individuals involved in the field.

1. *Develop appreciation for nature.* Today the majority of people in our urbanized society have limited opportunities for contact with the great outdoors. They have little chance to develop knowledge of and appreciation for nature's processes. Without such knowledge and appreciation it is difficult for people to become interested in the conservation and preservation of natural resources. For increasing numbers of people, the only contact with a natural environment occurs during outdoor recreation experiences on an occasional trip to the country or a visit to a nearby scenic or historic area. In view of this, it is important that outdoor recreation programs be aimed toward increasing people's knowledge of and appreciation for nature, and making them aware of the importance of sound conservation and preservation practices.

2. *Enhance individual satisfaction and enjoyment.* People participate in outdoor recreation primarily for joy and satisfaction. This contributes to happiness, the ultimate desire of all. Since people resort to the outdoors for satisfaction and joy, and since this achievement is desirable, then outdoor recreation agencies should try to enhance these qualities. Each agency involved in outdoor recreation ought to develop an aggressive program of identifying and developing those resources which have unusual potential for creating in people a feeling of satisfaction and well-being. Included should be areas which are significant from the standpoint of aesthetics, history, geology, archeology, biology (including wild life resources), and a certain amount of just "open space."

3. *Provide opportunity for diversion and relaxation.* For the most part people go to the outdoors to divert themselves from their usual rapid pace, routine patterns, and the restrictions under which they ordinarily live. Therefore, agencies should help them to achieve this much-sought-after diversion. This will become increasingly difficult as the number of users continues to increase at a rapid rate. In the outdoors, people must find opportunity to relax, to live at their own desired pace, to find time to identify their place in the scheme of things, and to renew and refresh themselves in preparation for a return to their usual patterns of living.

4. *Develop physical fitness.* The increasing lack of physical fitness has been recognized as one of the crucial problems facing the American society; and much emphasis is currently placed on remedying this situation. Many typical forms of outdoor recreation are vigorous in nature and tax participants far beyond their usual levels of performance. For instance, hiking, swimming, hunting, fishing, skiing, and camping often provide unusual physical challenges. In many instances, participants in such activities condition themselves to meet the occasion. Special attention should be given to promoting physical fitness through outdoor recreation. People should be encouraged to do a wholesome amount of hiking to points of interest and to participate in vigorous outdoor activities. The idea should be developed that in order to fully enjoy the outdoors one must become vigorous and somewhat "rugged."

5. *Develop desirable social patterns.* There was a time when if a man went to the outdoors he was alone, but for the most part those days are gone. Today the typical outdoor participant finds many people wherever he goes. Often he drives most of the way to his destination on a super highway where he passes thousands of cars in a day's drive. He fishes on a lake where boat traffic is so heavy that strict controls are required. He hunts where he sees more hunters than game, and each night he camps within a colony of other campers. The fact that today's outdoor recreationist must share his resources with many other people requires that desirable patterns of social outdoor conduct be developed. Attitudes of courtesy, consideration, and sincere interest in each other, must

be fostered. Each recreationist should recognize that others have come for essentially their own same purposes. Agencies involved in outdoor recreation must take the lead in stimulating desirable social conduct.

CHALLENGE TO THE RECREATION PROFESSION

Those who comprise this important profession will face much greater challenges in the future than in the past, because people today are attaching much greater significance to leisure time and they will expect more and better leisure time opportunities. This increase in expectations from the public, combined with increased financial and technical support from all levels of government, will place the recreation profession in an enviable position. In the future it is not going to be possible for people in the profession to sponsor and conduct pygmy programs amid giant opportunities, as has often been done in the past and which is still being done all too frequently. The public is not going to accept half-prepared, half-dedicated leaders who stumble through their responsibilities as if they related only to unimportant aspects of life. Leisure activities and the results they produce are going to be ever more prominent in the lives of individuals and communities.

In order to produce the kind of leadership that will be required, those teaching in college recreation curricula will have to be more thorough and penetrating in their study of the kinds of information and experiences that students need. Present options in the curricula will have to be more clearly defined and channeled more directly toward carefully thought out and well-defined objectives. The certification of recreation and park leaders will have to be accomplished on a broader scale than at the present. Further, procedures will have to be developed for the accreditation of professional preparation programs. As the profession becomes more prominent, and people's expectations of it increase, nonaccredited preparation programs will become less acceptable and noncertified leaders will become less employable.

REFERENCES

1. Jensen, C.: *Recreation and Leisure Time Careers*. Vocational Guidance Manuals, Louisville, 1976, p. 2.
2. La Gasse, A. B. and Cook, W. L.: *History of Parks and Recreation* (Bull. 56). National Recreation and Park Association, Arlington (Va.), 1965.
3. Jensen, C.: *Outdoor Recreation in America—Problems, Trends and Opportunities*. 3rd ed. Burgess Publishing Co., Minneapolis, 1977, pp. 8-10.

4

Conditions and Trends Which Influence Leisure and Recreation

Americans of only a few decades ago lived in a situation characterized by hard work on farms and in factories, comparative isolation from the rest of the world both in terms of transportation and communication, a simple morality and a simple social structure, relatively little government control, uncongested conditions in towns and small cities, a production-oriented economy, and a small amount of leisure time.

Today we live in a situation characterized by labor-saving machines which relate to a high level of technology and automation, more income for less hours of work, world integration in terms of transportation and communication, a complex social structure with enormous related problems, a population living predominantly in cities and suburbs, corporations and big business, big government and extensive government controls, a consumption-oriented economy, and a marked increase in leisure time. Change has followed change with bewildering rapidity—at no time in the history of the world have people lived under such changing conditions as Americans live under today.

Prior to the industrial revolution, which started in the mid-1800s, most people would enter and leave this life under circumstances that underwent very little change. Life-styles and living conditions were static. Once change started, however, it accelerated steadily; technology fostered industrialization, and in turn, industrialization fostered more technology. Step by step these two major influences contributed to a host of changes in practically all aspects of our lives. The trends toward still more technology and industrialization remain intact, and will apparently continue for the foreseeable future.

TECHNOLOGY

Technology is the development and use of mechanical devices and their energy sources. In our society, mechanical devices perform an increasing number of functions with unmatched precision and rapidity. Sophisticated computers, gasoline engines, electrical machines, and other such implements perform a phenomenal amount of work that results in the saving of human time and energy, and even influence how we use the time and energy they help us save. Comparing our present situation with the circumstances of previous societies, technical devices make it possible for each of us to have at our disposal the equivalent of 500 slaves. Visualize, for example, the amount of human energy that would be needed to propel an automobile 60 mph for one mile. Most of us drive an automobile several miles each day, and sometimes we drive several hundred miles in a day. Further, visualize the human energy that would be equivalent to the electricity used for running our refrigerators, disposals, electric lights, and heating or air-conditioning units over a 24-hour period. Think of the thousands of hours that would be spent making the calculations that can be accomplished on a computer in one hour. Even more impressive is the equivalent human energy spent by a four-engine jetliner streaking through space at 600 mph, or a 100-car freight train traveling at 40 mph.

These time- and energy-saving procedures are largely responsible for the increased leisure presently available. At the same time other technical devices influence how we use our leisure in recreational pursuits. For example, power boating and water skiing are newfound pleasures that depend directly upon technology. The same is true of downhill skiing, underwater motorized exploration, driving for pleasure, and

Figure 12. Technological advances have made snowmobiles available in large numbers for recreational use. (USDA Soil Conservation Service photo.)

recreation involving aircraft and off-road vehicles. Many other recreational pursuits are influenced less directly but substantially by the availability of electricity, better modes of travel to and from location, and new and better implements and objects involved in our varied forms of participation, such as sport implements, hunting and fishing equipment, etc.

Today American scientists can see real possibilities for developing service-free electric automobiles powered by lithium batteries, nonpetroleum aircraft fuel, abundant solar energy units for heating buildings, minicomputers that will be cheap enough to be in every office and almost every household, door locks which unlock at the sound of your voice and only yours, and controlled relaxation and sleep so that fewer hours will yield the same amount of rest. A technologist is truly a significant contributor to our life-styles both on and off the job.

AUTOMATION

Automation involves the use of mechanical or automated devices in the production of goods and services. Obviously it is closely associated with technology. The main influence of automation on recreation is in freeing people from long hours of manual labor, thus contributing to both voluntary and forced free time. Voluntary leisure time is that which a person earns through work and takes for his own choosing, whereas forced free time is the result of unwanted unemployment. These two kinds of time have widely different meanings for both the individual and society. It would be tasteless to refer to unwanted unemployment as leisure time, because this condition is not surrounded by the important characteristics of leisure. Thus, even though automation has had a generally positive influence on people's living conditions, its negative aspect is that it eliminates jobs and forces some people into new occupations or unemployment.

Producing an automated system does not merely mean replacing workers by machines to do the task that men and women once did. John Diebold,[1] one of our foremost authorities in automation, points out that an automated system is a way of thinking just as much as a way of doing. He states that in America it is no longer necessary to think in terms of individual machines, or even in terms of groups of machines. Instead, it is practical to look at an entire production as an integrated system and not as a series of individual steps.

Walter Reuther,[2] one of America's prominent labor leaders, believed that we would make more technical progress in the next 25 years than in the last 250 years. He felt that the new generation of computers coming on fast and strong did not allow us time to deal with the wholesale threat to job security already posed by automation, or to think through the revolutionary process of transforming a society based on work into a society which, if it is to remain democratic, must increasingly be given over to meaningful leisure. He foresaw complex computers that will be able to do a decade of work during a lunch break, with an impact felt not only by blue-collar workers but by skilled technicians as well.

The rapid increase of our work force while jobs are eliminated by automation causes our economists great concern. Robert Theobald[3] reminds us that in the past society claimed that its members were entitled to a living only if they carried on a task for which society was willing to pay. The creation of a society of abundance will make it possible to relax this requirement. Some people may be allowed to follow an interest they find vital even when society does not totally support it through the price mechanism. Needless to say this new mode will influence what we do for recreation, where we go for it and how much time we spend at it. The appropriate use of the time that people will have in the future because of automation will certainly present an interesting challenge to individuals and to leaders in all areas of the social sciences.

EDUCATION

In a general sense education can be defined as the preparation of individuals to live happily and effectively in society, and to contribute toward its improvement. This means that the content of education is strongly influenced by the values and living practices present in the environment, and by the knowledge and attitudes that people must have in order to perpetuate traditions and cultural values.

Education is of two general kinds, that which prepares a person to make a living and that which prepares him for living. We can be fairly sure that work in the future will be increasingly intellectual in nature, more highly specialized, more automated, and requiring more and better education. Occupational fields have become highly specialized and dependent upon thorough knowledge in specialized areas, while at the same time technology and automation have enhanced the teaching and learning processes so that people can now learn more expediently. Further, increased population and urbanization have caused a need for more and better social understanding and the pressures of our fast-moving society have brought increased attention to the psychological aspects of learning and adjustment. All of this has contributed immensely to the complexity of our educational system and to the need for a high percentage of young people to be successfully engaged in formal education. Further, people who are no longer young have been forced to pursue continuing education in order to keep abreast of their changing circumstances and to keep themselves employable.

A few decades ago only a small percentage of American youth completed high school. There was much less need for it then, and for most a college degree would have served very little purpose. Now about 87% of the school-age children and youth in America are enrolled in school, and more than 80% graduate from high school. Further, approximately 45% of our college-age youth are college students. The number of college degrees awarded sets a new record almost every year, and the number of master's and doctor's degrees is significantly higher than it was one or two decades ago. In connection with all of this it has been estimated that 80% of all of the highly specialized scientists that have ever lived are presently alive.

The vast changes that have taken place in our education have had, and are having, a significant influence on all aspects of life—including how we spend our leisure time and what we do for recreational fulfillment. In the future greater emphasis will need to be placed on education for the use of leisure.

MOBILITY

Traveling for pleasure has become one of the great American pastimes, and it can be a wholesome and developmental interest. Not only does travel represent a significant use of leisure time but it also enhances many other leisure activities by making it possible for people in large numbers to go where they need to go for participation in the activities of their choice.

Once it was extremely rare for an outsider to participate in a hunting expedition in Alaska. Now the number who travel to Alaska for this purpose has become so great that the supply of game is rapidly diminishing, and stringent controls are being placed on the harvest of game. Not many years ago the beaches of Hawaii and the Bahamas were sparsely used. Now, due largely to our great travel potential, many recreational areas in these locations are crowded almost to the point of congestion. Further, tourism by Americans to Europe, South Africa, Japan, Australia, New Zealand, Mexico, and numerous other places in the world has accelerated greatly during recent decades.

In terms of mobility closer to home, think of a picnic area in a nearby forest crowded with 300 visitors on a Sunday afternoon, with the average distance traveled being 20 miles. This amounts to 6,000 miles of travel for picnicking in a single location. It would not be unusual for 50,000 attending a single college or professional athletic contest to have traveled an average of more than 10 miles each for an accumulative total of 500,000 miles, the equivalent of 20 times around the earth. If it were not for our great mobility, Little League baseball could not continue, the beaches would not be nearly so crowded, the ski slopes would be almost vacant, museums would be sparsely visited and the major concerts would be fewer and poorly attended.

The automobile is the king of travel, being used to shuffle people about for all kinds of reasons and for a variety of distances. There are presently almost 100 million automobiles in America, enough so that the total population could be seated in them at one time with less than 2.3 persons per vehicle. Highways, roads and streets lace the landscape of almost the total nation.

In addition, people travel extensively by train, bus, ship and aircraft. Aircraft is the second most prominent mode of travel, and this dramatic form of transportation is growing the fastest in terms of percentage. The 600-mph jetliner has revolutionized our travel ability. It is an exciting fact that people who have the means can now travel to almost any well-developed area on earth in a day's time.

Cruises by ship to places of recreational and scenic interest now surpass transportation by ship for other reasons. Cruises in areas of the Mediterranean, Caribbean and other scenic locations are becoming increasingly popular. Further, in many locations high-speed surface-skimming vessels transport people on short runs in numerous special-interest locations. Riding one of these vessels is an exciting recreational experience in itself.

Metros and rapid train systems are either under construction or in the planning stages in several of our larger cities. In the future these mass transportation systems will shuffle people here and there around metropolitan and megalopolis regions at a greatly increased rate. Further, it is predicted that not too long from now *fast trains* which skim over a thin layer of air at 200 mph will be in use in the United States.

It is also true that in the future a single-person jet air unit for recreational travel into outer space and to the depths of the sea is within the realm of probability.

INCOME

Few aspects of life in America are more impressive than the tremendous amount of goods and services produced by our population. Americans today are financially richer than ever before, as indicated by the fact that the per capita income for every man, woman and child in the entire nation exceed $5500 annually. This represents an increase of approximately $2000 per capita in the last six years.

Certainly the purchasing power of each of us has not increased to this degree, because of the offsetting effects of inflation, but it is true that on the average Americans have slightly more purchasing power this year than last year, and the people of this era are financially better off than the people of any other era in recorded history. We are more able to buy goods and services of all kinds and for all reasons now than at any time in the past, and part of the goods and services that we buy are related to the uses we make of our leisure time.

In order to get a more complete picture of the improvement in financial status of Americans, consider these facts. In 1930 the average income per person was $1224 and by 1940 it had increased only $53, to a total of $1277. By 1950 per capita income had reached $1676, in 1962 it was $2016, by 1965 it had reached $2300, and in 1970 it was $3200. In the six-year span from 1970 to 1976 per capita income made a phenomenal leap from $3200 to $5500 per year.

Fifty percent of all families in America currently enjoy incomes in excess of $12,000 per year, and 25 percent have incomes of $15,000 or more. However, there are also those on the lower end of the income scale. In 1976 an estimated 10 million families received incomes of $4000 or less. These families represented about one-fifth of the total population.

Additional income per individual and per family has resulted in greater expenditure in all phases of life, but the greatest increase in spending has been on nonessential goods (luxuries) as opposed to food, clothing and shelter. Only a certain amount of money is required for food and clothing, and this amount does not change a great deal as salary improves; as income increases a greater proportion can be spent on special-interest and luxury items.

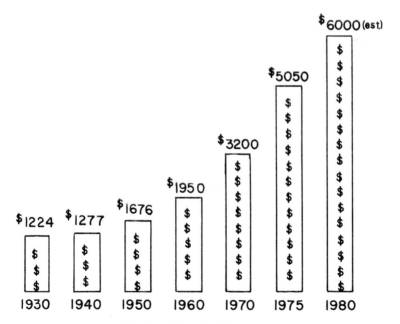

Figure 13. Trends in actual income per capita.

Certain forms of recreation have become possible and even popular because of our increased financial means. Among the more apparent examples are snow skiing, which is an expensive sport and one that is increasing in participation at the rate of 16% annually. Off-road vehicles have boomed in America, as have snowmobiles, camp trailers, power boats and sail craft, and a host of other expensive items that people use for leisure pursuits. Further, financial means have greatly enhanced travel both to nearby and faraway places. Today we can do many things that people could not afford previously, and we have developed an attitude toward doing them. We have become a consumption-oriented society.

POPULATION AND URBANIZATION

There are presently more than 220 million people in the United States. At the time our nation was born in 1776 there were less than 3

Figure 14. Expensive recreational equipment is one of the results of our improved economic status. (National Park Service photo.)

million. By 1850 the number had increased to 25 million. Then during the next half century (to 1900) the population increased to 85 million. During the first half of the twentieth century (1900-1950), it almost doubled to reach 151 million, and during the next 27 years it increased by almost 70 million. During the last few years, the percentage rate of growth had reduced significantly, and is presently only about half as great as it was 10 years ago. However, a small percentage applied to a large population still results in a large increase in number, about 3 million per year—an annual increase approximately equal to the total population at the time of the Declaration of Independence.

Approximately 75% of our population live in urban and suburban areas. This clustering together of people to form metropolitan areas and megalopolis regions has a significant influence on our life-style. Even though we are highly mobile we still live primarily in our immediate environment. If the environment is crowded or semicrowded, as it is for most Americans, then these are the conditions under which we do most of our work, our socializing and our recreational activities.

Urbanization has changed the social aspects of life in America by forcing us to live close together and to try to be compatible under these conditions. A much greater need for organized recreation activities of all kinds has developed. Further, urbanization has contributed to the need for structured or improved recreation facilities such as city parks and play fields, museums, recreation centers, concert halls and the like.

In addition, the increased population has required that the natural resources which have prime features for recreation—beachfront areas, wild and scenic rivers, attractive forest groves, and other places of special outdoor significance—be identified, acquired and set aside for present and future recreational use. As population and urbanization continue to increase, and they most certainly will, the influences that these factors have had on recreation will become more intense as a greater number of people occupy the same land area, causing the population density to increase.

While the general trend toward urbanization has been under way, some major changes have also occurred within the urban complexes; these changes will continue. The old and central portions of the cities have grown little in recent decades; indeed, some have lost population. In contrast the surrounding suburbs have expanded rapidly. Almost everyone in the United States has firsthand experience with some area of land which was a farm or a forest a decade ago and today is covered with houses, a shopping center or an industrial complex. Further, these population shifts from country to city and from central city to suburb have been highly selective as far as race, age income, education, and other characteristics are concerned.

Because of the large and sprawling suburban developments, some metropolitan areas are taking on dimensions of 100 miles or more. These are known as megalopolis regions, a term used to define an area where several metropolitan districts have grown together. In the foreseeable future the Atlantic seaboard, the Great Lakes region and the Pacific Coast area extending from San Francisco to San Diego will take on megalopolis characteristics.

In spite of the advantages enjoyed by urban dwellers, there is much criticism of large cities as places to live and to work. They are often attacked for their ugliness, lack of order and unity, congestion, poor sanitation and lack of open space. They are often breeding places of disaffection and violence. In many of our large cities, the central core suffers from blight. Furthermore, movement into the city for work and away from it for recreation and other qualities of good living causes severe transportation problems.

The number of people living in urban areas is expected to double during the next 30 years. The open spaces currently surrounding cities will turn into suburban developments with greater emphasis on condominiums and apartment complexes. Some of the present suburbs will incorporate high-rise apartments. Single-family units will become very costly and the lots will be small. Nature and its inspiring environment will become more remote from the day-to-day lives of people, which will tend to become more artificial (less related to nature and nature's processes). Social structure will become ever more complex, making social problems more prevalent and more difficult to solve.

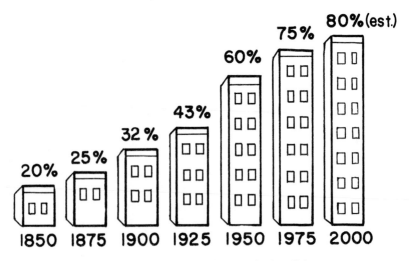

Figure 15. Trends toward increased urban living.

WORK AND LEISURE

The desire for increased leisure has become a reality of modern life in America. The former Secretary of Labor of the United States J. D. Hodgson has stated:

> Tremendous shifts in the work life of the average man or woman have occurred during the past century, with the result that the time free of the necessity of earning a living has increased spectacularly. The "sunup to sundown" working day, which was generally standard in the early 1800's, is now as rare as the horse-drawn buggy. . . .
>
> The American worker sees in leisure time the opportunity for a fuller life—an opportunity that his forebears were denied. Now that it is within his reach, he fully intends to make the most of it.[4]

While the average work week for Americans continues to shorten, leisure grows more rapidly than does our capacity to use it intelligently. Most Americans now work 40 hours or less per week. Compare this to the average work week of approximately 72 hours a century ago. Also, a hundred years ago we were still primarily an agricultural society, with the great majority of the population living in rural settings and devoting their work efforts to the agricultural industry. Now agriculture involves only about 10% of the work force of America, and only about 8% are actually farmers. The great shift from agricultural employment to industry and commerce is the main force that has caused America to become largely urbanized.

The trend toward less hours of work per week is still intact, but is moving at a slower rate than during recent decades. In the near future many workers in the *labor groups* will move to work weeks of less than

Figure 16. Mass urbanization has caused many problems, one of which is the provision of adequate space for recreational opportunities.

40 hours—36 hours and later 32 hours per week. Management and professional personnel will probably not experience such decreases in work hours until later, but even for these occupational groups the trend will probably continue. All members of the work force can expect more holidays, more vacation time, and earlier retirement.

Resources for the Future Incorporated projected that the average work week in America in 1985 would be 38 hours and in the year 2000 36.8 hours.[5] Cahn and Weiner predicted that by the year 2000 the work week will have declined to 31 hours,[6] and the National Planning Association in their 1967 projection supported this same idea.[7]

There is presently some experimentation among certain occupational groups with the four-day 40-hour work week. Working four 10-hour days instead of five 8-hour days would reduce the amount of travel time and expense and would result in a three-day weekend. A reduction in travel would help the gasoline shortage problem, traffic congestion, and pollution from automobiles. Those who favor three-day weekends claim that (1) families would have more time together, (2) there would be opportunities for more worthwhile leisure projects, and (3) increased job efficiency and better morale would result. Whether any of these advantages would actually occur only time and experimentation will tell.

It is interesting that four kinds of leisure are built around the work schedule: daily, weekly, annual, and retirement leisure. *Daily leisure* is represented by the amount of time left over each day after economic and biological requirements have been met. For the typical American this amounts to about four hours (24 hours − 8 hours of work and 12 hours for sleeping, eating, commuting, etc. = 4 hours). This four-hour period is choosing time, time when a person can participate in recreation of one kind or another, do service projects, or whatever else he chooses.

Weekly leisure is represented by the weekend. This period of two or three days permits involvement of time on a much different basis than a few hours a day.

Annual leisure is represented by vacation time, and full-time employees in America average about three weeks of this kind of leisure each year. Obviously certain forms of leisure time activities can be entered into during this time that are impossible during weekends or daily leisure periods.

The fourth kind of leisure is represented by *retirement*. Most people in America now retire from their regular occupations at about age 65, and some retire several years earlier. The trend toward earlier retirement is still progressing, and sometime in the not-too-distant future most people will be retiring by age 60. The average American now lives slightly more than 70 years. Many die before retirement, but those who reach retirement age live an average of eight to nine years beyond that age. Therefore most people reaching retirement age will have several years of leisure time on their hands, and some of them will have two or three decades. The cumulative affects of the gradual increases in these four forms of leisure will certainly have a significant impact on the amount of choosing time that people will have in the future. In turn this will have a marked affect on the amount and kinds of recreational opportunities that will need to be provided.

There has been, and currently is, a transition from older work attitudes among young people relative to work and leisure. Today many teenagers and young adults are hesitant to make early commitments toward work. They are more committed toward keeping themselves free to travel and experiment—to learn more of themselves and their environment. However, many middle-aged and older Americans find this unacceptable.

Another interesting light on contemporary work is the fact that, with assembly line procedures resulting in piecemeal forms of work, many workers never see the finished product. This is damaging to the workers' egos, and causes them to try to find compensating satisfactions in off-the-job activities. Traditionally, people's egos have been stimulated to expand through work, and for many people work has been the main satisfaction in life. Creative, challenging and meaningful work has long been one of man's significant needs. Fortunately, this is

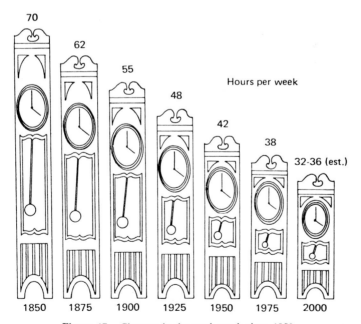

Figure 17. Changes in the work week since 1850.

still true to a large extent, but, because of the segmented character of much of our work, combined with increased opportunities for fulfillment during off-the-job hours, it is less true now than it has been in the past.

Time, whether involved with work or leisure, cannot be stored or saved or consumed at a rate faster than it is produced. Rich men have no more time than poor men, and no less. Like all other forms of time, leisure time must be consumed either by doing something or by doing nothing. For those with both affluence and leisure, who are anxious to put every moment to use, there are simply too many things to do. Overwhelmed by available goods and services and driven by an at-

Figure 18. Lawn bowling provides an interesting recreational outlet for many retired people.

titude of business, too many of us try to do too many pleasurable things at once. This is a condition known as "pleasure blindness."

Staffan Linder, a professor at the Stockholm School of Economics, stated "One may possibly buy more of everything, but one cannot conceivably do more of everything. To belong to a golf club as well as a sailing club is to spend half of one's time going from one to the other, and the other half observing all the social amenities that they entail." [4] Further, he points out that, because of the cost of belonging to both, one has to work more and has less time to enjoy either. Linder reminds us that Ralph Waldo Emerson stated, "If I keep a cow, that cow milks me." Linder argues that the same holds true of extravagant material possessions for use during leisure time. People become slaves of their possessions instead of creative users of their leisure. All of us know some people whose material goods for leisure enjoyment (boats, campers, snowmobiles, ski equipment, etc.) are so extensive that their lives are dominated by working more hours to pay for them. Certain people fall into this pattern because their pleasure is in possessing; the joy of participation is not one of their main objectives.

CHANGES OF ATTITUDES

Despite the many urgent problems that have accompanied the onset of technology and automation, these factors in our lives have brought with them a leisure mode which is taking its position in the usual evolution of events that occur in the development of a highly structured society. We have progressed from a state of feudalism based on a stable agricultural society, through industrialism based on a system of mass production, to a highly livable era characterized by more freely disposable time, money and materials than at any time in history. This additional time, money and materials offer new potential for service, creativity and further advancement of civilization.

Many people today accept the idea that the role of work is to make us masters of life's conditions, hence its constant discipline is essential to our grasp of reality. It is the function of work to provide us with a living, not necessarily for enlarging our capacities to consume but liberating our capacities to create. Release from excessive work affords us the opportunity to expand our horizons and involve ourselves in enriching experiences that otherwise would be impossible. Having been gradually liberated from the utilitarian process that for ages impoverished cultural and creative development, we find ourselves in an environment of new opportunity for personal enrichment and service to society.

There are social and psychological implications which relate to our adjustments to this new condition, because leisure and recreation have traditionally been viewed with suspicion and sometimes condemnation, while work has always been held as one of the higher values of American life. We have traditionally been influenced by the Protestant ethic that through work, man serves God and gains the essential values of the good life. Moreover, work has traditionally been associated with more than material accomplishments or economics. It has been a source of social and moral recognition.

Even though the attitudes of most people today, particularly the more responsible people, do not and should not minimize the values of work, they do include a greater appreciation for leisure and worthwhile recreational pursuits. The present attitudes as contrasted to previous attitudes are in essence a recognition that leisure time will become increasingly abundant, and as it does it will afford additional opportunities to the masses of the population to live fuller and more enjoyable lives. This will gradually but steadily increase the demand for leaders in the field of recreation and parks who have insight into the "good life," who know the needs of people and society, and who have the initiative and creativity to help large numbers of people achieve the qualities that contribute toward enrichment and satisfaction.

DETERIORATION OF OUR ENVIRONMENT

The interior portions of many of our large cities are old, poorly maintained, and polluted. Their deterioration has been a major cause of large population shifts, with the more affluent families moving out of the heart of the cities to suburban areas, and leaving the inner cities to the poor and the uneducated. The deterioration process is self-perpetuating, because replacement of the upper- and middle-class citizens by poor citizens contributes to further deterioration. The only curb to this trend is aggressive redevelopment action on the part of community agencies. Fortunately, there has been an awakening to this problem, and in many cities it is being dealt with more effectively than in the past. Community development and urban renewal projects, many of them partly financed by the federal government, have had a marked positive influence, but unfortunately many of them have not approached their expectations and some of them have proved outright failures.

The quality of our environment outside of the cities, particularly the "great outdoors," has also become a major issue, especially during the past two decades. This will continue to be a difficult issue because of the increased pressures that will continue to build up from population growth. The simple acts of experiencing natural beauty, breathing clean fresh air, and finding a reasonable amount of solitude can in themselves be cherished leisure time experiences, yet these experiences have become rare for many Americans because their environment has become noisy, ugly and polluted.

Pollution of the land, air and water is caused by people and the things that people do. Therefore, the only long-term solution to the environmental problem, both in our urban and outdoor areas, is to change the behavior of people. Just as we have polluted our environment, we can also depollute it. The depolluting process in many instances is going to be very expensive and it will take more time than most people want it to take. Prevention of pollution and depollution procedures will have to be built into all aspects of production systems and living patterns, and these procedures will have to be accepted, enforced and paid for, whatever the cost may be, because there is no other acceptable alternative. The trend toward pollution must be reversed.

Recreation and park agencies can play a major role in making both city and country life more livable. Not only can the leaders in the field help provide the needed areas but they can also stimulate and guide the establishment of policies and controls needed to combat pollution of the environment. This kind of leadership is one of the most significant responsibilities of recreation and park personnel.

Figure 19.   Too many people in too little space result in a certain form of poverty, whether in a neighborhood, a schoolground, or a national park.

PARKS AND OPEN SPACE

At the crux of the successful provision of parks and open spaces is the timely identification and acquisition of areas which have high recreation potential, in view of both their natural features and population concentrations. The overcrowding and congestion presently experienced in some of our large cities must be avoided in the development of new urban and suburban areas, because those areas will eventually become parts of large cities. It is urgent that adequate open space be acquired during the initial development of these areas, since once the space is filled with expensive structures it has become committed on a long-term basis. The lack of advance planning and timely acquisition always results in a big price to be paid by those who live there, both now and in the future. Of prime importance is the passage of needed land-use legislation, which in most areas is vital to the proper handling of pressures of industrialization, urbanization and population growth.

With respect to the great outdoors, it will be necessary for outdoor recreation planners to find methods of serving more people with basically the same amount of resources. This will be extremely challenging in the case of certain kinds of resources, such as fish and wildlife and nonrenewable natural phenomena such as those often found in national parks. An area can be utilized to a certain degree before it becomes impossible to preserve it in anywhere near its original state. Because of this there are already serious conflicts between the advocates of the use concept and the preservationists in many areas. Some resources, such as forests and fish and game, are renewable, given enough time, while other resources are absolutely nonrenewable. For instance, the Indian ruins in Mesa Verde National Park, the geysers in Yellowstone, the natural arches in Arches National Monument, and the Civil War trenches in several historical sights in the east could never be replaced. As a result areas within the national parks system are administered under the preservation concept, meaning that the resources are to be used but still preserved in their present state indefinitely for the enjoyment of the people.

Visits to national parks alone have more than doubled in the last 20 years and they are expected to double again in the next 25 years. Integrating this trend with the preservation concept in a workable combination is going to be increasingly more difficult.

Another matter that will continue to cause problems and heated discussions is the use of off-road recreational vehicles. In many instances these vehicles have become so damaging to the environment that additional regulations will have to be vigorously enforced in order to make their use acceptable.

Meeting the recreational needs of a growing and urbanizing society will continue to receive major emphasis from many quarters. Private citizens, working cooperatively with local, state and federal officials, will need to unify their efforts even more effectively in the future to meet the rapidly increasing park and open space needs of the people. Failure to successfully accomplish this would be disastrous to the protection of our environment, the development of our towns and cities, and the perpetuation of a desirable life-style.

VIOLENCE, VANDALISM AND REBELLION

Crime of practically all kinds is at an all-time high in America. Vandalism has increased at an alarming rate, to the point that in some localities it has become a major loss factor. Arson, deliberate breakage, and littering have made it necessary to close or severely restrict the use of some parks. Budgets for repairs have had to be increased, and sometimes personnel shifted from one locality to another, determined by ethnic factors.

Most vandalism is caused by juveniles. The widespread use of drugs and alcohol among young people has been a contributing factor to violence and vandalism, as well as being a problem in itself.

THE ENERGY CRUNCH

It appears certain that as time goes on we will face greater restrictions on certain forms of energy because of shortages of energy-producing raw materials and the need for additional control of the pollution that results from energy-producing processes.

This means that we are going to have to develop more conservative attitudes toward our uses of energy resources, and to some extent we will have to change our life-styles to accomodate energy conservation. In the meantime new and different sources of energy will be discovered and cultivated. Automobiles powered by electricity or hydrogen fuel will gradually replace gasoline-powered cars, solar energy will be captured for the heating of homes and other buildings, and several other known sources of energy will be perfected for everyday use.

In recent years a large number of motels, resorts, restaurant and travel agencies have lost business because of energy shortages, particularly of gasoline. Travel has been somewhat curbed by flight cancellations, the closing of filling stations, and the significant increase in cost of fuel. As a result, many would-be travelers have stayed closer to home, thus spending more of their leisure time and resources in close-to-home activities.

An associated factor, tight money, has also placed some restrictions on the development of new commercial recreation enterprises, and this has resulted in a greater load on the available facilities. The tight money problem fluctuates, but it appears that the energy shortage will be with us indefinitely.

THE NEED FOR MORE ACTIVITY

In the relatively short span of about 50 years the automobile and other modes of mechanical travel have so altered our way of life that walking, the most natural mode of locomotion, now seems almost incredible—yet a sufficient amount of walking each day is a healthful form of exercise for all age groups.

Motorized travel is not just a mechanical replacement for walking. It represents an entirely new attitude and a new set of customs, and it has ushered in an era of physical inactivity. Our passion for passivity extends even into sports, robbing some of them of their healthful characteristics. The golf cart, the power boat, and the trail bike are only three of numerous examples that could be given. We have become so engrossed with television that a major portion of our leisure time formerly spent in more active pursuits is now spent watching television. Further, remote control is making it unnecessary to leave the comfortable cushioned chair to change television stations. Where will it end?

All of these changes have been too swift for the human organism to adjust. Over many thousands of years, since before the dawn of civilization, our bodies have been geared to extensive physical activity. Now with dramatic suddenness that functional pattern has been broken, and our muscular and supporting systems are largely unemployed.

Certainly our technological advances are desirable, and they represent progress, but we must be intelligent enough to adjust our living practices to compensate for the disadvantages that accompany the advantages which afford us this new life-style. To do this we must recognize that our muscular system, as well as other systems of the human body, adheres to the *law of use* in a manner exactly opposite to that of mechanical devices. In the case of the human body the systems develop with use and deteriorate in the absence of use. In other words, the functional level of the organism as a whole, and of each specific physiological system, is influenced positively with use, whereas deterioration occurs when the systems are not used sufficiently.

The basic changes in life-style toward mechanization have not been concluded. The trends toward more conveniences to reduce the amount of exercise in our daily lives will continue. Leaders in the recreation and park profession are in a prime position to help combat the problem of physical inactivity. They can set examples, orient people toward the need for fitness, and provide many useful opportunities for wholesome and vigorous activity.

REFERENCES

1. Diebold, J.: *Automation: Its Impact on Business and Labor*. National Planning Association: Planning Pamphlet No. 106. Washington, 1969.
2. Reuther, W.: Freedom's time of testing. Saturday Review, August 29, 1964.
3. Theobold, R. L.: The man with the pencil of light. Saturday Review, August 29, 1964.
4. Hodgson, D.: Leisure and the American works. J. Health Phys. Ed. Recreat., 38-39, March, 1972.
5. Resources for the Future Incorporated: *Resources of American Future*. Johns Hopkins Press, Baltimore, 1963.
6. Cahn, X. and Weiner, X.: *The Year 2000*. Macmillan, New York, 1967.
7. National Planning Association: National Economic Projections Series Report 1967-nl. Washington, 1967.

5

Sociological and Psychological Implications

The world changes because the forces which cause social and technical change remake it day by day. These changes are not deliberately willed by us or thrust upon us, but result from events. Our discoveries and innovations keep the mainstream of change alive, and the mainstream of events causes numerous side effects that influence the lives of all of us.

New discovery and other forms of innovative change have three major phases—the creative idea, the practical application, and the diffusion through society. The time required for each of these phases is gradually shortening, and it is now recognized by psychologists and social scientists that the rate of change is perhaps a more pressing problem than direction of change. We have limits on our ability to adapt, and these limits are more closely related to speed than direction. The disorientation created by rapid technological and social change is uncomfortable to many and actually painful to some. Psychologists claim that many people in our society combat this problem by pretending that change really is not occurring, or that it is occurring at only a gradual rate, or that the changes that do occur will not affect them, when in reality the changes affect us all.

Patterns of human interaction and social stability are largely based on kinship, friendship, neighborhood and job associations, memberships in organizations and service relationships. Among these, recreation and park agencies have a significant potential for aiding people toward social satisfaction and social and psychological stability. When friendships and acquaintanceships are broken by job changes or relocation, assistance in creating an environment where new associations are readily possible is an important social service.

People must feel a sense of worth and a sense of belonging. It has long been recognized that group attachment and group unity can be effectively achieved through certain recreational activities. Even in

84

primitive societies use was often made of competitive activities and physical skills in important ceremonies and induction processes. To a large extent in our society, people of the past have had a sense of belonging and a feeling of worth fulfilled largely by significant work. Fortunately work will continue to offer this potential for many people in society, but it is a fact that technology and automation have helped to create many jobs that offer very little fulfillment. People occupying these positions strive harder than before to establish significance and a sense of belonging through off-the-job activities. Further, since all of us, on the average, have more off-the-job hours than our ancestors, activities that are engaged in during these hours make a greater contribution to our lives as a whole. Neal Maxwell expressed a meaningful statement in connection with this when he said in a speech:

> The thoughtful working person will provide some intervals between his tasks, like green belts of grass, trees, and water that we often need in our living environment to interrupt the asphalt. Each of us will be more effective if we plan some time for contemplation and renewal.

J. B. Nash also added meaning to the work-leisure relationship when he said:

> Work meets many of our psychological, social, spiritual and material needs. But we must also be recreated and maintain a healthy balance between work and play . . . recreation and work together contribute to fullness. To people who do not work, leisure is meaningless. To people who are over worked, leisure may become just as meaningless.[1]

The rhythm of life in our society has traditionally been based around the organization and accomplishment of work, and leisure opportunities have been geared primarily to this dominant rhythm—but not every person fits society's rhythm. Those who are cut off from life's normal rhythm find it difficult to enjoy the usual style of leisure. They may be the unemployed, the retired, minority blacks or Chicanos, or those whose jobs necessitate unusual hours. Their conditions of employment, cultural barriers, and ethnic factors sometimes render them incapable of full enjoyment of leisure. Society must find a way of better integrating such people into normal leisure activities.

The truly happy life is experienced by the person who responds with positive interests to a great range of objects, and who fulfills these interests by activities that bring enjoyment. If we were to sum up the good life in a few words, we would say that it is *the cultivation and fulfillment of positive interests* in which all the sides of man's nature— the volitional, intellectual, hedonic and passional—form a community, an organized unity, and in which all these interrelated parts are cultivated and fulfilled. *Self-actualization, which involves the fulfillment of a broad range of individual interests in recreation, is a prime value in life.*

SOCIAL ADJUSTMENT AND LEISURE ACTIVITIES

From one point of view the pursuits of leisure are great social levelers. Relationships of work are usually conditioned by job status, seniority, and graded expertise. In leisure activities these conditions are not usually so strong, and in ideal situations they are totally lacking. In leisure there is a possibility that relationships can be based upon shared interests without the artificial constraints of social and economic rules associated with job structure.

An important function of recreation is to improve the relationships among people of different racial, religious, or class backgrounds by giving them an opportunity to participate together in programs of mutual interest. Community recreation committees or neighborhood improvement associations may provide the medium through which people can express civic pride and community spirit. When the barriers of misunderstanding caused by lack of contact among people of different backgrounds are removed, intergroup relations may be markedly improved.

In addition, recreational programs may provide a medium for sharing customs, values, and folk traditions, thus helping to remove the stereotypes that account for much of intergroup hostility. In the early decades of this century, many social scientists characterized the American society as a "melting pot." Now it would appear that we seem to be achieving what has been called an American mosaic, in which citizens of different backgrounds maintain distinct subcultures (retaining national traits, customs, and values). Within such a mosaic, recreation can provide an ideal means for sharing folk culture and traditions while at the same time permitting each group within the society to retain its own pride and self-identity.

It is important to mention the significance of recreation as a means of establishing a healthy relationship between young couples in the casual precourtship dating of teenagers and young adults, and as an important activity of men and women during courtship itself and during the engagement period. The fun-filled activities of this period are useful as a means of becoming better acquainted, exploring common interests, and developing a natural and wholesome relationship, at whatever point of casual acquaintance or serious courtship a couple may be.

Very important also is the recreational life of young married couples who are in the preliminary period of adjustment. Changes are sometimes required in attitude and in relationships for their marriage to grow smoothly into the deep and fulfilling experience it should be. The light touch of fun and happiness in pursuing together pleasurable activities may be of importance in this period, as well as throughout the whole of married life. Married couples must always know how to have fun together.

Recreation fills a need of individuals for group association in uniquely satisfying ways because of both the pleasure that people get from the recreational pursuits themselves and the added pleasure from enjoying such pursuits in the company of others. The important role of competitive activities in recreation acknowledges the competitive strivings in individuals which define some of their social relations, and provides relatively benign forms for competitive expression. Human association in recreation also avoids much of the demand and strain of other associations, because of mutual interest and the pleasure each individual gains from the voluntary and pleasurable things he is doing with others, free from the requirements of many other associations.

A key value of organized recreation service is that it provides healthy and constructive outlets for many drives and interests which might otherwise be expressed in socially harmful or personally destructive activities. Venereal disease, drug addiction, compulsive gambling, and the highway accident rate are only four examples of the outcomes of the search for pleasure and thrills that dominate many in our society. Even though the mere provision of other forms of socially desirable recreation will not ensure that people will avoid harmful forms of play, it is essential that such alternatives be consistently provided.

Summing up, then, one of the purposes of recreation as a form of community service is to provide happiness and pleasure, to enable those of all ages and all conditions to enjoy their leisure in personally and socially constructive ways, to promote positive forms of social interaction in order to achieve community morale and a sense of unity, and to provide appealing alternatives to less desirable forms of activity.

RECREATION'S CONTRIBUTION TO HEALTH

Recreation is vital for the health of residents in American communities, both the overall population and those who have physical, mental, or social disabilities. Luther Terry, formerly Surgeon General of the U.S. Public Health Service, confirmed the value of recreation in this respect when he wrote of health as

> . . . the measure of man's capacity for coping with or adapting effectively to the physical, emotional, intellectual, social and economic demands of his environment. This is clearly a dynamic life process involving a variety of stimulus-response relationships. . . . Meaningful activity is important to health throughout the life span. In order to mature—physically, intellectually, emotionally, and socially—a child must be exposed to appropriate stimuli. And so too must the adult if he is to remain at his peak. Today, people are increasingly involved in leisure activity. . . . More and more people have time on their hands. Moreover, the injudicious use of leisure time is a characteristic feature of both maladjusted teenagers and adults, and of retired, elderly persons. Too often, because of ignorance, indifference, or inertia we are faced with the time-consuming and difficult task of reestablishing a human capacity which need never have been lost. Recreation has an important—and an increasing—role in rehabilitation.[1a]

A substantial number of mentally retarded individuals are believed to be the victims of environmental deprivation, in the sense that their initial disability has been seriously compounded by the lack of adequate stimulation, challenge, and instruction. Play, as a normal aspect of development, is often consciously lacking among retarded children. Stein writes:

> Mentally retarded boys and girls do not play spontaneously or innovate as normal children; they have to be taught to play whether the play be individual, parallel, or group. Many of the motor skills and abilities basic to play and recreation that most normal children learn from association and play with the gang on the block must be taught to the retarded.[2]

Several studies have explored the value of physical activity programs—including games and sports—for the mentally retarded. One study carried out in England by J. N. Oliver brought about marked improvement in athletic achievement, physical fitness, and strength (mentally retarded children are often poorly coordinated and obese), and also was responsible for an average 25% increase in I.Q. of its subjects.[3] Similar efforts with educable mentally retarded boys produced improved scores on the Wechsler Intelligence Scale for children after only 20 days.

Particularly in institutions which serve emotionally disturbed youth, recreation plays an important role in rehabilitation. Often it is found that disturbed youths who enter treatment centers are unable to play. Redl and Wineman write:

> It is . . . important that the institution as a whole and every person in it are openly and explicitly accepting of children having "fun." . . . By their very definition, our hyperaggressive and extremely destructive children are in need of a good deal of program activity which involves the happy discharge of surplus aggression, diversion of destructiveness into excited large-muscle activity.[4]

Such activities provide informal situations in which children can receive affection and trust from adults and begin to build ties of confidence and trust with them. They also provide situations in which children develop mechanisms for control of the group by its own members rather than always relying on the adult leader to stop misbehavior. Gradually, disturbed and delinquent youth learn to accept losing and failure with equanimity, to exert self-discipline, to have a sense of their own autonomy, and to place trust in others—and all these are purposes of recreational programs in such remedial settings.

People with disabilities have the same need for a full range of recreational opportunity as the nondisabled. Many disabled persons, however, are today unable to use public recreation facilities freely. According to the Bureau of Outdoor Recreation:

> Great numbers of disabled persons are not receiving the benefits of our nation's recreation resources. The severity of their disabilities, architectural barriers, nonacceptance by society, and slowness of the recreation profession to adjust its programs and facilities to their needs all have contributed to a serious lack of opportunity.[5]

Efforts have recently been made to provide full access to recreation facilities for persons with limited mobility and with wheelchairs, crutches, and braces. On the national level, the General Services Administration of the federal government has ordered that all new construction contracts permit easy access to the disabled, and the National Park Service and Forest Service are moving rapidly to make sure that the steps, curbs, doors, and other barriers of their hundreds of facilities are modified to permit entry to the handicapped.

Old people retain human needs and appetites, and if they are to be physically and emotionally healthy they must continue to have a full range of social and recreational opportunities which provide settings for friendship, social involvement, and creative activity. When these are not provided, many older persons tend to decline abruptly following retirement or serious personal losses.

One of the most important challenges facing us today is to make the lives of aging persons in the community as rewarding and happy as possible, to prevent disability, withdrawal, and institutionalization. It is particularly important that recreation activities for older persons be suitable for their stage of life, in terms of dignity and maturity. Too often, the programs provided in senior centers are juvenile and childlike. Often, the most meaningful activity may be in the area of community service, through which retired people with special skills help others. Such programs, which are often part of a total range of recreational and social activity, provide retired persons with a deep sense of satisfaction and continuing worth.

EMOTIONAL ADJUSTMENT AND STABILITY

During the early decades of this century, despite the growing interest in play on the part of many educators, it continued to be regarded by some authorities as an experience of dubious worth. For example, the 1914-15 edition of *Infant Care*, the official publication of the U. S. Children's Bureau, represented the infant "as a creature of strong and dangerous impulses":

> Playing with the baby was regarded as dangerous; it produced unwholesome pleasure and ruined a baby's nerves: "The rule that parents should not play with the baby may seem hard, but it is no doubt a safe one . . . . The dangerousness of play is related to that of the ever-present sensual pleasures which must constantly be guarded against."[6]

Gradually, however, in the decades that followed, the same publication came to regard play as natural and desirable, and it recommended that mothers play with their children. By the 1940s Ruth Strang, a leading child-guidance authority, was to write, "The play life of a child is an index of his social maturity, and reveals his personality more clearly than any other activity."[7] Similarly, two noted child psychologists, Gesell and Ilg, stated, "Deeply absorbing play seems to be essential for full mental growth."[8]

Psychologist Lawrence Frank wrote:

> Play, as we are beginning to understand, is the way the child learns what no one can teach him. It is the way he explores and orients himself to the actual world of space and time, of things, animals, structures, and people. Through play he learns to live in our symbolic world of meaning and values, of progressive striving for deferred goals, at the same time exploring and experimenting and learning in his own individual way. Through play the child practices and rehearses endlessly the complicated and subtle patterns of human living and communication which he must master if he is to become a participating adult in our social life.[9]

Another leading psychiatrist, Karl Menninger, who has pioneered in the use of play and recreation in the treatment of the mentally ill, views a well-rounded play life as essential in maintaining a healthy emotional balance. Play, in Menninger's view, provides the opportunity for many

Figure 20. An important purpose served by recreation is as an outlet for creative activity.

miniature victoriés which compensate for the injuries inflicted by the daily wear and tear of life. Under his direction, a study carried out at the Menninger Institute compared the hobby interests in the earlier lives of a number of seriously ill patients with those developed by a group of comparatively well-adjusted ones. It was found that the well-adjusted had pursued nearly twice as many hobbies as the maladjusted. Menninger comments that in his work with psychiatric patients he has consistently found them deficient in the capacity to play, and unable to develop balanced recreational interests and skills.[10]

The concern that has been widely developed in the United States about the value of play for emotional well-being has been strongly supported by a number of leading psychotherapists. Menninger has put it in these terms:

> If it were economically possible, beginning tomorrow, to relieve every man in the United States of half his present work requirements (or rather, his work opportunities) without decrease of income, the nation would be in peril. It would be absolutely impossible for the great majority of these people to utilize the suddenly acquired leisure in any psychologically satisfactory way, i.e. in play. *Some* of the energy thus released would undoubtedly be taken up with play, but most of it would be expressed in direct aggressiveness or in some form of self-destructiveness. People would begin fighting, drinking, and killing themselves and one another.[11]

Gans states the view that leisure and recreation are, comparatively speaking, relatively unimportant causal factors in achieving . . . mental health. He goes on, however, to describe "satisfying" leisure behavior as the kind of activity that provides the individual with physical and emotional relaxation, reduction of fatigue, restoration of energy lost elsewhere, and avoidance of activity with ill effects. He concludes:

> If satisfying leisure behavior as I have defined it is part of the good life, it would follow that it is a constituent part of mental health. Therefore, the recreation facilities which help to make leisure satisfying are necessary for the maintenance of mental health.[12]

EFFECTS OF PHYSIOLOGICAL IMPROVEMENTS

Numerous researchers have been suggesting that manipulations of physical fitness through a physical training program can be used to change psychological functioning in predictable directions. Although these studies contain a number of interpretational problems they have generally indicated that, as physical fitness increases, depression, anxiety and self-centeredness decrease and self-satisfaction and social adjustment increase; pertinent work includes that of Behrman, 1967; Cooper, 1968a; Hellerstein, Hornsten, Goldberg Burlando, Friedman, Hirsch and Mirik, 1967; McPherson, Paivio, Yuhasz, Rechnitzer, Pickard and Lefcoe, 1967; Popejoy, 1968; Stamford, Hambacher and Fallica, 1974.[13] These researchers would generally agree with

Ismail and Trachtman (1973) when they say ". . . physical activity can change the state of one's mind . . ." [13]

Many educators maintain that most adult Americans are illiterate physically. They know little about their bodies. They have never sensually experienced the thrills and feeling of confidence that come through physical activity. They lack confidence and self-assuredness when it comes to their bodies and how they are used. According to authorities in the field, this physical illiteracy is caused more by a lack of exposure and education in early movement activities than by incapacity.

New physical education programs in elementary schools are thus putting major emphasis on individual needs, individualized learning, and daily, year-round activities for all children. This approach is de-

Figure 21. Improving a child's skill has important implications physically, socially, and psychologically.

signed to give every child assistance in motor skill development, to adapt the classroom experiences and learning to every child's needs, not merely to those of the small percentage who eventually may become "athletes."

Visit a good elementary school today and you no longer find children standing in line to participate in some sport. They're moving! They're active! Time is being spent (at least 30 minutes a day) on activities that improve and develop coordination, that teach increasingly complex activity skills which give a sense of accomplishment and build self-reliance. Little emphasis is placed in the early years on competitive activities. According to Dr. Louis Browers,

> A child's self-image and his social interaction with others depends to a large extent on how he sees himself, his body, and what he can do with it. Through increasing the individual's range of movement, his control over his body in performance, and his confidence and interest in attempting new activities, he will perhaps see himself and others in his environment in a different light.[14]

Specialists have found that success in physical activities gives handicapped youngsters a sense of accomplishment, that such children are more likely to experience success in physical activities than in more complex social and vocational endeavors. In fact, they feel that without a foundation in basic motor skills and abilities, more complex learning skills are not likely to take place. In school systems with ideal physical education curricula, specialists work with young children to identify and correct perceptual motor lags. These corrective activities generally include body awareness exercises to develop muscle coordination, games such as tossing beanbags to develop eye-hand coordination, handclapping to specific rhythms to develop auditory response, sorting colored corn to develop small control. Most of the activities are designed so that all students succeed; there are no failures, only progress. Programs are primarily geared for learning readiness, to prepare children for normal classroom studies.

In reporting on the progress of one young girl in such a program the teacher said, "At the beginning of the year she seemed too shy to speak to her classmates. She appears to have a much better understanding of arithmetic concepts and really is doing quite well in our reading program. She seems much happier and has so much confidence in herself."

Participation in wilderness survival experiences has been found to be associated with a decrease in anxiety and socially maladaptive behavior (e.g. delinquency), and an increase in self-esteem (including perceptions of one's identity, self-satisfaction, behavior, physical self, moral-ethical self, personal self, social self, and value as a family member). The positive benefits of this rigorous physical and recreational activity were found to maintain themselves one year after the initial testing.[15, 16, 17]

INFLUENCE OF THE FAMILY

Waller and Hill stated some interesting observations about the family:

> The family is important in the life of the individual because it gets him first, keeps him longest, is his major source of cultural imperatives, and prescribes them with emotional finality.[18]

Cohen added further to the significant role of the family:

> Experiences in the family are the most important determinants of the frame of reference through which the child perceives, interprets and evaluates the world outside. And, the knowledge, habits, and skills which he acquires in the home help to determine his capacity for dealing successfully with situations outside.[19]

In the last several decades nearly every new force in our society has been instrumental in weakening family ties. Years ago it was nearly impossible to avoid contributing to and accepting from the daily lives of other members of the family. In early pioneer days, life was a cooperative family affair. The father farmed while the mother cooked and cleaned, the sister helped with the younger children, and the brother helped with the chores outside. Out of necessity, all family members were on the same team, working together to survive the hardships of the land. As a result, there was a keen sense of unity and belonging. When the work was done, leisure time was spent within the same closely knit circle, singing, reading, or playing games. The home was the center of educational, recreational and industrial life.

Families used to be bigger—not in terms of more children so much as adults: grandparents, uncles, aunts, cousins. Those relatives who didn't live with you lived nearby. You often went to their houses. They came as often to yours, and stayed for dinner. You knew them all—the old folks, the middle-aged, the older cousins—and they knew you. This had its good and its bad sides.

On the good side, some of these relatives were interesting people, or so you thought at the time. Uncle Charlie had been to China. Aunt Sue made the best penuche fudge on the block. Cousin Bill could read people's minds (according to him). And all these relatives gave you Christmas presents.

But there was the other side. You had to give Christmas presents to all your relatives. And they all minded your business throughout the years. They wanted to know where you had been, where you were going, and why.

The family is probably the most important structure in our society. Heaton states:

> All the organizations in the community cannot be much better than the family in which you were raised. You cannot rise much higher than the formative years which your family life has given you. The family leaves its mark upon you for life. The atmosphere of enjoying life and knowing what to do with it begins in the home.[20]

Statistics show that 60% of our interests were started below the age of ten and 70% started below the age of twelve, but where did we acquire these interests? An extensive survey taken by Nash showed that 70% of recreational interests started in the home, and in 44% of the instances the parents were the teachers. The survey showed that youth is the time to lay down basic behavior patterns, to learn skills that last a lifetime; the home is the place to learn new activities, and the home folks are the teachers.[21]

How does your family stand? Do you have a close relationship with other family members? Do you enjoy being together? How much love do you show toward one another? What could you do to make it better? Do you have more fun away from home than at home? A poll of 2,000 teenagers in Iowa revealed that 86% of the girls said they had more fun away from home. Yet it was also indicated that most of them added, a little wistfully, that they wished more home pleasures were available.[22]

Home is the strength of the individual, and each individual contributes to the strength of the country; this is why it is important to make home life a happy and growing experience. The success of the world depends largely on the success of each individual family. How do you have a successful home? Obviously you don't just get it; you have to make it. One important aspect is doing things together as a family, building memories and traditions, and being together as a unit. Recreation helps to strengthen family relationships by enriching the environment and content of family life. It helps point the way to solving problems which may exist between one another and toward making a happy home.

I am certain that practically all couples when starting their lives together share in many activities, and they too feel and know they are needed by each other. As time goes on and the length of their marriage increases, however, their interests diverge. This is supported by a statement made by Kenneth Cannon, "Some couples may be reasonably compatible at the start of marriage but change and development cause them to go in different directions or at different rates and in such development they lose their compatibility.[23]

Cannon goes on to say, "In a world as complex as this world is and where the everyday worlds of the marriage partners have less and less chance of binding themselves together, and where there are chances of turning elsewhere for the closeness that both partners desire and need, it is little wonder that divorce tends to be fairly common."[24]

Cannon believes that in urban families there tend to be no day-to-day activities which require husband and wife to share with each other. He feels this is a serious problem, and has theorized that sentiments (liking, love, etc.) among the members of a group are closely related to two other elements, sharing of activities and interaction (by which he means communication). He has the conviction that sharing of activities among group members is highly essential if they are to maintain close feelings of love and liking for each other.[25]

There are many ways in which wholesome recreation can help the family unit. The family that does interesting things together will be more likely to stay together. The child's memories of his family should be happy ones— memories that taught basic principles, and that brought him into the adult world with a feeling of satisfaction and accomplishment. The home should be a place where children learn to love and respect other people, by first learning to love and respect their family members. The home is a place where talents are learned, and a good self-concept is developed. The parents should analyze their children as well as participate with them so that they might understand and recognize the individual interests of each child.

Since the family is the basic unit of society, basic principles not taught in the home will probably not be taught at all. These principles are what the United States stands on—truth, honesty, responsibility, respect, and integrity—and should be learned in home situations. Also, when the family does things together as a unit the children are taught cooperation and respect for each other.

It seems little things that families do together are remembered as the most fun: a hike in the woods, an evening around the fire toasting marshmallows and talking, making a garden or building a birdhouse. Sons or daughters away from home are not likely to remember watching television as a fun family experience. They will remember the activities done as a family where cooperation, love, and happiness abounded.

Many people would be surprised at what can be learned from playing a game of basketball or touch football with family members. Children can learn importance of teamwork and cooperation as they figure out plays for their team. They can learn to be enthusiastic, and develop an appreciation for hard work. Further, they can learn good sportsmanship through proper adult examples. The parents can learn about their children through a game of basketball, observe their skill levels, and find out the skills the children don't have. When they discover what their children need, parents can better help them to improve.

DELINQUENCY AND CRIME

Two American criminologists, Sheldon and Eleanor Glueck, spent ten years in a study of the differences between 500 delinquent and 500 nondelinquent boys. Though they covered many aspects, the following is what they learned about family provisions for recreation:

> The poorer quality of home life enjoyed by the delinquents, as compared with the nondelinquents, is again revealed in the provisions made by the family for

recreation. Over half of the delinquents had no recreation facilities at home, except for an occasional book or toy. The same condition was found in 1 of 3 of the homes of the nondelinquents. Only 2 in 10 of the families of the delinquents permitted the boy to bring his friends home, while 4 in 10 of the other group of families did so. Only 1 in 3 of the families of the delinquents made a custom of having leisure-time activities that the whole family could enjoy together, as compared with 2 in 3 of the families of the nondelinquents. This reflects the lesser degree of family unity in the homes of the delinquents. When family unity is poor, a child is less likely to respect the parents' wishes or to show family pride.[26]

Ethel Shanas completed a significant research study some time ago wherein she stated in the findings:

> An analysis of the boys who committed delinquent acts during the period of the study revealed that those who attended supervised recreation committed fewer delinquent acts than those who did not attend. Nearly two-thirds of the delinquent acts were committed by boys who had no previous delinquency records. Of the nondelinquents studied, only 1.7% of those who participated in supervised recreation became delinquent during the period, whereas 5.1% of those who did not participate became delinquent. The proportion of the nondelinquents not in recreation who became delinquent was three times as high as the rate for nondelinquents in recreation.[27]

Defeat Produces Defeat

Numerous studies show that what matters most in producing a delinquent is not race, religion, or nationality; it is where the child grows up. Official delinquency data make it clear that children in disadvantaged areas of the city are more likely to become delinquent. The environment most apt to produce delinquency comprises a large city, a broken home, numerous children in the family, poor performance in school, and low economic and social status.

One important aspect of adolescence is to find out who one is, what one can do, and what one believes. Accomplishment of these primary tasks is much more difficult for a disadvantaged youth than for an advantaged youth. Among all the critical dimensions in which the disadvantaged differ from those enjoying advantage, none is more critical than the development of satisfactory self-image. The disadvantaged youth has difficulty in thinking well of himself. Often his physical and social environment conspire to convince him he cannot achieve any commendable goals. One learns to be successful by being successful; there is no other way. But for many disadvantaged youth success is a long time coming. Caught in the pressure cooker of poverty and social disorganization, the disadvantaged child grows up to expect defeat and frustration. He is rarely disappointed.

In the development of a stable and satisfactory self-image, adult models are important. The child is encouraged or discouraged in his development by people around him, and the people he associates with during his formative years help determine who he becomes. The child's life space is the home, the school, and the immediate community. If his home and school fail him, his only hope is the community. If the community fails to provide satisfactory models and opportunity for success, he soon learns to expect failure and frustration. He learns he is a nobody, decides he can do nothing, and believes the world is against him. Shortly this becomes a self-fulfilling prophecy.

A skillful and relevant recreation agency can do much for disadvantaged youth. It can provide suitable adult models. It can provide opportunities for young people to find out what they can do. It may help them learn what they believe, and, if it is particularly relevant and skillful, the agency may help them find out who they are. Disadvantaged youth are often dependent almost entirely on community sources for this kind of help.

If a youngster has friends that are delinquents, he will be more likely to become delinquent, too. Young people sometimes become delinquents because they are bored during their leisure time and are looking for excitement. If they do not find it in community approved activities, then they will look for it elsewhere, whether it be legal or illegal. With factors such as risk, and challenge to wit and speed, think of how a teenager can feel accomplishment if he "gets away with" some illegal act.

In order to understand the influence of recreation in helping to mitigate the extremes of delinquency, it is necessary to accept the truth that recreation of the right kind is a positive opportunity for growth and development and not basically a measure to correct social ills. The great potential of recreation is in the opportunity it provides for positive, personal development. It is not a time filler, but an avenue for self-expression and fulfillment. When attractive play and recreation opportunities for children and youth are provided, positive influences are brought to bear upon their lives.

Police-Sponsored Activities

Law enforcement agencies have provided important recreational services to youth as a supplement to delinquency control. Activities may include street programs, athletic leagues, special events and trips, summer camp-outs, and swimming. Through law-oriented programs for recreation, better understandings and impressions are made between law officers and the community they serve. This is expressed in the following:

> A major benefit of such programs (recreational programs) is the way they reorient the attitudes of children and youth toward law officers, whom they learn to know as friends rather than as threatening and punitive adults. . . . There are similar attitude changes with the police—that recreation is a tool for guiding youth.[28]

William Banks in writing a letter to Richard Kraus, author of *Recreation Today*, said concerning police-sponsored activities:

> These experiences provide the opportunity to compete with other young men in their own age group in a positive form of activity. They also tended to eliminate the feeling of being isolated which, I feel, is one of the negative aspects of many residential type settings which are set up to deal with youngsters from socially and economically deprived areas, school dropouts, underachievers, and emotionally deprived youngsters who are not psychotic. . . . The process of rehabilitation is expected to take place in environments quite different from ones in which the youths encountered their problems.[29]

The Salt Lake City and County Probation Units organized a softball league for boys on probation. This offered the boys a wholesome and positive participation activity in which not only to grow physically but to improve their emotional and mental stability. The program was successful and met the needs and wants of the boys in a way that would benefit them and help them to adjust to the rest of the community.

The SLC Police Department sponsors a baseball league entitled the Cops League. This league allows anyone to participate, whether delinquent or not. The officers themselves are the coaches. They try to instill into the boys that the law-abiding citizen is a great person and should be proud of that fact. They also provide a friendly relationship between the boys and those who enforce the laws.

J. Edgar Hoover spoke on the problem, saying:

> Unfortunately leisure in itself is not always conductive to productive development. Leisure put to this use (crime) is leisure misused—leisure becomes the highroad for the warping of the individual personality and the injury of society. The intelligent use of leisure, in large measure, is the key to happy worthwhile living.[30]

Correctional Institution Programs

Considerable progress has been made in providing wholesome recreation in correctional institutions, including games and sports, crafts, hobbies, music and club activities. If inmates have reached these institutions because of a wrong use of leisure time, it follows that they should be helped while there to find wiser uses for it. Recreation can do much to straighten out warped minds and alleviate bitterness. Thus recreation has become part of the rehabilitation programs in many correctional institutions, a type of therapy. Recreation is not only a use of time but a way to keep inmates physically fit, and it is not so much to relieve boredom of the inmates as to help them in the process of again becoming potential contributing, law-abiding citizens. It used to be that, when a person went to prison, he gave up all of his rights and privileges. This was part of the punishment. This is changing, and positive rehabilitation is becoming more successful.

The Detached

The abnormal wandering of youth (and adults) is as much a psychological as it is an economic problem. It becomes a problem of leisure as well. With little to do, and away from home, youth search for adventure and diversions. The very fact that they move from place to place indicates that they do not find what they want in their homes and communities. Many of them are "lost souls," having become detached from their original moorage. Being on the road subjects them to many temptations. Perhaps the worst evil is that they lose purpose and ambition, become shiftless and morally degenerate. It is difficult to provide recreational services for transients and hobos, yet this part of our population needs guidance in leisure and facilities for wholesome recreation. It is most disheartening to see homeless people idling away their time, often just sitting listlessly, brooding over their predicament and giving in to despair.

THE DRUG PROBLEM

Why are so many people today terrified by consciousness? Joyce Oates, a college teacher of English literature, explained:

> Last year in one of my classes an extremely articulate, intelligent young man explained quite frankly his liking for drugs: You must take drugs, he said, because life is so boring. The class was on modern fiction, and all year long we had been reading the works of writers like Dostoevski, Camus, Kafka, and Ionesco—men who wrote out of the despair of their times, men who felt they must come to grips with the horror of existence. Life to such men is not boring, in fact, it is hellishly violent. It is struggle, strife, probable defeat. Yet my student, who was well-groomed and not obviously a drug freak, could state quite calmly that life was boring, at least to him, and that only artificial stimulants could make it worth living.[31]

An escape from boredom is not the only reason for drug use. Drugs also offer an obvious escape from parental and school pressures. A Radnor High senior from Chicago said that she smoked marijuana three or four times a day because there was so much pressure at home. "Ever since the eighth grade all I heard from my parents was 'you have to get into a good college.' There was really no interpersonal communication in my family—and grass gave me that outside with my friends."[32]

A need for communication and friends also brings about drug use. There are some groups of people whose common interest is dope, and to be a part of that group you must use it. For them smoking marijuana is the "in" thing, like wearing mod clothes, observed a Newton High senior from Chicago. A senior girl from Philadelphia admits she "first smoked marijuana because I didn't want my friends to think I was scared or straight. . . ."[33]

According to information from the Smith, Kline and French Laboratories:

> Addicts have an inherent inability to develop meaningful interpersonal relationships. Others have said that addicts are persons who are unwilling to face the responsibility of maturity. Adolescent addicts may have suffered childhood deprivation or overprotectiveness. Or, they simply may not be able to cope with the physical and emotional change accompanying this period. It is significant that many addicts have their first drug experience in their teens.[34]

Youngsters cannot be using their leisure constructively (as in wholesome recreation) and get into trouble at the same time. Trouble usually arises when there is nothing to do. It is in their desperate hunt for amusement that young people become court cases. The absence of enticing relaxation and interesting recreation is often the underlying cause of drug abuse, and it is believed that the problem of drug abuse could be reduced if people were introduced and helped to acquire constructive leisure time activities. This places even more stress on the importance of teaching useful skills, interests and appreciations at an early age. Louria says that:

> If we are to minimize the abuse of drugs, we must involve our children early in constructive activity and in the problems of our society, for those who are so committed tend not to use drugs.[35]

Researchers have found that the most fundamental solution to drug abuse is better communication within the family and closer family ties and unity. In addition to this, the school can provide opportunities for encountering challenges appropriate to the middle years of youth. If a child can find ego satisfaction in wholesome activities, he is not likely to turn to drugs. Among such activities are sports, directed play activities, skill training and hobbies where there is the possibility of continued improvements in performance. Equally rewarding is working at tasks involving study, advancement, and group recognition and leading to more complex and difficult undertakings.[36]

We know that one of the attractions of drug abuse for many children of the middle years is that it is a challenging game, in which they can outwit parents, teachers, and police. Many other games and challenges which afford excitement and gratifications, and are not so destructive to the youth and to the community, can and should be provided through home and school.[37]

Another problem, of the same nature as drug abuse, which deserves mention is drinking. What is the relationship of drinking to leisure and recreation? Most of the drinking is during leisure and much of it is done in connection with social events, such as cocktail parties and social gatherings, and in connection with eating. The places that distribute liquor are more than dispensers of intoxicants, for some have become centers for dining and amusements. Millions of Americans spend much of their spare time, as well as their spare money, in liquor-dispensing centers.

In connection with both the drug and drinking problems, it should be kept in mind that any person who is by nature bored, dull, uninterested and, as a result, uninteresting; who is passive toward life; who demands that he be entertained while he does nothing more intelligent or creative than just sit there, would be amazed and delighted to discover that there are hundreds of subjects in which he could find real, deep interest and excitement—things that would cause him to get up eagerly in the morning and hate to go to bed at night.

URBAN PROBLEMS

The best and the worst things in human experience have often happened in cities. Cities provide the conditions and the opportunities for the most creative and most resourceful and the most primitive and least civilized behavior of humans.

More than 75% of us live in cities and, as importantly, the ideas, values and life-styles of the cities provide a common culture even for those who continue to live in nonurban environments. More people are now trying to live a good and gratifying life in the city at the very time that cities are failing to provide the social organization necessary to keep people in effective committed relationships to other people, and to the values and directives that maintain the sense of community, common cause and common goals. Administratively and politically, cities are becoming more inept and more impotent at the very time when they should become more responsive to social and individual needs.

Even with the advancements in leisure and recreation opportunities, a class in our society still feels reluctant to use the facilities and participate in the programs. Poor Americans, roughly defined, equal about 50,000,000. They tend to represent extremes in society: over 8 million are 65 and older, while 8 million others are 18 and under. The poverty stricken are often lonely, uninvolved, and apathetic toward life in general. They are hard to reach through social work, and do no know how to help themselves. It is society's responsibility to study the poor, finding out how to reach them in order to allow them equal opportunity to experience wholesome participation and involvement.

The poor automatically are prevented from enjoying commerical or private recreation because of lack of money. In addition to this shortage of funds, they do not usually understand the concept of constructive personal leisure; therefore, they do not take advantage of the many available opportunities, and they do not know how to make opportunities. Often within the slum the only kind of leisure involvement which is available and attractive is of the pathological type—crime, delinquency, alcoholism, drugs, vice, and gambling. Life is lived mostly on the streets because rooms are small, dingy, and unappealing. People are looking for a way out, but work is hard to get so the bars do a business all day. People simply stand and talk in the streets, play sidewalk crap games, or amuse themselves with other time fillers or time wasters.

A study done by the National Advisory Committee on Civil Disorder confirms the fact that deprivation in recreation and park services and facilities is a major source of dissatisfaction among ghetto residents. The study of cities where serious riots have occurred indicates clearly that there is a reservoir of major grievances in slum neighborhoods. Twelve of the most serious of these were identified, and recreation was ranked on the second level of intensity.

First Level
1. Police practices
2. Unemployment and underemployment
3. Inadequate housing

Second Level
4. Inadequate education
5. Poor recreation facilities and programs
6. Ineffectiveness of the political structure and grievance mechanisms

Figure 22. Children and youth will play wherever they can. If there are no playgrounds, they will use the streets.

Third Level

7. Disrespectful white attitudes
8. Discriminatory administration of justice
9. Inadequacy of federal programs
10. Inadequacy of municipal services
11. Discriminatory consumer and credit practices
12. Inadequate welfare programs

Grievances concerning municipal recreation programs were found in a large majority of the 20 cities that were studied: typically, references were made to inadequate facilities (parks, playgrounds, athletic fields, gymnasiums and pools) and the lack of organized programs. Throughout the study, examples were given of cities where recreation had been a focus of demands by ghetto residents: Chicago, Tampa, Cincinnati, Atlanta, and a number of cities in northern New Jersey—Newark, Elizabeth, Plainfield and New Brunswick. It was documented that this was a concern of long standing. For example, in a study carried on in Detroit by the University of Michigan (this was before the bloody Detroit riot of 1967), ghetto residents expressed major dissatisfactions which included the following:

> A significant proportion believed municipal services to be inferior; 35% were disatisfied with the schools; 43 percent with the city's contribution to the neighborhood; 77% with the recreational facilities; 78% with police services . . .[36]

The important role played by recreation in urban communities was stressed by a federal official in the Department of Housing and Urban Development, who commented that political leaders in every city should realize

> that the recreation or parks department is one of the most important communication links with the inner city—with the ghetto. . . . Few other agencies have the opportunity to work inside ghetto neighborhoods on a day-by-day and people-by-people basis. Few other city programs offer opportunity for direct participation in all phases of program development and execution by the neighborhood people themselves. In better ways than the police, and schools, recreation programs can reach large numbers of people and bring city government face to face in friendship with individual families and people, bridging economic barriers, ethnic differences, age differences and neighborhood boundaries.[38]

Perhaps the most important reason for recreation in the ghetto is the chance it gives participants to interact with other people. A friend is truly a most valuable possession. Friends playing or working together in a wholesome, uplifting atmosphere are excellent therapy for those suffering under mental strain, and present an opportunity to get to know yourself as well as others—to know what your capabilities really are.

EDUCATION FOR WORTHY
USE OF LEISURE

It has been found that the adolescent's self-image is closely related to participation in extracurricular activities. A study of over 5,000 high school students of varying social, religious, and national backgrounds revealed that those with a high degree of self-esteem tended to take part actively on sports teams, in musical organizations, publications staffs, outdoor recreation, and social activities. Those with a low degree of self-esteem were much less involved.

Youth need to be guided into effective uses of free time. If they are trained in this when they are young, they will have the resources all through life. Youth have more free time than any other group of people, and therefore need more to keep them effectively engaged in useful free-time activities. Much of this kind of education ought to occur in the home, and among family members, but the schools must also play a key role. In Chapter 1 it was pointed out that most hobbies and other recreational pursuits start in the environment of the home, and the immediate family members are the teachers. The schools rank second to the home as the place where leisure interests originate. Most interests and associated skills are developed early in life.

Some leisure time interests and skills are learned in other settings. In Olympia, Washington, a camp was organized to take elementary students out of their classrooms. High school students are used as counselors; in this way both high school and elementary school children benefit and learn as well as have fun. This idea of outdoor education has been expanded to summer programs as well. The Quinault Summer Education Program is one example. They use the "learning by doing approach." It was decided that experience was most important, and the camp was designed to give each person a variety of educational experiences. Science is studied by learning about the floor of the forest, watching insects and observing spiders. Field trips to fish hatcheries are planned. Arts and crafts include mounting plants and making slide creations. The children who attend a camp like this not only enjoy themselves but also learn more about the real world in which they live, and they tend to remember much of what they learn.

Many Indian children have problems in school because they do not understand English. Their parents speak one language at home and they are faced with another when school starts. A summer camp was designed to meet this need. The program emphasizes active enjoyment and stresses the positive rather than negative. The children learn much faster in the camp than in a classroom, and by being exposed to good English even when they are playing they remember it longer. Taking school out of doors is happening more often. Outdoor education to some extent is becoming a reality, and recreation is playing a vital role in helping it succeed.

What are the particular merits of games played as a learning process? Coleman suggests that games constitute an approach to learning that

starts with a fundamentally different premise from traditional method-
ology:

> The first premise is that persons do not learn by being taught; they learn by
> experiencing the consequences of their actions. Games which simulate some as-
> pects of reality are one way a young person can begin to see such consequences
> before he faces the real actions and the real consequences as an adult. A second
> premise underlying the development of these games is that schools find it difficult
> to teach about the complexity that characterizes modern society, with the result
> that the students have had little or no experience to prepare them for facing a
> multitude of decisions and problems in adult life.[39]

Teaching through the use of games helps the student become aware
that each of his actions has direct consequences and that he has the
power to affect his own future.

Because of the rapidly increasing numbers of retired people, our
nation needs to concern itself with educating the retired for leisure
centered living. Retired people are searching for fulfilling activities,
service, fellowship, fun and comradeship. Their concern is not merely
one of recreation, but of creation. They have the desire to do something stimulating and worthwhile. Meaningful activity is the keystone
to happy living at any age.

After retirement it is found that those who were most involved in
leisure activities tend to be the persons with the more favorable outlook on their own life situations. Retirement comes as a shock to many.
Recreation has an important responsibility in helping these people gain
the confidence and assurance they need to adjust to this new situation.

Since it is recognized that older citizens are as diverse in their interests as any age groups, emphasis should be placed on the need for
initiating, extending and implementing a broad range of programs. A
variety of public and private resources, including clubs, social and
cultural activities, travel, camping, library service, information and
education services, should be available to the senior society.

Paul Weiss sums up the necessity of education for leisure in one
paragraph:

> Leisure, then, is the time when men can be at their best, making it possible for
> them to make the rest of their day as excellent as possible, not only by enabling
> one to work with more zest or efficiency but by enabling one to give a new value
> and perhaps a new objective to whatever is done. The good life is a life in which a
> rich leisure gives direction and meaning to all else we do.[40]

It is imperative that people be educated both in thinking and living.
Education for leisure takes upon itself the role of educating the individual for living. A person who is educated in both thinking and living
has a definite advantage over his uneducated neighbors. The future will
belong not to the educated person but to the one who is educated to use
leisure time wisely in self-satisfaction and personal development.

REFERENCES

1. Nash, J. B.: Philosophy of Recreation and Leisure, 2nd ed. William C. Brown Publishing, Dubuque, 1967, p. 151.
1a. Terry, L.: Recreation in treatment centers. American Recreation Society, Hospital Section, September 1965, p. 3.
2. Stein, J. U.: The mentally retarded need recreation. Parks and Recreation, July 1966, p. 574.
3. Stein, J. U.: *Op. cit.,* p. 575.
4. Redl, F. and Wineman, D.: *Controls from Within: Techniques for the Treatment of the Aggressive Child.* Free Press, Glencoe (Ill.), 1952, p. 54.
5. Bureau of Outdoor Recreation: Outdoor recreation planning for the handicapped. Technical Assistance Bulletin. Washington, p. 1.
6. LeShan, E. J.: The perfect child. New York Times Magazine, August 27, 1967, p. 63.
7. Strang, R.: *An Introduction to Child Study.* Macmillan, New York, 1951, p. 495.
8. Gesell, A. and Ilg, F.: *The Child from Five to Ten.* Harper, New York, 1946, p. 360.
9. Frank, L. K.: In *The Complete Book of Children's Play* (Hartley, R. E. and Goldenson, R. M.). Thomas Y. Crowell, New York, 1963, p. 43.
10. Menninger, K.: *Love against Hate.* Harcourt, Brace and World, New York, 1942, p. 185.
11. Menninger, K.: *Op. cit.,* p. 184.
12. Gans, H. J.: Outdoor recreation and mental health. In *Trends in American Living and Outdoor Recreation,* Vol. 22. Report of the Outdoor Recreation Resources Review Commission. U.S. Government Printing Office, Washington, p. 235.
13. Heaps, R. H.: Proceedings of the 80th Annual Convention of the American Psychologists Association, Boston, 1973.
14. Browers, L.: Gaining self-confidence through P.E. Des Moines *Register,* September 4, 1972.
15. Thorstenson, C. T., Heaps, R. A. and Snow, R.: The effects of a twenty-nine day wilderness survival experience on anxiety and hearing sensitivity. Therapeutic Recreation J. 117, 1975.
16. Thorstenson, C. T. and Heaps, R. A.: Outdoor survival and its complications for rehabilitation. Therapeutic Recreation J., 31, 1973.
17. Heaps, R. A. and Thorstenson, C. T.: Self-concept changes immediately and one year after survival training. Therapeutic Recreation J., 61, 1974.
18. Waller, W. and Hill, R.: *The Family: A Systematic Introduction.* Dryden Press, New York, 1951, p. 23.
19. Cohen, A. K.: *Delinquent Boys: The Culture of the Gang.* Free Press, Glencoe, 1963, p. 77.
20. Heaton, A.: Recreation Education 371X. Dept. of Home Study, Brigham Young University, 1970, p. 185.
21. Nash, J. B.: *Op. cit.,* pp. 15-16.
22. Lancaster, R.: *Recreation in our Families.* Herald Publishing, New York, 1956, pp. 31-33.
23. Cannon, K. L., et al.: *Developing Marriage Relationships.* Brigham Young University Press, Provo, 1972, p. 431.
24. *Ibid.,* p. 433.
25. *Ibid.,* p. 342.
26. Stevens, A. J.: What role does community, church, and family recreation play in juvenile delinquency? Unpublished research, March 1974.
27. Shanas, E.: *Recreation and Delinquency: A Study of Live Selected Chicago Communities.* Chicago, 1942.
28. Miller, N. and Robinson, D.: *The Leisure Age.* Wadsworth Publishing, California, 1963, p. 324.
29. Kraus, R.: *Recreaction Today.* Appleton-Century-Crofts, New York, 1966, p. 330.
30. Nash, J. B.: *Op. cit.,* p. 151.
31. Oates, J. C.: The fact is, we like to be drugged. McCall's, 69, June 1970.
32. What's wrong with the high schools? Newsweek, 65-67, February 1970.

33. *Ibid.,* pp. 65-67.
34. Smith, Kline and French Laboratories: Drug abuse: escape to nowhere. Philadelphia, 1967, p. 461.
35. Louria, D. B.: Cool talk about hot drugs. Readers Digest, 117, November 1967.
36. Winick, C.: Drug addicts getting young. P.T.A. Magazine, 6-8, September 1970.
37. *Ibid.*
38. Rettie, D. F.: Urban Affairs Seminars. Congress on Recreation and Parks, Seattle, 1968.
39. Coleman, J. S.: Learning through games. National Education Association J., 70, January 1967.
40. Weiss, P.: A philosophical definition of leisure. In *Leisure in America: Blessing or Curse?* (Charlesworth, J. C., Ed.). American Academy of Political and Social Science, Philadelphia, 1964, p. 29.

6

Physiological Implications

A fundamental problem associated with leisure is that it is never inherently good or bad; it has tremendous potential for either. Leisure is a key that unlocks new doors and provides new opportunities, and it unavoidably involves the making of choices. My own expression of significance of these choices is as follows:

> During leisure man may choose to eat and drink. The wisdom of his choices in relation to his needs may determine his capacity to live fully, to be only half alive, or to contribute to his own destruction.
>
> During leisure man may also seek spiritual sustenance. He may do this through organized religion, or he may establish certain values by which he chooses to live. Outlets for spiritual activity must be a part of a man's leisure hours. . . .
>
> Another pursuit of leisure is the maintenance of a sense of physical well being. . . . Still another component is the recreative process through which man seeks to refresh himself, to relax, or as the word itself means, to be created anew.

Attempting to reach and maintain a desirable level of physical fitness can, in one sense, be compared to taking a journey. If you are travelling from San Francisco to Miami you would obtain a road map to determine the route to follow. The journey to fitness should be approached in a like manner, but most people are not well informed about fitness road maps. Therefore, it is important to obtain guidance from a qualified specialist or learn from printed material prepared by someone who knows the route. The most popular and best source available is the book entitled *New Aerobics*, by Kenneth Cooper. This and other selected sources are listed below:

Cooper, K. H.: *New Aerobics.* Bantam Books, New York, 1970.
Barney, V., et al.. *Conditioning Exercises.* 3rd ed. C.V. Mosby, St. Louis, 1973.
Allsen, P., et al., *Fitness for Life, An Individualized Approach.* William C. Brown. Dubuque, 1976.

The ordinary tasks of daily living no longer provide enough vigorous exercise for most people to develop and maintain a satisfactory level of cardiovascular fitness, good muscle tone, or the recommended body weight. Inactivity combined with poor personal health practices on the part of many Americans has resulted in a massive nationwide physical fitness problem.

In homes and factories and even on farms, machines now supply the power for most of the work. Machines have virtually eliminated the necessity of extensive walking, running, lifting or climbing. One modern machine—TV—holds people in captive idleness for an average of 22 hours a week. Further, electrical devices, gasoline engines and computers are able to perform work so extensively and rapidly that the uses of the physiological systems of the human body have been greatly diminished. As desirable as these circumstances might seem from some points of view, they present serious problems relative to fitness with which Americans must deal. One of the best opportunities for dealing with these problems is through the active use of leisure.

Heart disease is a national disaster. Every year about one million Americans die from heart and blood vessel diseases—a death rate higher than that of any other country. About 100,000 people, or one every 50 seconds, die from coronary disease alone. Millions more are partially crippled by heart attacks. To make matters worse, the disease seems to be reaching out to younger people. Men in their forties and even in their thirties are dying at an alarming rate, and as in most everything else the women are catching up with the men. Death from heart disease in young American women is also the highest of any country in the world. Perhaps this whole situation explains why the longevity of American men is 17th and that of women is 20th among the major nations of the world.

Coronary heart disease has a number of causes: heredity, stress, diet, smoking, and inactivity. Some of these causes cannot be changed, but patterns of inactivity definitely can. Fortunately more and more people are starting exercise programs during their leisure time as a means of practicing both preventive and rehabilitative medicine.

Approximately 55% of the deaths in the United States result from cardiovascular diseases, many of which are associated with obesity and inactivity. Heart attacks alone cost industry approximately 132 million work days annually (4% of the gross national output). More than 100,000 people, many of them at the peak of their value to their employers, will die of heart attacks this year.

Obesity is a major health hazard. If all deaths from cancer were eliminated, two years would be added to the average life span of Americans. If all deaths related to obesity were removed, it is estimated that the average life span would increase seven years. Some authorities indicate that life expectancy decreases approximately 1% for each pound of excess fat carried by an individual between the ages of 45 and 50.

Even such seemingly minor things as the common backache, far less dramatic than a heart attack, is often a result of physical degeneration. Once again the price is high. According to the National Safety Council, backaches cost American industry one billion dollars annually in lost goods and services, and an additional 225 million in workman's compensation.

The human body is a marvelous and intricate machine. From two cells contributed by a mother and a father develop millions of cells that make up the blood, bones, muscles, nerves, skin, and other portions of the organism. We start to grow old at an early age. Physical vitality begins to decrease at about age 20, then at more rapid rates depending on living practices and individual rates of degeneration. Much research supports the idea that regular participation in vigorous exercise can retard the rate of physical deterioration and bring about the following benefits:

1. Physically active individuals are less likely to experience heart attacks or other forms of cardiovascular disease than sedentary people, and an active person who does suffer a coronary attack will probably have a less severe form and will be more apt to survive the experience.

2. Physical activity is as important as diet in maintaining proper weight, and overweight has a serious detrimental effect on overall well-being. It is related to several chronic diseases, shortened life expectancy and emotional problems. Medical authorities now recommend that weight reduction be accomplished by a reasonable increase in daily physical activity along with the necessary dietary controls.

3. Medical authorities and fitness specialists generally agree that exercise helps a person look, feel and work better. Various organs and systems of the body are stimulated through activity and as a result they function more effectively. Posture can be improved through proper exercises that increase the tone of supporting muscles. This not only improves appearance but can decrease the frequency of problems in the lower back.

4. Perhaps the greatest benefit maintaining physical fitness is the degree of independence it affords. This is an asset to be prized in later years. There is a great psychological and financial advantage in having the ability to plan and do things without depending on relatives, friends or hired help. To drive your own car, to succeed with do-it-yourself projects rather than pay someone else for the service, to go and come as you please, to be an aid rather than a liability in emergencies—these are forms of personal freedom well worth exercising for.

FITNESS APPRAISAL

Ask the average American about his automobile and he will be able to give you miles per gallon, the proper oil weight, piston displacement and a flood of other information. Ask him about his fitness and he will be hard pressed for an answer that has an acceptable level of exactness and reliability. Of course, most people have a generalized concept of their state of fitness as compared to what they thought it was five or ten years ago or even last year, and most individuals have a generalized impression of how their fitness compares with that of their associates. Still, the average American is sadly uninformed about his exact state of fitness. What is even worse, most people do not know where to acquire this information. The most important aspects of physical fitness appraisal are *cardiovascular endurance, proper body weight* and *muscle conditioning*.

Cardiovascular Endurance

One of the best indicators of cardiovascular endurance is the amount of oxygen the body can use, because this indicates the oxygen delivery capacity of the circulatory-respiratory system and the oxygen utilization capacity of the cells. This characteristic can be measured accurately in a laboratory using a treadmill or bicycle ergometer, with the proper measuring devices. The inspired and expired gases are collected and analyzed to determine oxygen consumption. It is obvious that such cumbersome laboratory procedures are too time consuming and impractical for mass use. Therefore, simpler but less exact testing methods have been devised, the best of which is Cooper's 1.5-mile run test. The time that it takes for a person to run 1.5 miles is applied to Cooper's interpretation table and the fitness level is read from the table. Despite the simplicity and ease of administration, this field test is highly accurate when compared to laboratory measurements. By this method an individual can quickly assess the cardiovascular fitness category for himself or anyone else, and by repeating the test periodically he can determine the direction and rate of change of his fitness.[1]

Muscle Condition

Muscle condition involves the status of strength, endurance and tone, with strength being the primary component; the other two are natural by-products of strength. Strength is defined as the ability to exert force against resistance. Many people think that strength is necessary only for athletes and others who are required to do heavy muscular work. Of course, near *maximum* strength is not important for most people, but a reasonable strength level can add to everyone's ability to deal more effectively with the rigors of everyday life and to be more effective in active pursuits. Adequate muscle conditioning will result from living a generally active life or by doing specific exercises against sufficient resistance to stimulate the muscles to maintain the desired strength level. The exercises can be in the form of calisthenics, weight training or vigorous sports participation. The relatively few who want or need an unusually high level of strength must participate regularly in a structured strength training program based on the concepts of *heavy load* and *progressive resistance*.

Strength can be measured rather accurately with specific strength measuring devices, but these are not available to most people. Fortunately the condition of the muscular system can be quite easily evaluated by the individual himself by making two kinds of observations: (1) the tone of the muscles as indicated by proper shape and firmness, and (2) the relative amount of strength that is apparent compared to the amount that was available previously—last year, five years ago, or ten years ago. For example, how many pushups can you do now, compared to how many you used to do?

Body Weight

Most people depend on height-weight charts to determine proper body weight. There is no reason not to use these, but it must be recognized that the information on the charts is generalized and does not apply with accuracy to all individuals. An important factor to be considered is how much of the total weight is fat. It is not impossible for some people to fit the height-weight table while actually carrying from 15 to 20 pounds of excess fat. The optimum weight and optimum percent body fat are those which are most conducive to good health. Unfortunately we are not yet able to predict exactly for a given individual what these optimum values are, but it is certain that it is undesirable to weigh a great deal more or less than average. Between these two extremes there is a fairly wide range of individual "desirable weights."

Figure 23. Exercise gyms are used extensively for fitness development. (Xerox Corporation photo.)

A standard of 12 to 15 percent body fat for men and 15 to 20 percent for women has been generally accepted as desirable. Laboratory techniques for measuring percent body fat involve hydrostatic (underwater) weighing or skin fold tests. Skin fold tests are by far simpler and more expedient than hydrostatic weighing, but even these simple procedures must be done by someone who can interpret the measurement and has the use of skin fold calipers.

Fortunately, within reasonable limits, proper body weight is quite apparent. Usually each individual is generally aware of how his or her body weight compares with the norm, and how it has changed from what it used to be. By these guidelines most people can evaluate rather accurately the extent to which their body weight deviates from the desirable level. Unfortunately many people who are moderately overweight either will not admit it or lack the motivation and the will power to correct it. Usually the approach to reducing body weight is a combination of sensible dieting and increased exercise, living a more active life.

DEVELOPMENT OF FITNESS CHARACTERISTICS

In order to develop and maintain an acceptable level of fitness it is necessary to use the physiological systems of the body regularly and to exercise them at a high enough level to stimulate the desired level of fitness. If the *cardiovascular system* is to function efficiently it must be kept healthy, and used regularly at a demand higher than that which results from passive or sedentary living; if the *muscles* are to maintain a reasonable level of strength and endurance and remain well toned, they must be contracted regularly against a sufficient amount of resistance; and if the body is to be maintained at the *proper weight*, with no more than the recommended proportion of fatty tissue, it is usually necessary to be selective about the kind of food eaten and prudent about the amount. The right combination of total body exercise and proper diet, both in terms of amount and dietary balance, will result in an optimum level of fitness. In turn, the fitness will contribute toward a healthier, longer and more satisfying life.

Developing Cardiovascular Endurance

Cardiovascular endurance is the body's ability to continuously provide oxygen to the cells while they perform work for extended periods of time. This depends primarily upon the effectiveness and efficiency of the circulatory and respiratory systems. Activities that stimulate increased oxygen transportation and utilization are sometimes referred to as aerobic exercises. Examples of aerobic activities are swimming, jogging, handball, basketball, bicycling and vigorous walking. As the muscles utilize more oxygen with active participation, changes occur in the oxygen supply system and the result is increased cardiovascular endurance. This condition contributes to overall health and fitness.

Anyone interested in taking a systematic approach to increasing cardiovascular endurance needs to become acquainted with two important variables: *intensity* and *duration* of exercise. A fairly reliable indicator of intensity of an activity is the increase in heart rate it produces. Duration refers to the amount of time spent in continuous participation. An increase in one or the other of these variables will result in an increased stimulus for cardiovascular endurance.

When a person begins to engage in a cardiovascular improvement program, two questions that are often asked are: (1) How much exercise should I do? (2) Which activities are the best for developing cardiovascular endurance? Unfortunately there are no clear-cut answers because each person's program must be individualized in light of his present cardiovascular condition, the extent of the improvement he wants, and the rate at which he wants to improve. The best advice that can be given is to refer to Cooper's book on aerobics. This small and easy-to-read book will furnish you with a wealth of information on how to proceed with an effective cardiovascular fitness program.

Improved Muscular Condition

A reasonable level of muscular condition is important in many occupations, as well as in housework, childbearing and recreational activities. In vigorous pursuits the overall effectiveness of the body depends largely upon the condition of the large muscles of the legs, trunk and arms. In fact, if you wish to pursue the "good life" adequate strength levels in these muscle groups are imperative. If all else remains equal, increased strength will consistently improve performance in vigorous activities.

The most effective method of achieving strength gains is to follow a well-designed program of progressive resistance exercise. However, such a program is not necessary for most people because they do not want optimum strength gains, but only a reasonably well-developed muscular system with a medium level of strength. This can be achieved through regular active participation in vigorous and semivigorous activities, or by regular involvement in a variety of calisthenic exercises. Some people's jobs provide adequate muscle conditioning, but most Americans do not have such occupations. Therefore, the best opportunity to gain and maintain an acceptable level of muscle conditioning is through activity during leisure hours.

Women and teenagers in particular are often fearful that muscle training will produce unsightly bulging muscles. A sufficient amount of research indicates that this is not so. Inherent differences of males and females, such as the secretion of the hormones testosterone and estrogen, along with morphological characteristics, determine femininity and masculinity—not physical activity. Girls and women can set aside any fears that regular active participation or even structured muscle conditioning programs will affect their appearance in any way except beneficially. The end results will be better muscle tone, a replacement of fatty tissue with firm muscles and improved overall fitness.

Achieving Proper Body Weight

"You are what you eat." Even though genetic information dictates the organization of the material that constitutes each of our bodies, these materials are all derived from the food, water, and air taken into the body. This obvious concept has vast implications for health and well-being. Through better nutrition we can improve the quality of life. Since we control the kinds and amounts of foods that we eat we alone are ultimately responsible for our body's nutritional state.

Nutrition has a significant effect on health because nutrients from foods are necessary for every heart beat, nerve sensation and muscle contraction. Not only does good nutrition contribute to prevention of deficiency diseases such as scurvy and anemia but it also improves resistance to infectious diseases and plays a part in the prevention of chronic diseases. Good nutrition is a certain form of preventive medicine.

Most of the useful information about nutrition available today has been discovered since the turn of the century. The discovery that vitamins, trace minerals and amino acids (building blocks of protein) are essential for the body's growth and health has made us increasingly aware of the complexity of our diets. Today more than 40 different nutrients are known to be essential to man.

Figure 24. Participation in vigorous dance activities can contribute to both physiological conditioning and creative expression.

In contrast to the problem of undernourishment that affects many parts of the world, the health of many Americans is negatively affected by overnourishment, resulting in excess fat. Obesity has become a national health problem in the United States, and it has also become a national obsession. Regular coverage by newspapers, magazines, radio and television indicates that nutrition and weight control are increasingly prominent topics of concern to Americans. This concern by the general population is shared by health professionals who associate excess body fat with incidence of disease and mortality. The prevalence of obesity among Americans may partly be due to the increased mechanization of our society, resulting in decreased activity and increased leisure time. However, insufficient knowledge and lack of motivation toward proper diet are also reasons for the prevalence of this condition.

Reliable statistics show a significant association between obesity and early mortality from a number of diseases. Obesity may increase the risk of developing some diseases or may aggravate diseases caused by other factors. For example, diseases of the heart and circulatory system are frequently associated with obesity, as are high blood pressure and hardening of the arteries. In addition to contributing to health problems, obesity leads to general discomfort and inefficiency. Even though other factors influence weight to some degree, in essence weight control is determined by the amount of calories taken in as opposed to the amount expended on a regular and continuous basis. If a person consistently consumes more calories than he utilizes he will gradually become obese, whereas if the reverse is true he will gradually lose weight. This means that there are two variables that must be controlled: (1) the amount of calories that are consumed on a daily basis, and (2) the amount of exercise, which influences the caloric expenditure.

Gene Mayer, M.D., states,

> Inactivity is the most important reason behind the problem of overweight in modern western society. The regulation of food intake was never designed for the highly mechanized sedentary conditions of modern life. If a person is to live a sedentary life without getting fat, he will have to step up his activity or be hungry all of his life.
>
> Studies indicate that fat children often eat less and are much less active than children of normal weight. The same conclusion has been derived from controlled animal studies.[2]

It is true that weight can be controlled by diet alone, but this is a slower and much less desirable method of reducing than a combination of diet control and exercise. It should be emphasized that a daily program of activity is much better than an inconsistent and sporadic program. The most natural and long-term effective method of weight control is to discipline yourself to a diet that is effective and acceptable both in terms of content and amount, and combine this with an active life.

For a great many people in America the only opportunity to balance their sedentary lives with a sufficient amount of exercise is during leisure hours. For these people active leisure pursuits should be used to advantage for improved health and longer and happier lives.

Calorie Expenditure per Minute for Various Activities (From Consolazio, F., et al.[3])

| | Body Weight | | | | | | | |
	90	108	125	143	161	187	213	240
Archery	3.1	3.7	4.5	4.9	5.5	6.4	7.3	8.2
Badminton (recreation)	3.4	4.1	4.8	5.4	6.1	7.1	8.1	9.1
Badminton (competition)	5.9	7.0	8.1	9.3	10.4	12.1	13.9	15.6
Baseball (player)	2.8	3.4	3.9	4.5	5.0	5.8	6.6	7.5
Baseball (pitcher)	3.5	4.3	5.0	5.7	6.4	7.4	8.5	9.5
Basketball (half-court)	2.5	3.5	4.1	4.7	5.3	6.2	7.0	7.6
Basketball (moderate)	4.2	5.0	5.9	6.7	7.5	8.8	10.0	11.2
Basketball (competition)	5.9	7.1	8.2	9.4	10.6	12.3	14.0	15.2
Bicycling (level) 5.5 mph	3.0	3.6	4.2	4.8	5.4	6.2	7.1	8.0
Bicycling (level) 13 mph	6.4	7.7	8.9	10.2	11.4	13.4	15.2	17.1
Bowling (nonstop)	4.0	4.8	5.6	6.3	7.1	8.3	9.5	10.6
Boxing (sparring)	3.0	3.6	4.2	4.8	5.4	6.2	7.1	8.0
Calisthenics	3.0	3.6	4.2	4.8	5.4	6.2	7.1	8.0
Canoeing, 2.5 mph	1.8	2.0	2.3	2.7	3.2	3.7	4.7	4.8
Canoeing, 4.0 mph	4.2	5.0	5.9	6.7	7.5	8.7	10.0	11.2
Dance, modern (moderate)	2.5	3.0	3.5	4.0	4.5	5.2	5.9	6.7
Dance, modern (vigorous)	3.4	4.1	4.7	5.4	6.1	7.1	8.1	9.1
Dance, fox-trot	2.7	3.2	3.7	4.2	4.7	5.5	6.3	7.1
Dance, rumba	4.2	5.0	5.8	6.6	7.4	8.6	9.8	11.0
Dance, square	4.1	4.9	5.7	6.5	7.3	8.5	9.7	10.9
Dance, waltz	3.1	3.7	4.3	4.9	5.5	6.4	7.3	8.2
Fencing (moderate)	3.0	3.6	4.2	4.8	5.4	6.2	7.1	8.0
Fencing (vigorous)	6.2	7.4	8.6	9.8	11.0	12.8	14.6	16.4
Football (moderate)	3.0	3.6	4.2	4.8	5.4	6.2	7.1	8.0
Football (vigorous)	5.0	6.0	6.9	7.9	8.9	10.3	11.8	13.2
Golf, 2-some	3.3	3.9	4.5	5.2	5.8	6.7	7.7	8.6
Golf, 4-some	2.4	2.9	3.4	3.9	4.3	5.1	5.8	6.5

Calorie Expenditure per Minute for Various Activities (continued)

	90	108	125	Body Weight 143	161	187	213	240
Handball	5.9	7.0	8.1	9.3	10.4	12.1	13.9	15.6
Hiking, 40 lb. pack, 3.0 mph	4.1	4.9	5.7	6.5	7.3	8.5	9.7	10.9
Horseback riding (walk)	2.0	2.4	2.8	3.1	3.5	4.1	4.7	5.3
Horseback riding (trot)	4.1	4.8	5.6	6.4	7.2	8.4	9.6	10.8
Horseshoe pitching	2.1	2.5	3.0	3.4	3.8	4.4	5.0	5.6
Judo, karate (vigorous)	7.7	9.2	10.7	12.2	13.7	16.0	18.2	20.5
Mountain climbing	6.0	7.2	8.4	9.6	10.7	12.5	14.3	16.0
Paddleball, racquetball	5.9	7.0	8.1	9.3	10.4	12.1	13.9	15.6
Pool, billiards	1.1	1.3	1.5	1.7	1.9	2.2	2.6	2.9
Rowing (recreation)	3.0	3.6	4.2	4.8	5.4	6.2	7.1	8.0
Rowing (machine)	8.2	9.8	11.4	13.0	14.6	17.0	19.4	21.8
Running, 11-min. mile 5.5 mph	6.4	7.7	9.0	10.2	11.5	13.4	15.2	17.1
Running, 8.5-min. mile 7 mph	8.4	10.0	11.7	13.3	14.9	17.4	19.8	22.3
Running, 7-min. mile 9 mph	9.3	11.1	13.1	14.8	16.6	19.3	22.1	24.8
Running, 5-min. mile 12 mph	11.8	14.1	16.4	18.7	21.0	24.5	27.9	31.4
Stationary running, 140 counts/min.	14.6	17.5	20.4	23.2	26.1	30.4	34.6	38.9
Sprinting	13.8	16.6	19.2	21.9	24.7	28.7	32.7	36.8
Sailing	1.8	2.1	2.4	2.8	3.2	3.8	4.3	4.8
Skating (moderate)	3.4	4.1	4.8	5.4	6.1	7.1	8.1	9.1
Skating (vigorous)	6.2	7.4	8.6	9.8	11.0	12.8	14.6	16.4
Skiing (downhill)	5.8	6.9	8.1	9.2	10.3	12.0	13.7	15.4
Skiing (level, 5 mph)	7.0	8.4	9.8	11.1	12.5	14.6	16.6	18.7
Skiing (racing downhill)	9.9	11.9	13.7	15.7	17.7	20.6	23.4	26.4
Snowshoeing (2.3 mph)	3.7	4.5	5.2	5.9	6.7	7.8	8.8	9.9
Snowshoeing (2.5 mph)	5.4	6.5	7.5	8.6	9.7	11.2	12.8	14.4
Soccer	5.4	6.4	7.5	8.5	9.6	11.1	12.7	14.3
Squash	6.2	7.5	8.7	9.9	11.1	12.9	14.8	16.6
Swimming, pleasure 25 yds./min.	3.6	4.3	5.0	5.7	6.4	7.5	8.5	9.6
Swimming, back 20 yds./min.	2.3	2.8	3.2	3.7	4.1	4.8	5.5	6.2
Swimming, back 30 yds./min.	3.2	3.8	4.4	5.1	5.7	6.6	7.4	8.5

Calorie Expenditure per Minute for Various Activities (continued)

	90	108	125	Body Weight 143	161	187	213	240
Swimming, back 40 yds./min.	5.0	5.8	7.0	7.9	8.9	10.4	11.9	13.3
Swimming, breast 20 yds./min.	2.9	3.4	4.0	4.6	5.1	6.0	6.8	7.7
Swimming, breast 30 yds./min.	4.3	5.2	6.0	6.9	7.7	9.0	10.3	11.5
Swimming, breast 40 yds./min.	5.8	6.9	8.0	9.2	10.3	12.0	13.7	15.4
Swimming, butterfly 50 yds./min.	7.0	8.4	9.8	11.1	12.5	14.6	16.6	18.7
Swimming, crawl 20 yds./min.	2.9	3.4	4.0	4.6	5.1	5.8	6.8	7.7
Swimming, crawl 45 yds./min.	5.2	6.3	7.3	8.3	9.3	10.9	12.4	13.9
Swimming, crawl 50 yds./min.	6.4	7.6	8.9	10.1	11.4	13.2	15.1	17.0
Table tennis	2.3	2.8	3.2	3.7	4.1	4.8	5.5	6.2
Tennis (recreation)	4.2	5.0	5.8	6.6	7.4	8.6	9.8	11.0
Tennis (competition)	5.9	7.0	8.1	9.3	10.4	12.1	13.9	15.6
Timed calisthenics	8.8	10.5	12.2	13.9	15.6	18.2	20.8	23.9
Volleyball (moderate)	3.4	4.0	4.8	5.4	6.1	7.1	8.1	9.1
Volleyball (vigorous)	5.9	7.0	8.1	9.3	10.4	12.1	13.9	15.6
Walking (2.0 mph)	2.1	2.5	2.9	3.3	3.7	4.4	5.0	5.6
Walking (4.5 mph)	4.0	4.7	5.5	6.3	7.1	8.2	9.4	10.6
Walking 110-120 steps/min.	3.1	3.7	4.3	5.0	5.6	6.5	7.4	8.3
Waterskiing	4.7	5.6	6.5	7.4	8.3	9.7	11.1	12.5
Weight training	4.7	5.7	6.7	7.5	8.4	9.9	11.1	12.6
Wrestling	7.7	9.2	10.7	12.2	13.7	16.0	18.2	20.5
XBX, 5BX, Chart 1*	5.0	5.9	6.9	7.9	8.6	10.3	11.8	13.2
XBX, 5BX, Chart 2*	6.2	7.5	8.7	9.9	11.1	12.9	14.8	16.7
XBX, 5BX, Chart 3, 4*	8.8	10.5	12.2	13.9	15.6	18.2	20.8	23.4
5BX, Chart 5, 6*	10.0	11.9	13.9	15.8	17.8	20.7	23.6	26.7

* Canadian Ten Basic Exercise and Five Basic Exercise Programs in Royal Canadian Air Force, Royal Canadian Air Force Exercise Plans for Physical Fitness. New York, Essandess Special Editions.

In order to have a clearer concept of the relative effects of different activities on the expenditure of calories, a chart of calorie expenditure per minute is presented. In reading the information from the chart, it is important to keep in mind that these values are only for the time spent actually engaged in the activity. For example, if you spent an hour at the swimming pool but only ten minutes swimming, you would calculate caloric expenditure for ten minutes and not for one hour.

The complete information prepared by the original authors included caloric expenditures for 22 different body weights with the weights listed at nine-pound intervals. Only 8 of the 22 weights are listed here, because this is all that is necessary to provide the reader with a concept of relative caloric expenditure of the different activities.

REFERENCES

1. Cooper, K. H.: *The New Aerobics.* Bantam Books, New York, 1970.
2. Mayes, G.: *Overweight: Causes, Cost and Control,* Prentice-Hall, Englewood Cliffs, 1968, p. 83.
3. Consolazio, F., et al.: *Physiological Measurements of Metabolic Functions in Man,* McGraw-Hill, New York 1963, pp. 331-332.

7

Federal Government Involvement

The federal government's role in recreation includes: (1) the management of federally owned property, such as national parks, forests, wildlife preserves and refuges and reservoir areas, and (2) technical and financial assistance to states and their political subdivisions. The involvement of the government in public recreation dates back to the Civil War. The principal justification for involvement is contained in the Preamble and Article I Section 8 of the Constitution, where it is stated that one of the purposes of government is to "promote the general welfare."

In 1864 an act of Congress granted Yosemite Valley and the Mariposa Big Tree Grove to the State of California for recreational purposes. This was the first act of the federal government that was clearly in support of public recreation, though there were certain other previous actions by the government that were recreation related. In 1872 President Grant signed a bill creating the Yellowstone National Park—the first national park in the world. Subsequently the federal government steadily expanded its involvement in the park and recreation field, until now almost every major division of the federal government is involved in public recreation in some way.

Actually the federal government is in the recreation business to a much greater extent than most people realize, and the leaders of a few decades ago would be surprised at the degree of involvement. In large measure government agencies have been forced into recreation beyond the point they had anticipated or desired. For example, only a few decades ago the National Park Service planned its services to handle 25 million visitors per year. In 1960 they crowded in 60 million; in 1970 the parks received 105 million visitors, and in 1976 more than 143 million people visited national park areas. Similarly the U.S. Forest Service had 6 million visitors in 1926; in 1960 the number reached 60 million; in 1970, 100 million; and in 1976, 138 million. Numerous other federal agencies, such as the Tennessee Valley Authority (TVA), the Bureau of Reclamation, the Corps of Engineers, and the Bureau of Land Management, have experienced similar visitor growth patterns. An overview of the involvement of different agencies of federal government follows.

Federal government involvement with recreation and parks was scant during the first century of the country's existence. Basic policy, however, was indicated early by decisions to create battlefield memorials. The first of these was a monument in 1776 to General Richard Montgomery, which is now a national historic landmark. The battlefield monument and memorial movement received considerable impetus from private organizations such as the Bunker Hill Battle Monument Association, the Gettysburg Battlefield Memorial Association, and several other such associations.

During the last half of the 1800s a few isolated incidences of federal involvement occurred—the establishment of the Hot Springs Reserve in Arkansas and the creation of Yellowstone and Yosemite National Parks. However, the participation of the federal government in this field was greatly accelerated during the presidential years of Theodore Roosevelt. His 1908 conference with governors and the appointment of a national conservation commission led to an inventory of the nation's natural resources in 1909. He also took executive actions to set aside vast acreages as forest reserves, wildlife refuges and national monuments.

The 1920s saw the first dedication of wilderness, probably originally envisioned by George Tatlan, artist and hunter of the 1830s, then Henry David Thoreau in the mid-1800s and later promoted by John Muir, Aldo Leapold and several others.

The 1930s, though clouded by economic depression, saw the Blue Ridge Parkway created as the nation's first designated scenic highway. The Tennessee Valley Authority, created to provide hydropower and flood control in one of the country's most depressed areas, brought planning and development of numerous park and recreation areas. The Civil Conservation Corps (CCC) and other work project groups carried out construction, tree planting and other conservation measures which have proved beneficial to local, state and federal parks.

Although the 1940s were dominated by World War II, the Bureau of Land Management was formed and in the Flood Control Act of 1944 recreation was identified as one of the purposes which should receive attention from the U.S. Army Corps of Engineers.

The decade of the 1950s is especially noted for the creation of the Outdoor Recreation Resources Review Commission (ORRRC) by Congress. The National Park System began it ten-year Mission 66 program to renovate and revitalize the park system. Subsequently the U.S. Forest Service began its Operation Outdoors program with similar goals for the national forests. Congress authorized a national Cultural Center for the Performing Arts at Washington, D.C., along the Potomac River, later to become the John F. Kennedy Center.

The 1960s will be remembered for gains in resource conservation, particularly for outdoor recreation, and for the beginning of intensified environmental programs. Numerous legislative acts and programs of this decade will be referred to in the subsequent sections of this chapter. It was our most significant period in terms of much-needed progress in the field of outdoor recreation and natural resource conservation; we saw the establishment of the Bureau of Outdoor Recreation, the Land and Water Conservation Fund, the National Foundation for the Arts and Humanities, the National Historic Preservation Program, the National Trails System, and the National Wild and Scenic Rivers System.

Even though the roots of the new environmental era were in the 1950s and 1960s, the formal growth began with the passage of the National Environmental Policy Act signed into law Janurary 1, 1970. During the 1970s several other significant federal government moves have been made toward environmental pollution control. The year 1973 marked the release of the first nationwide outdoor recreation plan, "Outdoor Recreation—A Legacy for America."

BUREAU OF OUTDOOR RECREATION

The Bureau of Outdoor Recreation was created in 1962 within the Department of the Interior as an outgrowth of an extensive national study done by the Outdoor Recreation Resource Review Commission, which was organized in 1958. The Bureau serves as the federal focal point to assure prompt and coordinated action at all levels of government for: (1) planning and financing public recreation, and (2) encouraging and assisting all governmental and private interests to conserve, develop and utilize outdoor recreation resources for the benefit and enjoyment of present and future generations. In brief, the Bureau of Outdoor Recreation is the:

1. banker of the Land and Water Conservation Fund
2. coordinator of the National Wild and Scenic Rivers System and the National Trails Program
3. federal coordinating agency for the use of land and water for recreation
4. national outdoor recreation planning agency
5. conveyor of federal surplus property for parks
6. main source of federal recreation technical assistance
7. agency principally responsible for reviewing the environment from the recreational point of view

The BOR is not a natural resource management agency. Its functions emphasize coordination, planning, and technical financial assistance. It has a relatively small staff stationed at the headquarters office in Washington, D.C., and in the offices of its six regions.

NATIONAL PARK SERVICE

The national park system of the United States comprises nearly 300 areas covering more than 31 million acres in 49 states, the District of Columbia, Puerto Rico and the Virgin Islands. Each of these areas is of such national significance as to justify special recognition and protection in accordance with various acts of Congress which define the scope of the system. The first area to be included was Yellowstone National Park, in 1872. The founding of Yellowstone Park began a worldwide national park movement. Today the movement has spread to more than 100 nations, which have established more than 1,200 national parks or equivalent preserves. However, the national park system of the United States is still significantly larger and more prominent than that of any other country.

The National Park Service, a division of the Department of the Interior, is the administrative agency for the national park system. The NPS was not established until 1906, and prior to that time lands belonging to the national park system were administered by the Secretary of the Interior.

The diversity of the parks is reflected in the various titles given to them. They are given such designations as national park, national monument, national memorial, national historic site, national seashore, national battlefield park, and national recreation area. Each area is established because of its national significance in terms of one or more of the following criteria: *natural features, historical significance, or recreational value.*

A statement from the act establishing the NPS in 1906 is quite descriptive of the purpose of the national park system:

> The Service thus established shall promote and regulate the use of federal areas known as national parks, monuments, and reservations. . . . By such means and measures as conform to the fundamental purpose of the said parks, monuments, and reservations which purpose is to conserve the scenery, the natural and historical objects and the wildlife therein, and to provide for the enjoyment of the same in such manner and by such means as will leave them unimpaired for the enjoyment of future generations.

The use of the areas of the national park system has more than doubled in the last 16 years (60 million visitors in 1960 and 143 million in 1976), and the rate of use is still increasing rapidly.

Some of the recreationists and resource user groups have objected to the strong preservation concept exercised by the National Park Service, while at the same time some of the preservationists have criticized the NPS for being too much recreation oriented. In connection with these conflicting concepts it must be remembered that many of the resources in areas of the national park system are *nonrenewable*, while others are renewable after a long period of time. For instance the ruins of Mesa Verde and the geysers of Yellowstone are not renewable and they are prone to easy destruction with use. Also many of the wonders of the Grand Canyon and Glacier National Park are not renewable, but these are not prone to easy destruction. Trees such as those found in Sequoia National Park and stalactites and stalagmites found in many of our park caves are slowly renewable, but only after many centuries of work by nature. Because of the lack of renewability of a great many of the resources that are significant in areas of the national park system, the preservation concept must remain dominate. Use will be governed by limitations imposed by adhering to the preservation concept.

U.S. FOREST SERVICE

The first federal forest reserve, established under an act of Congress in 1891, was originally known as the Yellowstone Timberland Reserve. It was later named the Shoshone National Forest (Wyoming). After its initiation the forest reserve system grew rapidly. Only two years after the original act was passed, more than 13 million acres of forest had been placed in the reserve. Through the years other land has been identified and added piece by piece to the system, until now there are

Figure 25. Backpacking in national parks is a popular recreational pastime. (National Park Service photo.)

more than 187 million acres included in 124 different national forests in 44 states and Puerto Rico. Because of its natural characteristics, much of the national forest reserve has high recreation value.

In 1905 the U.S. Forest Service was established as a division of the Department of Agriculture for the purpose of administering the forest reserve system. Prior to that time the reserve had been administered by the Secretary of Agriculture. At the time the U.S.F.S. was established the Secretary of Agriculture issued a set of instructions which laid the basis for the Forest Serice policy. Among these instructions were:

> (a) all the resources of forest reserves are for use and this use must be brought about . . . under such restrictions only as will assure the permanence of these resources . . . , (b) in the management of each reserve, local questions will be decided upon local grounds . . . , and (c) . . . the dominant industry will be decided first but with as little restrictions to minor industries as may be possible . . . where conflicting interest must be reconciled, the question will always be decided from the standpoint of the greatest good to the greatest number in the long run.

These instructions have since remained the watchword for the U.S. Forest Service administration. The concepts of *conservation, multiple use* and *decentralized administration* still form the foundation of U.S.F.S. policy.

Even though the U.S.F.S. has never been aggressive about promoting recreational use of forest lands, it has been forced into an active role in managing recreation in order to minimize forest fires, stream pollution, and hazards to the recreationists themselves. Forest Service personnel apparently adapted themselves to the situation, and in so doing have caused the official policy of the U.S. Forest Service to become one of encouraging recreational use of the forests. Now the U.S.F.S. even prepares posters, movies, pamphlets and other media to carry the message. "The National Forests, America's Playgrounds."

National forests are used for many different recreational activities. Probably the most common of these are pleasure driving and sightseeing. However, consider from the following facts the variety and extent of other forms of recreation: One-third of the big game animals in the U.S. live all or part of the time in the national forests. In 1976 about 17 million visitor days of fishing occurred in the 180,000 miles of streams and in two million acres of lakes on the national forests. There are more than 5,500 developed camp and picnic areas, 230 developed ski areas, over 400 recreational resorts, approximately 18,500 summer homes, 96,000 miles of hiking and riding trails, 152,000 miles of scenic roads, and 96 wilderness and primitive areas.

The national forests have been administered under the concept of *multiple use* ever since the establishment of the service in 1905. However, the multiple use concept became more official by the passing by Congress of the Multiple Use Act of 1960. The act describes that national forests shall be used for five basic purposes: *recreation, timber, range, wildlife and fish*, and *watershed*.

In order to effectively accomplish its objectives the U.S. Forest Service has established some significant guidelines:

1. Recreation resources are to be made available to the public insofar as this is consistent with overall management of the forests.
2. Within reason all measures are taken to assure the safety of users.
3. Care is taken to prevent unsanitary conditions, pollution and forest fires.
4. Provision is made for the best possible wildlife habitat and best hunting and fishing, consistent with the other uses.
5. Only those facilities suitable to the forest environment are invited.
6. Operation of service facilities such as resorts, motels ski lifts, filling stations, and the like by concessionnaires is under the supervision of the Forest Service.
7. Lands that are mainly valuable for their wilderness qualities are protected.
8. Preferential private uses, e.g. summer homes, are allowed only where lands are not needed or are not suitable for public use.

The amount of recreation use of forest lands, as measured by number of annual visitors, has almost paralleled the use of the National Park Service areas. In 1960 about 60 million people visited the forests, and in 1976 that number had more than doubled to approximately 138 million.

BUREAU OF RECLAMATION

The Bureau of Reclamation was established within the Department of the Interior in 1902 for the principal purpose of applying the receipts from the sale and disposal of public lands in certain states and territories to the construction of irrigation works for the reclamation of arid lands. Early reservoirs constructed by the Bureau were for a single purpose—storage of irrigation water. Gradually other purposes were added: power, municipal and industrial water, flood control, and most recently recreation and fish and wildlife preserves. The early projects received no appropriation of funds for recreation or fish or wildlife; therefore, no official attention was given to these aspects. Beginning in 1949 with the Weber Basin Project (Utah), certain basic recreation facilities have been authorized on reclamation projects, including access roads, parking areas, picnic areas, drinking water, sanitation, and boat-launching ramps.

The Federal Water Project Recreation Act of 1965 verified the idea that the Bureau of Reclamation has both the authority and the obligation to enhance the recreational opportunities on its projects, and to cooperate with other federal agencies and state and local agencies to further this enhancement. The Bureau also cooperates whenever possible with the Bureau of Sports Fisheries and Wildlife in the planning of facilities to mitigate damages to and for the enhancement of fish and wildlife resources on reclamation projects. When reservoirs are within

U.S. Forest Service boundaries, the Bureau cooperates with the Forest Service in the development of recreation facilities.

By 1976 the Bureau had constructed 221 reservoirs with over 9,700 miles of shoreline. These areas support over 45 million recreation visits per year. This represents a significant increase over the 6.6 million visits in 1950, and the trend of increase in recreation business still continues.

Figure 26. There are many thousands of miles of fishing streams in our national forests. (U.S. Forest Service photo.)

U.S. FISH AND WILDLIFE SERVICE

The United States Fish and Wildlife Service in the Department of the Interior is the principal federal agency through which the government carries out its responsibilities for conserving the nation's fish and wildlife resources, and for the preservation of species. The responsibilities of the U.S.F.W.S. reach back over 100 years to the establishment in 1871 of a predecessor agency, the Bureau of Fisheries. A second predecessor agency, the Bureau of Biological Survey, was established in 1885. The two agencies were consolidated in 1940.

The responsibilities of the Fish and Wildlife Service include the management of wildlife refuges and fish hatcheries, the controlling of predators and rodents, the conducting of studies of water development projects and the submitting of recommendations thereon, the making of efforts to save rare and endangered species, cooperating with state and fish and wildlife departments, and the promoting of research on a wide variety of matters relating to fish and wildlife management.

In the efforts of the Fish and Wildlife Service to enhance outdoor recreation opportunities, the following kinds of problems are faced:

1. preservation of adequate wildlife habitat
2. provision of adequate public access to water and wildlife areas
3. prevention of water pollution
4. use of insecticides
5. provision of adequate visitor facilities at refuges and hatcheries
6. control of predators that diminish the wildlife resources
7. coordination of the various agencies interested and involved in wildlife, and
8. promotion of public hunting and fishing on private lands.

With the steady increase in population, combined with increased interest in fish and wildlife activities and probable decrease in suitable fish and wildlife habitat, it seems certain that the Fish and Wildlife Service will be under ever-increasing pressure. In the future the U.S.F.W.S. and the corresponding state agencies will find it extremely difficult to maintain adequate amounts of fish and wildlife to meet the needs and interests of the public.

THE CORPS OF ENGINEERS

The evolution of the U.S. Army Corps of Engineers has led the Corps from its early strictly military function to one including civilian works. The civil functions of the Corps of Engineers started in 1824 with passage of the first Rivers and Harbors Act. Several other pieces of legislation have influenced the civil functions of the Corps. The 1944 Flood Control Act authorized the Corps of Engineers "to construct and maintain and operate public park and recreation facilities in reservoir areas as part of multiple purpose projects." The act also specified "the water areas of all such reservoirs shall be opened to public use generally without charge . . . and ready access to and exits from such water areas . . . shall be maintained for general public use." On the basis of the 1944 act the Corps has become extensively involved in the installation of basic recreation facilities, including over-look stations for viewing the projects, public sanitary facilities, parking areas, access roads, guard rails, fences, informational signs, camping and picnic facilities and boat-launching ramps. The Corps of Engineers encourages state and local governments to assume responsibilities for additional construction and maintenance of the recreation facilities on projects constructed by the Corps.

In 1962 the President of the United States approved Senate Document No. 97, which specifies that full consideration be given to the opportunity and need for recreation and fish and wildlife enhancement in planning water projects and land use development.

Since World War II the recreational use of the Corps of Engineer projects has experienced a phenomenal increase. In 1946 visits to these projects totaled only 5 million, and then came the boats. By 1959 the number of visits exceeded 100 million, and in 1964 they exceeded 155 million. In 1976 over 250 million people visited Corps of Engineer projects, mostly for boating, fishing, picnicking and sightseeing.

BUREAU OF LAND MANAGEMENT

The Bureau of Land Management (BLM) was established in the Department of the Interior in 1946 through the combining of the General Land Office and the Grazing Service. The BLM is the manager of the "public domain," the great federal land reserve. The public domain is that part of the original public lands of the United States still under federal ownership and which has not been set aside for other uses, namely, national forests, parks, etc. Approximately one fifth of our nation's land is under the jurisdiction of the BLM.

The use of the public domain for recreation is increasing rapidly. Recreation is becoming an important partner with livestock grazing, mining, timber production and other traditional uses of the land. The recognition of recreation as a primary objective has resulted in the operation of a number of recreation areas on BLM lands. These areas now include over 170 camp-picnic sites, 1,000 family picnic units, 1,300 family camp units, 298 trailer spaces, 46 swimming beaches, and 30 boat-launching ramps. Also, more than 120 areas of unusual natural attractions have been identified on public domain lands.

TENNESSEE VALLEY AUTHORITY

The Tennessee Valley Authority (TVA) is a U.S. government corporation which was created in 1933 as a regional resource development agency. It is based on the concept that all the resources of a river basin are interrelated and should be developed under one unified plan for maximum effectiveness. To put the Tennessee River to work, the TVA built a system of multipurpose dams, with the primary goals being flood control, navigation and electric power production.

Even though the original TVA act made no specific reference to recreation, it did authorize surveys, plans and demonstrations for fostering an orderly and proper physical, economic and social development of the Tennessee Basin and the adjoining territory. TVA officials apparently interpreted this to include planning and developing the recreation and scenic potential, because these have received serious attention since the beginning of the TVA project.

The lakes created by the TVA cover over half a million acres and have shorelines totaling over 10,000 miles. These large man-made bodies of water attract over 65 million recreation visits per year, and the visits have been increasing annually by almost 2.5 million. Boating,

Figure 27. Kyacking through white water in the Tennessee Valley. (Tennessee Valley Authority photo.)

fishing, picnicking and camping are popular activities. There are more than 13,000 private vacation homes, several organized camps and numerous major recreation resorts.

BUREAU OF INDIAN AFFAIRS

Indian lands total some 51 million acres—an area slightly larger than the state of Kansas. The Indian reservations contain more than 3,600 ponds and lakes with a water surface area of approximately 750,000 acres. There are 6,600 miles of rivers and streams, some of which have high fishing value. About one-half of the total of the Indian land has been classified as hunting area. Each year approximately 700,000 man days are spent in fishing and about 290,000 man days in hunting on Indian reservations. Recreation visits for all purposes total about 3 million annually. In recent years significantly increased emphasis has been placed on the recreational development of Indian lands, both for the recreational use of the reservation occupants and for profit-producing purposes.

FEDERAL HIGHWAY ADMINISTRATION

As the road building agency for the federal government, the Highway Administration, within the Department of Transportation, administers funds for or directly handles engineering and construction of roads on federal lands. These roads include forest highways, park roads and parkways, and other kinds of roads on government lands. This agency also builds access roads into facilities of national fish hatcheries and game refuges. Highways linked together can make more accessible the public recreation, historic, and scenic areas. The tremendous increase in the use of federally owned recreation resources during the past years has been partially prompted by such accessibility. For example, it is estimated that over 95% of the visitors to Yellowstone, Glacier, Grand Canyon and Smokey Mountain National Parks come by private automobile.

OTHER FEDERAL AGENCIES

The *Agricultural Stabilization and Conservation Service* is a division within the Department of Agriculture which has participated extensively since 1962 in a cost sharing program with private land owners to preserve wet lands for migratory birds and natural habitat for other wildlife. Also it has participated in the construction of more than 3 million farm ponds, many of which stock fish.

The *Soil Conservation Service*, a division of the Department of Agriculture, provides technical assistance to land owners in planning and installing certain kinds of outdoor recreation enterprises. The SCS also provides technical help on the recreational use of land and water areas owned and operated by local units of government or nonprofitable organizations. Also, under authorization of the Flood Prevention Act of 1954 (Small Watershed Act), the SCS may share up to half the cost with state and local government agencies of the construction of basic facilities needed for public recreation and fish and wildlife on small watershed projects.

The *Cooperative Extension Service* of the U.S. Department of Agriculture is the educational branch of that department. In addition to carrying on many specific programs related to recreation through the 4-H Clubs, the Extension Service also provides advisory service to states and political subdivisions on recreation matters. The Extension Service now has approximately 100 recreation specialists and more

Figure 28. Water skiing is a popular activity on the many lakes under the jurisdiction of the Tennessee Valley Authority.

than 25 wildlife specialists working full time throughout the country in recreation and related activities.

The *Department of Defense* becomes involved through the fact that approximately 27 million acres of land are administered by that agency, and recreation facilities for service personnel are provided by most of the 220 military installations. Outdoor recreation use on military installations exceed 2 million visits per year.

The *Department of Health, Education and Welfare* (HEW) is involved in several ways, as:

1. The Bureau of Education for the Handicapped, a division of HEW, provides grants to institutions for the training of physical education teachers and recreation leaders for the handicapped
2. HEW is authorized to provide grants to improve and extend community schools which ordinarily include strong recreational components

The *Department of Housing and Urban Development* (HUD) is involved in a variety of programs which assist in the planning and development of park and recreation areas in and around housing developments. As part of HUD's efforts to improve living conditions, it becomes much involved in environmental improvement and recreational opportunities.

In the Department of the Interior, in addition to the agencies already discussed, three other agencies have obvious roles related to recreation. They are the *Federal Water Pollution Control Administration*, the *Geological Survey* and the *Office of Water Resources Research*.

Independent agencies not administratively attached to a major department of federal government that become involved in recreation are: the *Appalachian Regional Commission*, the *Federal Power Commission*, the *General Services Commission*, the *Office of Economic Opportunity*, the *Public Land Law Review Commission*, the *Small Business Administration*.

Numerous other federal agencies become involved in recreation on a project basis or as a supplementary role to another agency. For example, within the Department of Commerce, the *Bureau of Census* recently conducted a special study for the Bureau of Outdoor Recreation and one for the Bureau of Fisheries and Wildlife. The *Bureau of Domestic Commerce* involves itself regularly in studies and the provision of information as to the manufacturing of recreation equipment, and the operation of resorts, ski lifts, golf courses, sport areas and other recreation facilities. The *Economic Development Administration* (also a division of the Department of Commerce) can provide a maximum of 75% of the cost of parks and recreation projects to public or nonprivate organizations which qualify under the Economic Development Program.

NATIONAL OUTDOOR RECREATION PLAN

Early in its existence the Bureau of Outdoor Recreation was charged with the responsibility of developing and maintaining a national plan, and for coordinating the outdoor recreation effort at the national level in accordance with the plan. After much groundwork, the BOR produced the written form of the plan in 1973—"Outdoor Recreation—A Legacy for America."

The plan explains how governmental and private institutions manage resources to provide outdoor recreation opportunities for the public. It provides a basis for establishing the roles and responsibilities of the various levels of government and the private sector in meeting outdoor recreation needs. Also, it identifies the actions necessary to achieve effective and creative use of recreation resources and programs. The plan looks at recreation as an important element in land use planning, and places outdoor recreation in context with this process. As part of the system of the plan, each state is required to have a comprehensive outdoor recreation plan which correlates with the national plan. It is required that the national plan and the individual state plans be kept current. Further, the developments initiated by the federal government and the individual state governments must be in accord with the respective comprehensive plans. This system of comprehensive plans will undoubtedly give much more direction to the total outdoor recreation effort than has previously existed.

RECENT GOVERNMENT LEGISLATION
AND SPECIAL PROGRAMS

In recent years recreation has gained much support from governmental agencies. Legislation has been passed and programs have been initiated which have had and will continue to have significant influence on recreation opportunities for the total population. Great changes have occurred in the emphasis toward recreational use of land and water owned by federal and state agencies. To a large extent a new system of values toward recreational use of the nation's natural resources has taken place. Accordingly new government policies and programs have been established.

Listed here are the acts of Congress and presidential proclamations passed in the last two decades which have resulted in significant impact on the recreation field. If you want to know more about a particular act or program you can obtain a copy of the public law from the Superintendent of Documents, Washington, D.C., or from any federal legislator's office, or you can refer to the descriptions given by Jensen in *Outdoor Recreation in America*.[1]

1958—Establishment of the Outdoor Recreation Resources Review Commission (OORC) by proclamation of the President

1961—Passage of the Small Reclamation Projects Act (PL 84–984)

1962—Establishment of the Bureau of Outdoor Recreation by directive from the President

1964—Establishment of the Wilderness System (PL 88–577)

1964—Passage of the Federal Water Projects Recreation Act (PL 89–72)

1964—Passage of the Water Resources Research Act (PL 88–379)

1964—Passage of the Economic Opportunity Act (PL 88–452)

1965—Establishment of the Land and Water Conservation Fund Program (PL 88–578), amended 1968 and 1974 (PL 90–401 and PL 93–303)

1965—Passage of the Water Quality Act (PL 89–234)

1965—Passage of the Highway Beautification Act (PL 89–285)

1965—Passage of Section 707 of the Housing and Urban Development Act (PL 89–117)

1965—Passage of the Public Works and Economic Development Act (PL 89–136)

1965—Passage of the Older Americans Act (PL 89–730)

1965—Passage of the Higher Education Act (PL 89–329)

1965—Passage of the Elementary and Secondary Education Act (PL 89–10)

1966—Passage of the Natural Historic Preservation Act (PL 89–665)

1966—Establishment of the Green Span Program (PL 89–321)

1967—Passage of the Air Quality Act (PL 90–148)

1968—Establishment of the Wild and Scenic Rivers Program (PL 90–542)

1968— Establishment of the National Trails System (PL 90–543)

1970—Passage of the Environmental Education Act (PL 91–516)

1970—Passage of the Water Quality Improvement Act (PL 91–224)

1970—Passage of the Environmental Quality Improvement Act (PL 91–224)

1970—Passage of the National Environment Policy Act (PL 91–190)

1971—Passage of the Federal Safety Act (PL 92–75)

1973—Passage of the Endangered Species Act (PL 93–205)

1974—Passage of the Water Resources Act (PL 93–251)

1974—Passage of the Housing and Community Development Act (PL 93–341)

1974—Passage of the Forest and Rangeland Renewable Resources Planning Act (PL 93–376)

1975—Passage of the Eastern Wilderness Act (PL 94–28)

During the last two decades numerous other acts affecting recreation have been passed, but are not included here because of their local or temporary application. Among such acts are those providing funds for recreation and related developments, and establishing new parks and forest reserves or expanding existing parks and reserves.

REFERENCES

1. Jensen, C. R.: *Outdoor Recreation in America,* 3rd ed. Burgess Publishing, Minneapolis, 1977.

8

State Government
Role in Parks
and Recreation

A state has been described as an institution created by the people to enable them to do collectively what they would be unable to accomplish individually. It is one of the principal organizations through which people have been able to promote education and health, improve living and working conditions, expand ways and means of communication and transportation, and achieve many other ends that contribute to an orderly society.

A century ago state government was relatively simple and was concerned with only a few functions. Many of the present services such as education, health and welfare were initiated and carried on for a time by private agencies. As their need and value became more recognized certain phases of these services were gradually given more attention by state authorities, and special agencies were created to sponsor and administer them.

In the early history of our nation recreation was considered of little or no public concern, and the early attempts to provide recreational opportunities were through private initiative and funds. During the last century, however, state governments have gradually accepted certain recreation-oriented responsibilities, and have developed them along the same historical patterns as education, health, and other well-established public services. States are now involved in a variety of recreational functions. State forests, parks, game refuges and other areas with recreation value now total 40 million acres.

The tenth amendment to the Constitution gives the separate states authority to provide recreational services as the need for such services becomes evident. This amendment, commonly referred to as "state's rights," is also the authority by which state governments provide public education and various social services.

All of the 50 states now have one or more agencies with major responsibilities for park development and/or recreational services. These responsibilities are not consistent throughout the states, and neither is there consistency among the organizational plans for administering them. Each state is unique in its organizational structure and the services it provides. It is important for recreation and park professionals in a particular state, therefore, to be familiar with the contributions and services provided by state agencies, and to know how these agencies cooperate with local agencies to better serve public needs.

The first clear-cut involvement of a state in the field of recreation was in 1864, when Congress granted to the State of California a large portion of public domain which included Yosemite Valley and the Mariposa Big Tree Grove, under the condition that the areas ''shall be held for public use, resort and recreation . . . for all time.'' In essence this became the first state park. Unfortunately California at the time was unable to manage those resources adequately. Later the federal government repossessed the areas, and in 1884 the Yosemite National Park was established. In 1872 the federal government declared Yellowstone a national park, providing 25,000 square miles of land which was placed under the supervision of the territory of Wyoming. This proved unsuccessful, and subsequently Yellowstone was supervised by the military for 32 years.

The State of New York was actually the first state to make a clearly successful effort related to recreation when in 1885 it established a state forest reserve in the Adirondacks. Later this preserve became Adirondack State Park. Also in 1885 Fort Mackinac was given to the State of Michigan. It has since developed into a significant recreational attraction.

In 1894 the New York Constitution was amended to provide funds to purchase forest lands under the Forest Preservation Act of 1885. This resulted in enlargement of the preserves known today as the Adirondack and the Catskill Reserves. In 1898 Pennsylvania followed New York's lead and took measures to protect selected forest areas from exploitation.

In the 1890s the beautiful Palisades of the Hudson River were recognized for their utility as raw material for concert, and their defacement began to proceed rapidly. Women's groups can claim the initial credit for halting this destructive action, because in 1899 the New Jersey Federation of Women's Clubs convinced the New Jersey legislature to pass a bill allowing the governor to study the situation. Subsequently on Christmas Eve of 1900 an interstate agreement between New York and New Jersey was signed to save the scenic value of the Palisades.

Illinois is credited with establishing the first state agency for managing a state park system. In 1903 Illinois acquired Fort Massac as a state park. In 1909 the state legislature appointed a commission to study the use of state lands for public parks. In 1919 the Illinois Division of Parks and Memorials was established within the Department of Public Works and Buildings. Indiana followed Illinois' lead by establishing a Division of State Parks, Land and Water within the Department of Conservation in 1919.

During the decade after World War II both federal and state governments made positive moves to improve their park and recreation services. The Surplus Property Act of 1944 was amended in 1948 to allow certain federal lands to be used for developing state park and recreation facilities. Under this act surplus property could be transferred at 50% of its fair appraised value to states and local governments for park and recreation areas.

In 1960 New York became the first state to go to the public with a substantial bond issue to support the development of the state park system. In that same year California published a two-volume state recreation plan.

The Open Space Program, authorized in 1961 under the Housing and Home Finance Agency, provided for financial assistance to state and local governments to acquire and improve open space areas. Since the inauguration in 1964 of the Land and Water Conservation Fund, revenue to state governments for the acquisition and development of recreational areas has greatly accelerated. In connection with the utilization of these funds, every state has been required to complete and keep updated a comprehensive state recreation plan.

STATE EDUCATIONAL SYSTEM

In the early days of America, education for leisure was unplanned and was not considered a direct responsibility of the schools. However, in view of the vast changes that have occurred in our living conditions, education for the wise use of leisure has become more broadly accepted as a responsibility of fundamental importance to society. This was expressed as early as 1917 when "the worthy use of leisure" was stated as one of the seven cardinal principles of education. State educational systems have generally assumed responsibility for this phase of education, but, like certain other aspects of education, this responsibility needs increased attention and improvement.

State colleges and universities (as well as certain private institutions) offer professional preparation programs for recreation and park leaders, and some institutions offer general education courses oriented toward recreational pursuits. Also, a large number of universities provide consulting services by their specialized faculty members to state and local government agencies. Further, the State Cooperative Extension Services of the land grant colleges were among the first state agencies to provide leadership in recreation. The Extension Services have for a long time conducted recreation training courses, sponsored state-wide conferences, provided consultation services and published resource materials. The state department of education in every state has on its staff at least one specialist in health, physical education and recreation whose responsibility it is to help improve these phases of public education.

ENABLING LEGISLATION

Through enabling legislation states permit local political subdivisions to conduct recreation programs under the administrative and organizational arrangements described in the legislation. The first enabling act of this kind was passed in 1915 in New Jersey, and by 1947 34 states had such laws. The other states have passed recreation enabling acts since then, and now all states allow local governments to sponsor recreation programs and manage areas and facilities. It is important for the recreation professionals in a given state to be acquainted with the enabling legislation of that state, to be informed of the legal circumstances under which the local programs are managed. In some cases it is important to lobby for improved legislation to provide a legal structure that will better enhance recreation services.

When writing legislation, it is advisable that experts from the recreation profession as well as lawyers who have had training in drafting such proposals be selected. New laws must be consistent with other forms of legislation, and careful consideration must be given to objectives and basic principles. Recreation practices which are enacted into law should always be: (1) consistent with the spirit of the law, (2) consistent with other legal principles, (3) comprehensive or inclusive, (4) peaceably agreed to, and (5) neither obscure in meaning nor merely implied.

Following are some key paragraphs taken from a typical piece of state enabling legislation (Official Utah Code). These paragraphs will serve as examples of the kinds of statements included in state enabling park and recreation laws.

Supervision

May provide entertainment facilities for citizenry

Local authorities may organize and conduct plays, games, calisthenics, gymnastics, athletic sports and games, tournaments, meets, and leagues, dramatics, picture shows, pageants, festivals and celebrations, community music, clubs, debating societies, public speaking, story telling, hikes, picnics, excursions, camping and handicraft activities, and other forms of recreational activities that may employ the leisure time of the people in a constructive and wholesome manner.

Recreation board

Authority to supervise and maintain any of such recreational facilities and activities may be vested in any existing body or board, or in a public recreation board, as the governing body of any city, town, county, or school district may determine. If it is determined that such powers are to be exercised by a public recreation board, such board may be established in any city, town, county or school district and shall possess all the powers and be subject to all the responsibilities of the respective local authorities under this chapter.

Number of members—selection—term

Such recreation board shall consist of five persons. When established in a city of the first or second class, two members shall be selected from the board of education of the school district therein, and when established in any county two members shall be appointed from the board of education of that county; provided, that in counties having two or more school districts one member shall be appointed from each county school district therein. The members of such board shall be appointed by the appointing authority of the city, town, county, or school district and shall serve for a term of five years, and until their successors are appointed; provided, that the members first appointed shall be appointed for such terms that the term of one member will expire annually thereafter. Vacancies in a board occurring otherwise than by expiration of term shall be filled in the same manner as original appointments for the unexpired term. The members of the recreation boards shall serve without compensation.

Funds

Cooperation between school districts and cities, towns, and counties

Any board of education of any school district may join with any city, town, or county in purchasing, equipping, operating, and maintaining playgrounds, athletic fields, gymnasiums, swimming pools, and other recreational facilities and activities, and may appropriate money therefor.

Expenses—payment of—authority to appropriate and tax-rate limitation

All expenses incurred in the equipment, operation, and maintenance of such recreational facilities and activities shall be paid from the treasuries of the respective cities, towns, counties, or school districts, and the governing bodies of the same may annually appropriate, and cause to be raised by taxation, money for such purposes.

Special taxes and licenses

They (cities) may fix the amount, terms and manner of issuing licenses, and may, consistent with general law, provide the manner and form in which special taxes shall be levied and collected.

Borrowing power—warrants and bonds

They (cities) may borrow money on the credit of the corporation for corporate purposes in the manner and to the extent allowed by the constitution and the laws, and issue warrants and bonds therefor in such amounts and forms and on such conditions as they shall determine.

Borrowing power—issuance of bonds—payment of interest

The board of trustees of any town may borrow money on the credit of the town for corporate purposes in the manner and to the extent allowed by the constitution, and issue warrants and bonds therefor in such amounts and forms and on such conditions as the board shall determine. . . .

Areas and Facilities

Powers of local authorities to designate and acquire property for

The governing body of any city, town, school district or county may designate and set apart for use as playgrounds, athletic fields, gymnasiums, public baths, swimming pools, camps, indoor-recreation centers, or other recreational facilities, any lands or buildings owned by such cities, towns, counties, or school districts that may be suitable for such purposes; and may, in such manner as may be authorized and provided by law for the acquisition of lands or buildings for public purposes in such cities, towns, counties, and school districts, acquire lands and buildings therein for such use; and may equip, maintain, operate and supervise the same, employing such play leaders, recreation directors, supervisors, and other employees as it may deem proper.

Cooperation between school districts and cities, towns and counties

Any board of education of any school district may join with any city, town, or county in purchasing, equipping, operating, and maintaining playgrounds, athletic fields, gymnasiums, baths, swimming pools, and other recreational facilities and activities, and may appropriate money therefor.

Expenses—payment of—authority to appropriate and tax-rate limitations

All expenses incurred in the equipment, operation and maintenance of such recreational facilities and activities shall be paid from the treasuries of the respective cities, towns, counties, or school districts, and the governing bodies of the same may annually appropriate, and cause to be raised by taxation, money for such purposes.

STATE PARKS

At the time of the first national conference on state parks in 1921 at Des Moines, Iowa, 19 states had at least one park. This marked the beginning of an organized state park movement. National parks were proving successful and the states and the public were asking the first director of the National Park System, Stephen T. Mather, for more national parks. Mather saw state administration as an alternative to protecting some areas until he could gather political and financial support to bring a few of these parcels into the national park system. As a result of these concerns Mather was a dynamic influence in organizing the Des Moines meeting.

Since its inception, the National Conference on State Parks has been the foremost professional group in the development of our present state park systems. This organization encourages states to seek suitable lands and funds to improve their state parks. The Conference has also been successful in encouraging cooperation among the states and the National Park Service.

A few states have been successful in finding wealthy philanthropists to help finance the state park systems, and the federal government has been helpful to states through the authorization of various programs whereby the states have been able to acquire selected sites of public domain at a very low cost. Also under certain programs the federal government has cooperated in the direct financing of areas and facilities. Still, financing has been a traditional problem for state park systems. One of the major solutions has turned out to be bond issues. In 1960 the State of New York passed a bond issue for $75 million to acquire state park and recreational lands. In succeeding years the totals grew. California in 1964 approved bonds for $150 million, Michigan in

1968 for $100 million and New Jersey in 1974 for $200 million. Several other states have passed bond issues for similar or lesser amounts, totalling approximately $300 billion since 1960.

All of the 50 states now have state park systems. In most states, the park agency is a separate department of government. However, in several of the states, it is a division within a larger department, and in a few states which have small park systems the parks are administered by an agency the primary function of which is something else.

The state park systems in the 50 states administer a combined total of approximately 3,500 areas, covering 8 million acres. These parks with an annual patronage which exceeds 450 million, are second only to municipal areas in number of visitors per year.

State parks are the most prevelant in states which have large populations: New York—205 areas; Pennsylvania—202 areas; California—174 areas. Some of the less populated states, such as Rhode Island, Kansas and Idaho, have only 20 to 30 areas in their park systems.

For the most part state parks are intermediate areas, leaning more toward the wilderness than municipal areas, while they are more user-oriented than national parks and forests. Parks take a variety of forms even within the same state, and they vary immensely among states. The particular kind of terrain of a state, combined with the amount of scenic areas and culturally and historically significant areas, strongly influences the numbers and kinds of state parks. Often state parks contain significant natural features with some man-made improvements in the form of picnic and camp sites, eating accommodations and various sports facilities. The location and accessibility of a park to a particular segment of the population can influence markedly the amount and kind of facilities needed. Further, it can be said that the availability and accessibility of federal areas, such as national parks and forests, influence significantly the need for state park areas in a particular locale.

STATE FISH AND WILDLIFE AGENCIES

Every one of the states has either a separate department or a major division within a department for the propagation, control, and management of fish and wildlife resources. Generally these agencies have responsibility for game animals, fur-bearing animals, game birds, and game fish. They manage fisheries and game refuges and reserves, issue licenses for hunting, fishing and trapping, and have a broad responsibility for regulating and improving hunting and fishing as forms of recreation. These state agencies work closely with their counterpart at the federal level, the U.S. Fish and Wildlife Service. They also have working relationships with each other, and with certain local agencies.

More than 35 million people participate annually in fishing and hunting in the United States, and many nonhunters and nonfisherman, such as photographers, nature hikers and sightseers, also enjoy their own forms of recreation in connection with fish and game.

Ordinarily associated with these agencies is a state board of control that sets policies and procedural guidelines. The department or division is usually administered by a chief selected by the controlling board or appointed by the governor.

Figure 29. Many people consider game hunting an exciting form of recreation. (U.S. Fish and Wildlife Service photo.)

STATE FORESTS

Most of the 50 states, but not all of them, have state forest systems. In many cases this system is administered by a separate department or a division of state forests. However, in a few states where the systems are rather meager, they are administered by other land management agencies. The extensiveness of any given state forest system is strongly influenced by the amount of national forest reserve in the vicinity. In some states, particularly in the intermountain region and the western states, practically all of the desirable forest land is in the national reserve, leaving little opportunity and little need for the development of an extensive state forest system. Conversely, in eastern and midwestern states there is a minimal amount of national forest reserve, and ample need and opportunity for the development of state forests. State forest systems are especially well developed in Pennsylvania, Ohio, Indiana, Kentucky, Tennessee and other states in the eastern and southeastern portions of the nation.

STATE HIGHWAY AGENCIES

Travel has become a popular recreational activity. In fact, travel for pleasure accounts for the greatest single recreation expenditure in America. Roads which are built and maintained under the responsibilities of state highway agencies enhance a significant portion of this travel.

In addition to the contribution of state highway departments to pleasurable travel, roads are built and maintained specifically for recreation access. Among these are roads to winter sport areas, water recreation areas, access roads for hunting and fishing, etc. Also, the state highway agency is often responsible for the construction of roads on state-owned lands—state parks, state forests, and state fish and wildlife areas.

OTHER STATE RECREATION FUNCTIONS

State departments of tourism, health departments, water resource control agencies, and land boards are among the several other agencies which contribute to recreation. The number of "other state agencies" and the prominence of their roles in recreation vary among the different states.

STATE CONSULTATION SERVICES

Several states, including North Carolina, New Jersey and California, provide consultation services to local governmental units, and to nonprofit organizations and private individuals, for the purpose of helping these organizations and individuals be more successful in their efforts to provide park and recreation facilities and programs to the public. In addition, as mentioned in a previous section, consultation services are provided in many of the states by recreation specialists who are staff members of the State Cooperative Extension Services which are affiliated with land grant universities.

Also, as stated earlier, every state has one or more specialists in the area of health, physical education and recreation on the staff of the state department of education, who is usually referred to as the state director of this phase of education. Practically all of the work of these specialists is in connection with the public school programs.

STATE RECREATION PLAN

As explained in the previous chapter, the federal Bureau of Outdoor Recreation has completed a national recreation plan and, in connection with the plan, every state has been required to furnish a current and comprehensive plan in order to be eligible for participation in the benefits of the Land and Water Conservation Fund. Every state has completed its plan, and each plan contains outdoor recreation development guidelines pertaining to state agencies, political subdivisions and non-government interests. A copy of the plan for any particular state may be obtained from the State Outdoor Recreation Liaison Officer who is housed in the State Office Building.

Figure 30. Swamplands are far from a waste in the minds of some recreationists. (Soil Conservation Service photo.)

9

Local Government
Recreation and Park Systems

According to George Butler, "The term local government is considered applicable to any local unit of state government such as a county, city, village, or township, or school park and recreation districts."[1] Further, Butler explains that *municipal recreation* is an inclusive term which covers all public recreation and park programs sponsored through local government agencies. Unlike that provided by private, semiprivate and commercial agencies, municipal recreation is for all people. In large measure it is equally available for rich and poor, for people of various ages, racial backgrounds, social status, political opinions, and religious preferences, for boys and girls and men and women. It gives to everyone the opportunity to engage in activities of his choice. Municipal recreation generally conforms with the American spirit and way of life. *Community recreation* is a commonly used term that means essentially the same.

When recreation is provided as a local government service, it must be sponsored within a framework of desirable social values, and must be designed to achieve significant social goals that will benefit the community at large as well as the individuals. Municipal recreation consists of those programs presented at the local level which are designed to provide constructive and enjoyable leisure experiences for the participants. Individuals take part in municipal recreation programs during their free time and generally within a framework of free choice, either because of the pleasure they provide or because of certain desirable outcomes such as physical, social or emotional benefits which they hope to obtain.

Municipal park and recreation programs have a long but spotty history in America. The Pilgrims brought with them a concept of the "commons," and fortunately the "village green" or "church green" was not one of the many old-world customs that were rejected. Initially the village commons was multifunctional and served important purposes for social, economic and military activities. The Boston Commons, established in 1634, is recognized as the first "city park" in the United States.

William Penn's plan for Philadelphia in 1682 provided for five community squares to be used for public affairs, and also included provisions for timber reserves to be maintained within the city. For every five acres of timber cut, one acre was to remain.

It is questionable whether the colonial public open spaces were used very much for recreational activities; the Puritan work ethic was very strong and rigidly enforced. However, football, probably a form of rugby or soccer, is recorded as early as 1686.

Washington and Jefferson showed considerable insight into the well-landscaped city when they guided Major L'Enfant in drawing the plan for Washington, D. C.

The colleges were the first to provide gymnasiums, at first outdoors and later indoors. In 1891 the Salem Latin School opened the first of these facilities with little equipment and no supervision. Within a decade several other colleges followed suit.

With the development of Fort Dearborn Park in Chicago in 1839 and Central Park in New York in 1853, the trend was established and the stage was set for the development of a broad and continuous municipal park and recreation movement. There have since been many significant events in this movement, too many to mention here, and they have led us to our present position relative to local recreation and park programs.

In order to effectively develop recreation opportunities on a continuing basis at the local level, certain responsibilities must be fixed and the essential tools—finances, leadership, facilities, equipment and supplies—must be provided systematically and continuously. Usually it is desirable to have an active citizen's council representing various interest groups, with a board or commission officially responsible for direction of the recreation and park system. As part of the complete community plan, voluntary, private and commercial agencies can provide additional opportunities for individual and group recreation.

In cities, towns and villages throughout America, people have demonstrated their interest in public recreation programs by supporting the use of tax funds for facilities, programming and leadership. The extent and quality of a program in any community are measures of an expressed interest on the part of the people and an expressed commitment on the part of local government officials.

LOCAL SPONSORING AGENCIES

Numerous groups and agencies participate in meeting the recreation and leisure time needs of the people of a community. The sponsoring groups and agencies can be generally classified into: *private, voluntary, commercial* and *public*.

Private groups, such as clubs, fraternal, social and church organizations, are ordinarily financed by the membership. In every community of much size a variety of private organizations offer various kinds of recreational opportunities, usually restricted to members of the private group. They include private golf clubs, tennis clubs, yacht or sailing clubs, chess and bridge groups, athletic or sports clubs, and a host of others. These organizations serve a valuable purpose in rounding out the recreational opportunities in the community, and serving special interest needs. Such organizations should be encouraged and fostered to the extent that they contribute to the overall welfare of the community. As part of their total contributions, such groups often involve themselves in valuable community service projects.

Voluntary agencies are usually service oriented, and in many cases they are geared toward serving youth. Ordinarily they are supported by membership fees, sometimes supplemented by community funds and donations. Included in this group are such organizations as the Boy Scouts, Girl Scouts, YMCA and YWCA, girls' and boys' clubs, and certain church-sponsored programs. Usually recreational service is only one of the purposes of these organizations, while education of one sort or another is usually the prime objective.

Commercial recreation is sponsored primarily for the purpose of gaining a profit. Unfortunately some commercial forms of leisure activities are undesirable to the development of individuals and to the welfare of the community, but they continue because they are financially profitable. On the other hand there are commercial enterprises that offer desirable forms of recreation and contribute to the overall recreation opportunities in the community. The public recreation department ought to encourage and support the desirable commercial enterprises, and to discourage undesirable commercial activities.

Public sponsored programs are offered by local government agencies, and they are usually under the auspices of a recreation and park department sponsored through the government of the city, school district or county. The kinds of facilities ordinarily managed by public recreation agencies are parks, playgrounds, athletic fields, recreation buildings, golf courses, community centers, cultural arts centers, aquatic facilities, and sometimes zoos, gardens, museums, camp areas, waterfront areas, and winter sport areas.

LEGAL ASPECTS

Local government sponsorship of park and recreation programs is dependent upon state enabling laws. Within the framework of these laws local charters and ordinances provide the structure for a local sponsoring agency. Enabling laws are *permissive legislation*, not mandatory. They authorize local government agencies to establish and operate park and recreation systems, but local governments are not required to do so under such laws. They also permit local governments to acquire land and use public funds to construct buildings and sponsor programs. Other powers are also sometimes granted, such as the authority to join with other local government agencies in cooperative efforts. Some examples of state enabling laws were presented in the preceding chapter, which has to do with the functions of state government.

Local charters and ordinances are the legal instruments used to establish a department or agency at the local government level, and to describe the framework within which it is to function. The next section of this chapter describes charters and ordinances in more detail.

In some states, such as California and Utah, the state enabling law specifies rather exact elements of the organization that must be established to administer the local program, and rather exact descriptions of how the program will function. Some other states allow much more flexibility on these matters. In North Carolina, for example, the enabling statutes applicable to cities, counties and towns provide that local park and recreation systems may be conducted just as any other function of local government; however, local elected officials are authorized to create recreation boards and commissions by ordinance or resolution if this appears to be in the best interest of the people.

In all fifty states enabling laws allow local governments to acquire land and buildings for park and recreation purposes by negotiated purchase, donation, bequest or lease. In most cases local governments may condemn land for park and recreation purposes; this is known as the *right of eminent domain*.

In most states enabling laws empower school districts, municipalities, counties and other units of local government to join with one another to establish, own, operate, and maintain recreation and park systems. For example, the Utah and California laws permit any two or more units of local government to join in providing recreation facilities. The expenses of the joint operation are portioned among the participating agencies. The laws of most other states permit similar arrangements. The Iowa law, which is unique among the states, authorizes the creation of a county conservation board, and permits the board to cooperate with appropriate state and federal agencies, as well as with cities, towns, villages or other county conservation boards, to establish and maintain park and recreation systems.

LOCAL CHARTERS AND ORDINANCES

Local governments operating under *home rule charter* have the authority to establish and operate park and recreation systems under their general power "to promote the welfare, the safety, health, peace and morale of the citizens," (in other words the police power). In some instances the original charter includes a description of the provisions under which a park and recreation system should be established and administered, whereas in other cases the charter provides only the authority, and an *ordinance* must be written for official action.

A local government not acting under a home rule charter may, by use of an *ordinance*, create a park and recreation system and a governing board, provided it is authorized by state enabling legislation. Ordinances usually indicate the manner in which the park and recreation director and the board are selected, and define their power to pass regulations and rules pertaining to uses of areas and facilities, speed limits inside parks, closing hours of the facilities, and the kinds of conduct permitted. Following are some specific features that are essential in a *charter* provision or an *ordinance* used to establish a recreation and park department:

1. Name of the department
2. Designation of the managing authority (board, commission, council, etc.)
3. Outline of the powers, responsibilities and duties of the managing authority
4. Authorization and provisions for hiring and supervising personnel
5. Authorization for cooperative agreements and relationships with other agencies
6. Authorization for the acquisition and management of areas and facilities
7. Authorization for methods of financing the department
8. Description of limitations in programming, if any
9. Description of the nature of records and reports to be kept by the department, and of how the records are to be handled

Following is a sample of a city ordinance that could be used to establish a recreation and park commission. The exact provisions included in an ordinance of this kind would vary in accordance with the specifics of state enabling legislation and the preferences of the local officials initiating the action, but this model can serve as a general guide as to the kinds of information ordinarily included.

An Ordinance Creating a Recreation and Park Commission Prescribing Terms of Members, Organization, Powers, and Duties
Be it Ordained by ＿＿＿＿＿＿＿＿＿＿＿＿＿＿＿＿＿＿
of the City of ＿＿＿＿＿＿＿＿＿＿＿＿＿＿＿＿

1. Under the provisions of Section ＿＿＿＿ of Chapter ＿＿＿＿ of the General Laws of ＿＿＿＿, there is hereby established a recreation and park commission. This commission shall consist of five (5) persons serving without pay who shall be appointed by the mayor. The term of office shall be for five (5) years or until their successors are appointed and qualified, except that the members of such commission first appointed shall be appointed for such terms that the term of one member shall expire annually thereafter. Vacancies in such

commission occurring otherwise than by expiration of term shall be filled by the mayor for the unexpired term.

2. Immediately after their appointment, they shall meet and organize by electing one of their members president and such other officers as may be necessary. The commission shall have the power to adopt bylaws, rules, and regulations for the proper conduct of a public recreation and park system for the city.

3. The parks commission shall provide, conduct, and supervise public playgrounds, athletic fields, recreation centers, and other recreation facilities and activities on any of the properties owned or controlled by the city, or on other properties with the consent of the owners and authorities thereof. It shall have the power to conduct, or to cooperate with other agencies in conducting, any form of recreation that will employ the leisure time of the people in a constructive and wholesome manner.

4. The commission shall have the power to appoint or designate someone to act as superintendent who is trained and properly qualified for the work and such other personnel as the commission deems proper.

5. Annually the commission shall submit a budget to the city governing body for its approval. The commission may also solicit or receive any gifts or bequests of money or other personal property or any donation to be applied, principal or income, for either temporary or permanent use for parks, playgrounds or centers or other recreation purposes.

6. The recreation and park commission shall make full and complete monthly and annual reports to the governing body of the city and other reports from time to time as requested.

7. All ordinances, resolutions, or parts thereof, in conflict with the provisions and intent of this ordinance are hereby repealed.

Passed and Adopted this _____ day of _____
19 _____

THE MANAGING AUTHORITY

There are several possible kinds of managing authority at the local level. Most often the parks and recreation system is administered under a single department, which is separate from any other department—a department of parks and recreation. Sometimes parks and recreation are administered through two separate departments—a recreation department and a parks department. School districts sometimes manage recreation programs as a function supplementary to the public education program. Sometimes the county government becomes involved, and sometimes special districts are formed. A study conducted by the National Recreation and Park Association in 1970 showed that 76% of the local recreation and park programs are sponsored by city (or town) governments, while counties sponsor 9%, special districts 8%, schools 2%; multijurisdiction and other arrangements are involved in 5%.

No one authority is best suited to administer the recreation and park system in all cases. Conditions which vary in different localities must be considered in order to determine the best administrative arrangement: (1) The existing state enabling legislation must be examined to determine the permissible options. (2) Since the funding of the program is basic to its success, consideration must be given to the financial advantages under the different options. (3) The public attitude toward the organizational options must be considered, because public support for the sponsoring agency is important to success. (4) The facilities that are controlled by each agency must be considered, because this can influence significantly the availability of already existing facilities.

A Combined Department

As stated earlier, this is by far the most common of the different forms of organization, and is increasing the fastest. It is especially popular among small and medium-sized communities, whereas divided departments are more frequently found in large cities where these functions are more extensive and complicated. Perhaps the strongest points in favor of consolidation into a single department are: (1) increased efficiency, (2) better coordination of the use of areas and facilities, and (3) less potential conflict between park management and recreation programming. Generally the combined department results in financial savings and improved services, and it is usually the preferred organizational structure.

Separate Departments

Numerous large cities and some smaller ones maintain separate park and recreation departments, each with its own administrator and its own defined responsibilities. Sometimes the two departments are under the control of the same governing board, and sometimes they have separate boards. Some people advocate this separation because: (1) they claim that more direct and expedient attention will be given to both aspects of recreation and parks by having a specialist in each area administering the department and reporting directly to the municipal officials and (2) they think that a combined park and recreation system in a large city is too unwieldy to administer effectively through one department.

The disadvantages of separate departments are: (1) they generally compete for budgetary support, (2) often the leaders of the two departments are unwilling or unable to coordinate the efforts of the two units effectively, and (3) the departments are often (but not always) more expensive to operate because of duplication of equipment and personnel.

In the early development of the movement, the establishment of park departments preceded government interest in recreation programming. When recreation programs did begin to develop, this function was usually added to either the parks department or the school system. Later, after the need for recreation programs became better recognized, a few separate departments for this purpose were established, and gradually it became popular to combine recreation programming and park management into a single department. In some cases separate departments have continued to exist. In Cincinnati, Ohio, the officials believe that the duties of each department are sufficiently diverse to justify the two departments. Another kind of separation is illustrated in Monroe County, New York, where the county coordinates major land purchases and leaves programming, which varies considerably in different localities, in the hands of the communities. Obviously this approach would require very close cooperation and coordination between the governments of the county and the cities within the county.

School Administration of Recreation

It is important to recognize that the school system usually has a large amount of both indoor and outdoor facilities. By putting these facilities to effective use, they need not be duplicated in the form of community centers, playgrounds, athletic fields, etc. Further, school personnel represent a valuable source of leadership that can sometimes be available during the summer, and on a limited basis during the school year.

However, school districts are usually not able to adequately manage a balanced recreation and park system because, in addition to the recreation facilities and activities that are closely related to the school program, a complete recreation program involves nonschool facilities—golf courses, aquatic facilities, picnic areas and sometimes such specialized facilities as cultural art centers, boat-launching ramps, winter sports areas, zoos, aquariums, and museums. In other words, even though many aspects of recreation are closely aligned with school programs and facilities, some aspects are not. It is true that a school district dedicated to doing a good job in sponsoring recreation can make a significant contribution, and this is sometimes a good method of administration, so long as one or more local agencies supplements the school's recreational efforts.

Many professional recreation and park planners have strongly encouraged recreational use of school facilities and school use of recreation facilities. This approach has been advanced under the "park-school" and "community-school" concepts. The "park-school" is a facility that consists of one or more school buildings constructed on or adjacent to a park site. The "community-school" is a modern concept in which the school is conceived of as an agency that makes maximum use of its facilities and other resources to serve both the educational and recreational needs of the community. It is a "lighted-schoolhouse" concept.

The most efficient method of implementing cooperative school and community use of facilities is through joint recreation, park, and educational planning. That is, each recreational and educational facility or area is originally planned and constructed for joint use by the two departments. Even though this approach is a valuable one, it is apparent that all the recreation and park needs of the people cannot be satisfied through cooperation with the school system. Opportunities for golf, swimming, boating, hiking, picnicking, cultural arts, usually must be provided through other community agencies.

County Administration

The most frequent involvement of county government is in the provision of physical facilities such as parks, golf courses, playgrounds, athletic fields, and recreation centers which are used in support of community sponsored programs. In counties where a large number of people live outside the boundaries of the incorporated communities (a large rural or semirural population), it is important that the county government provide recreation opportunities for these people in addition to supporting community efforts.

In Iowa the legislature delegated to the county board of supervisors the responsibility for appointing a five-member conservation board to finance land purchase and development. The board of supervisors can levy annual taxes of not more than one mill on the assessed valuation of taxable real and personal property. Almost all of the 99 counties in Iowa have become involved in the purchase and development of park lands under the authority of this state law.

Special Districts

In some states special park districts are legal political subdivisions, and consequently are separate from any city or county government. Such special districts are regional complements to local recreation and park systems. They are permitted to levy taxes and issue bonds. Special districts have some unique characteristics:

1. They are usually organized to perform a single function
2. They can enter into contracts and own and dispose of property
3. They have fiscal and administrative independence from other political subdivisions
4. They are frequently exempt from the tax and debt limits imposed on city and county governments

Examples of such districts are the North Jefco Metropolitan Recreation and Park District, an 84-square-mile rural area in the northeast corner of Jefferson County, Colorado, and the Cleveland (Ohio) Metropolitan Park District, which is concerned primarily with land acquisition, development and maintenance. Generally special districts are best avoided, but under certain unique circumstances a special district might offer the most effective solution to the recreation and park needs of the locale.

FINANCING

Once a community has accepted the sponsorship of a recreation and park system as a governmental function, sufficient and consistent financial support must be supplied in order to provide adequate facilities, services and programs. To a large degree the budget determines the magnitude, the scope and the quality of the services that can be offered. Funds are needed to acquire areas and facilities, to employ qualified leaders, to purchase supplies and equipment, and to maintain the parks, community centers and other sites that are essential for a well-rounded program.

Financial needs are normally of two kinds: *current operating expenses* and *capital outlay*. The current operating funds ordinarily come from appropriations, special recreation taxes, and fees and charges. The funds for capital outlay usually come from bond issues, special assessments, donations, and government grants.

Figure 31.   The performing arts are important to the overall community program.

Appropriations from the General Fund

Tax funds may be appropriated for the support of recreation and parks on the same basis as for other services of local government. Decisions are made by local government officials (city councilmen, county commissioners, or whatever), and are not voted on by the members of municipality. This is the most widely used method of financing local park and recreation systems, and other methods of financing are usually considered supplementary to it.

The amount of appropriated funds that can be obtained each year depends to a large extent on the ability of the administrator to win approval of his program by the governing authorities of the community—those who determine the allocation of funds. If the budget proposal is well prepared and well justified, and if the governing authorities are contemporary thinkers and civic minded, the recreation and park department will probably receive its just share of appropriated funds. How well those funds are used in providing important services will then probably have a strong influence on the amount of funding that can be acquired the next year.

Figure 32. Creative playground equipment. (Chicago Park District photo.)

Special Tax

In some states, in accordance with enabling legislation, a municipality can levy a special tax for the particular purpose of financing the park and recreation system. In some states the special tax can be levied by decision of the municipal officials, whereas in other states the tax must be approved by the voters. The main advantage of acquiring funds by this method is that the money can be spent only for the purpose for which it was raised. In reality the special tax is a property tax expressed in terms of a certain number of mills on each dollar, or cents on each $100 of assessed valuation of real property. In some states the enabling legislation places a ceiling on the tax, whereas in other states it does not, thereby leaving the amount to the discretion of local officials.

Fees and Charges

Two approaches can be taken on fees and charges: (1) the use of special fees not related to recreation such as revenue from parking meters or local taxes on certain items such as cigarettes, or (2) admission and use of fees from recreation area facilities such as golf courses, swimming pools, museums, zoos, aquariums, etc., and profits from concessions.

It is important to realize that parks and recreation can no more be self-supporting than can public education. But collection of certain fees can be justified, and this can certainly help to offset the total cost of the program.

Bond Issues

Local governments ordinarily have the authority to issue bonds to finance capital acquisitions and improvements, including park areas and recreation facilities. The issuing of bonds must be approved by the voters of the municipality, and a limit to bond indebtedness is placed by state law. The issuing of bonds is actually a form of borrowing, and it is not a substitute for appropriated funds or revenue. The bonds must be paid off over a period of years, as a mortgage on a home. The sale of bonds is often used in connection with the acquisition and development of large park areas and the construction of swimming pools, community centers and golf courses.

Special Assessments

Special assessments are sometimes used to finance permanent improvements which are paid in whole or in part by the property owners in the area especially benefited. This method is not used widely, but under certain circumstances it is a desirable approach. The positive feature is that it places the cost of services on those who benefit and are willing to pay. However, if this becomes a common method of financing the low economic areas of the community which often need facilities and improvements the most generally are neglected.

Donations and Gifts

Donations, gifts and bequests constitute a major form of income for some departments. Philanthropic organizations and wealthy civic-minded individuals have, in some cases, been very kind to park and recreation departments. However, in most communities this is not a significant source of income, and it is never a regular source because this form of financing is usually in the form of a gift of valuable property that can be developed into a park, or the donation of funds for a community center or a boys' or girls' club, and may happen only once in a decade or perhaps only once in a lifetime. In their long-range plans, however, recreational authorities should be alert to this possible source of financial assistance, and be prepared to utilize it if it becomes available.

Government Grants

The federal government, and in some cases state government agencies, can grant money to local governments for certain approved purposes having to do with the park and recreation system. This is explained in the two chapters covering the involvement of federal government and state government agencies. By far the most prominent source of grant money in recent years has been the Land and Water Conservation Fund, which is administered by the federal Bureau of Outdoor Recreation. This fund has been a boon to many municipal recreation and park systems since it was instituted in the mid-1960s. A large number of tracts of land have been purchased and developed by local governments through such financing that could never have been purchased or developed otherwise.

PROGRAMMING

It is not enough to provide areas and facilities for recreational use. People need programmed opportunities for participation under effective leadership. In determining the content of the recreation program, certain valuable principles ought to be considered:

1. The recreation program should attempt to meet the basic recreational needs of both individuals and groups in the community.
2. The program should be diversified in order to give balance relative to people's needs, interests and desires.
3. The program should provide approximately equal opportunity for all people regardless of race, creed, social status, economic needs, sex, age, interests or intellectual and physical capacities.

4. The activities in the program should be offered at a variety of times in order to accommodate the diverse living schedules of the population.
5. The various activities in the program should be planned and coordinated to make the best use of community facilities and personnel resources.
6. Adequate leadership should be recognized as the backbone of a successful recreation offering.
7. The procedures and methods involved in the program should adequately assure the safety and health of the participants and the employees.
8. The program content and methods should be evaluated regularly, and creative approaches should be consistently applied toward improvement of the program.

A community recreation program can include a great variety of activities and special interests. The kinds of opportunities most often included are: field and gymnasium sports and games, aquatic activities, arts and crafts of various kinds, dance instruction and performance, dramatic productions, music activities, social events, camping and outdoor experiences, tours of zoos, museums, aquariums, etc., special community events, community service activities, and special interest or hobby groups.

PROVIDING AREAS AND FACILITIES

One of the major responsibilities of the park and recreation sponsoring authority, and one which has long-term impact, is the planning and development of areas and facilities. In a large system the following kinds of areas and facilities are usually included:

Large multipurpose parks
Small neighborhood parks and playgrounds
Athletic and play fields
Forest or nature reserves
Zoos, aquariums and gardens
Museums and galleries
Street and area beautification
Facilities for the performing arts
Swimming facilities and waterfront areas

One of the most important challenges to park and recreation officials is the provision of adequate areas and facilities for both the immediate and long-term needs of a growing population. It is absolutely essential that planning and acquisition be kept well ahead of the growth of the community. Otherwise land becomes committed to shopping centers, parking lots, industrial areas, residential districts, and roads and streets. The escalation of land prices has made it increasingly difficult to acquire and develop the needed amount of space. Acquisition well in advance can help avoid price escalation caused by demand as the area grows.

Contrary to the beliefs of many, American cities and towns are not blessed with an abundance of park and recreation space. By European standards, where many cities are spotted with attractive parks and beautiful city squares, many American cities are impoverished in this regard. The land acquisition programs of the faster growing cities—Los Angeles, Salt Lake City, Dallas, Denver, and Phoenix—are coming nowhere near keeping pace with increased growth.

It is important for park and recreation leaders to keep in mind that the amount of land available for all uses is essentially fixed, while demands for it continue to increase. As our population expands, so does the need to use the same tracts of land for competing purposes. Land is being consumed for subdivisions at an alarming rate. For example, the open space report published by Fairfax County, Virginia, indicates that if the present rate of space consumption (approximately 188 acres per 1,000 new residents) continues for two more decades the entire county will be consumed by urban sprawl. Many other areas across the nation are in the same fix.

The price of land, especially sites suitable for parks, is increasing at a spectacular rate. Some public officials believe a crisis is developing. The Bureau of Outdoor Recreation, in its publication "Recreation Land Price Escalation," reports that values generally are rising throughout the nation at the rate of 5 to 10% annually, and the value of land suitable for recreation is increasing at even a higher rate.

Land for public use is obtained in a variety of ways, and resourceful public officials will explore the use of all of them. The most successful and widely used method is negotiation with the owner on price and then *cash purchase*. In some cases payments can be spread over a long period by agreeing to buy the tract on installments. Tax-delinquent land, usually marginal in character and value, is often acquired for certain purposes at very low prices. Occasionally it is necessary for local governments to exercise the *right of eminent domain*, which is a provision in the law allowing agencies of government to condemn privately owned land and acquire it for public use at the appraised market value. This right is usually used as a last resort, but sometimes it serves as a useful protective measure on behalf of public interest. *Donation* is another form by which local governments acquire land that is particularly suitable for park and recreation development. Some departments have been able to acquire a large portion of their park land by this method. Where law permits, local officials have often enacted subdivision regulations demanding *dedication of park sites* in new subdivisions or *cash payment* in lieu thereof.

In addition to acquiring complete title to a tract of land, some local officials have experimented with buying less than full title rights through the use of *scenic easements, right of way accesses,* and *conservation easements*. Also, property and buildings are sometimes *leased* by local governments on long-term agreements.

PLANNING AND ZONING

One of the most important steps toward achieving an adequate recreation and park system is the development and implementation of a plan which establishes priorities for the acquisition of areas based on existing and projected needs. The responsibility for such a plan is usually entrusted to one of two public agencies—the local planning agency or the park and recreation agency. In a survey conducted by the National Association of Counties, park and recreation directors replied that most plans are prepared by the planning agency in cooperation with the park and recreation agency. The planning agency has access to population data and other basic information. In addition it is well situated to dovetail the park and recreation plan with other elements of the comprehensive plan for the total community. Naturally each agency of local government, including parks and recreation, would have significant input to the overall plan.

Community planning cannot be static. The plan furnishes guidelines, but the guidelines must sometimes be altered to fit new needs influenced by changing situations. Although no one has developed a single best method of developing a plan, many planners agree that the procedure generally can be separated into three major phases: (1) collection of data on the present recreation supply and demand, including existing facilities, areas and programs, and people's expressed interests and needs, (2) an objective projection of future park and recreation needs, and (3) formulation of proposals to meet both near and long-term future needs.

Little is accomplished by comprehensive planning unless *implementation* occurs. Acreage must be obtained and developed as called for in the plan. Such things as a defined timetable for the plan, a financial structure to support it, and cooperation of other agencies and of the citizenry are important aspects of the implementation.

In view of our increasing population and the strong trend toward urbanization, it is essential that zoning ordinances be established and enforced to prevent overcrowded and disorderly conditions. Adequate zoning for parks and open space can greatly improve living conditions and result in increased property values.

In many cities and counties local officials have adopted *land dedication ordinances* which require subdivision developers to dedicate a portion of the subdivision as permanent open space, or to make a cash payment to the local government in lieu of dedication of the land. Such ordinances are predicated on the grounds that each subdivision increases the demand for park and recreation areas, and that each subdivider should be required to furnish open space for the community in relation to the need he creates by building homes. This is justified on the same basis as the requirement to install streets, sidewalks and other community improvements in connection with subdivisions. Theoretically the developer recovers the monetary cost of contributing land or money by raising the price of his homes. Thus the home owners who will benefit most from the open space actually pay for it.

In some localities officials are now taking steps to preserve open space in residential areas by enacting *cluster or density zoning ordinances*. A cluster zoning ordinance establishes an overall density for the area, usually in terms of acreage for each dwelling unit, but it allows the developer to adjust the lot sizes and group the homes as long as the overall density is maintained. One section of tract may be developed at a high density and the remaining portions at a low density, or all development may be centered in one section with the remaining open space preserved for park and recreation purposes. These ordinances stipulate whether the open space is to be retained in private ownership or dedicated to the local government. Both the community and home owners may reap aesthetic, recreational, and economic benefits from cluster developments. Local government officials find cluster developments a practical way to preserve adequate open space.

THE STATUS OF MUNICIPAL RECREATION

In 1975, the National Recreation and Park Association and the International City Management Association cooperated in an extensive survey of municipal recreation and park services and programs. The survey was restricted to U.S. cities over 10,000 population. The following important points of information resulted from the survey:

1. The vast majority (88%) of the cities responding to the survey provide full-time year-round recreation and park services. The larger the city, the more likely it is to have a full-time year-round program.

2. The majority (66%) of the cities which provide services function under a combined park and recreation agency.

3. Ninety-six percent of the cities that responded cooperate with the local school system in the use of school facilities, but only about half have a formal written agreement with the school system.

4. Generally, the larger cities tend to provide services to special groups more often than do the smaller cities. Such special groups include mentally retarded, physically handicapped, senior citizens, preschool children and the socioeconomically disadvantaged.

5. Many cities, particularly the larger ones, are now attempting to provide services to individuals who are excluded from traditional programs for such reasons as confinement to home, correctional institutions, orphanages or hospitals.

6. It was found that, in many cities, services are generally unavailable to citizens with a typical 8-to-5 work day. This suggests that recreation personnel also work a typical day.

7. The percentage of cities that do not provide services on weekends is significant, yet weekends may be the best time for many citizens to participate in municipally sponsored activities.

8. Local public appropriations, primarily revenue from property taxes, was the greatest source of income for park and recreation services, comprising more than 50% of all available revenue.

9. The survey showed that recreation and park employees have been a part of the trend toward collective bargaining and 41% of all of the agencies that responded have organized employee bargaining units.

10. The acquisition of community open space, especially in densely populated urban areas, continues to be of vital concern to local park and recreation leaders, and it was indicated that diligent efforts are being made to handle this problem.

COMMUNITY SCHOOL CONCEPT

Today the community school concept, which is being fostered primarily through the efforts of the Mott Foundation (Flint, Michigan), is making significant progress toward promoting better community use of school plants. A large portion of any community school program is recreational oriented. However, the program is much more inclusive than recreational activities alone. The modern community school fosters the idea that facilities and other school resources be put to optimum use by serving the educational and recreational needs of the community. Flint, Michigan, has served as the model city for this kind of development. It is considered more advanced in this respect than any other city in the country. Therefore, the community school concept can best be understood by describing how it has been implemented in Flint.

Each public school in Flint is open for service to people from early morning until late at night each school day and on Saturday during the entire 52 weeks of the year. Some schools are in service on Sunday for church programs, concerts, lectures and other cultural events.

The community school, as conceived in Flint, includes the core program as well as all segments of the voluntary program. Hence, each school day is 14 to 16 hours in length and includes more than just the 6-hour core program segment. The Flint Board of Education is responsible for the total program and pays for all staff and other expenses involved in the informal program as well as the core program. However, the Board of Education receives money from the Mott Foundation to support much of the informal program.

From 7:30 to 8:30 a.m. many children engage in such programs as sunrise singers, language study, shop, and art and crafts, while adults hold breakfast meetings, committee meetings and conferences at the schools. From 3:30 to 5:00 p.m. of the regular school day, on Saturday, and during the summer, children engage in a variety of enrichment activities, many of which develop positive attitudes toward and supplement the required formal work. Each child engages in the activities of his choice, and can select activities that are academic, cultural, aesthetic, service oriented, recreational or social in nature. The most commonly selected are: reading for fun, arithmetic for fun, science projects, arts and crafts, shop, homemaking, junior police, bachelor's club, dramatics, music, puppetry, typewriting, foreign language, free play, sports and games, gymnastics, bike hikes, roller skating, swimming, radio plays, interpretive dancing, track races, and Scouting.

The heaviest use of school facilities by adults occurs during the 5 to 10 p.m. period. Adults, like children and youth, also use the facilities on Saturday and sometimes on Sunday. Adults have a number of activities early in the morning before classes begin for the children. Frequently the community room and sometimes regular classrooms are used by adults during the formal portion of the day. There are over 1,200 different courses and activities available to adults in the areas of basic education, arts and crafts, clothing construction, business education, economic education, home arts and foods, mechanical skills, retailing, music, speech and dramatics, trades and industry, clubs for men and women, recreational athletics, college level work, mother-daughter and father-son nights, senior citizen programs, book reviews, lectures, town hall meetings and concerts.

During the late afternoons and on Friday and Saturday evenings a number of programs are conducted for family groups—family potlucks, family roller skating, family work bees, family shop programs, family swim nights, and cultural programs designed for the enjoyment and learning of the entire family.

As the Graduate Training Office of the Mott Foundation puts it: In summary the community school in Flint is a human engineering laboratory serving the basic needs of people throughout life—from the cradle to the grave—the learning center where:

Expectant parents receive instruction in prenatal care and parenthood
Babies are brought for clinical checkup
Preschool children get ready for the experiences of kindergarten
Undernourished children receive a wholesome breakfast
Mothers learn how to purchase, prepare and conserve food
Mothers learn how to launder clothes and to construct and care for clothing
Children give expression to their creative talents during optional periods
Teenagers engage in wholesome cultural, social, recreational and service activities
Teenagers are reclaimed as a part of society
School dropouts are reclaimed through the Personalized Curriculum Program
Mothers dependent on public assistance learn to become self-supporting
Adults learn to read and write and to acquire other basic skills
Men displaced by automation learn new salable skills
Adults study in any field of learning of their choice
Referrals are made to other agencies for help with basic needs
Hobbies are learned and pursued to meet leisure time needs, in some cases to produce income
Groundwork is laid for community leadership and community development
People get ready to meet changing conditions in the community
Health needs of all are cared for or referred

The cultural needs of people are fulfilled
Older citizens learn that they too are still a part of society
All the resources of the community are brought to bear upon the learning process[2]

DEPARTMENTAL GOALS

A local recreation and park department ought to have clearly stated goals which are challenging to the department, and yet realistic from the standpoint of achievement. If the goals are well stated, they become descriptive of what the departmental leaders hope to accomplish, and if the goals are realistic they are definitive of what will be achieved. Following are the goals of the Oakland City, California, Parks and Recreation Department;

> The Oakland Parks and Recreation Commission helps the citizens of Oakland discover and analyze needs and opportunities for worthy leisure-time pursuits for all. It seeks to provide public facilities, professional leadership, flexible programs and services, democratic planning and firm policies to help citizens meet these needs in order of greatest importance, according to sound principles of recreation planning and administration.
>
> The Commission seeks to provide recreational experiences which are socially satisfying, physically healthy, mentally stimulating, aesthetically pleasing, and culturally creative. The Commission believes that equal opportunity should be available to all citizens for discovering and enjoying the skills and benefits of athletics, games, swimming, art, drama, dance, music, outdoor living and camping, social recreation, social and hobby clubs, public festivals, and many other facets of our great American culture.
>
> The Commission recognizes that the recreation services and citizen contacts carried on daily by full-time professional staff in adequate neighborhood recreation centers are essential for serving the citizens in all areas of the city. Also recognized is the need for establishing certain programs and recreational services on a city-wide basis, when this is a more effective way to meet certain special needs.
>
> The Commission recognizes a special obligation to serve children, youth, the aged, and individuals with special problems. It is particularly aware of the potential influence of recreation on character development and good citizenship. Because trained personnel are in daily contact with large numbers of citizens in the neighborhoods in which they reside, there is a special opportunity to influence the attitudes of citizens toward their city government as a whole.
>
> The Commission recognizes its obligation to acquire, control, and safeguard for continued use of the general public those recreation facilities and services which should be publicly owned, controlled, or operated in the best interests of the total community.
>
> The Commission recognizes the necessity for cooperating with, serving, and assisting community organizations and agencies, business concerns, public schools and other public departments which are providing large segments of the over-all leisure time and recreation program within the community. The Commission is aware of its obligations to know vividly what is happening in the community, and to help in establishing community cohesiveness and harmony through the total operation of an adequate and dynamic Parks and Recreation Department as a vital unit of municipal government.[3]

COORDINATION AMONG AGENCIES

Coordination and cooperation among local agencies and between local and state agencies are essential to an adequate park and recreation system. Local divisions of government such as planning, personnel, finance, purchasing, law enforcement, and roads and streets play important supportive roles. Also the cooperation and support of civic groups and of local citizens, particularly the local leaders, are important to the success of the recreation and park program. Further, the municipal recreation and park agency should coordinate as well as possible its efforts with the efforts of private, volunteer and commercial agencies.

REFERENCES

1. Butler, G. D.: *Introduction to Community Recreation*, 5th ed. McGraw-Hill, New York, 1976, p. 68.
2. *A Look at Flint's Community Schools*. Graduate Training Office, Mott Foundation, Flint, 1976.
3. *Bulletin of the Parks and Recreation Commission*. Parks and Recreation Department, Oakland City, 1975.

10

The International Scene of Leisure and Recreation

Anthropologists and historians generally agree that athletics, outdoor sports, dancing, games, music, folklore and such other leisure time activities existed in some form and to some degree in every culture that we know about. These are "cultural universals" which apparently grow out of basic human needs, and serve a somewhat common purpose to all people regardless of the time of their existence or the cultural group to which they belong. Extensive efforts have been made to determine what underlying identities between various people are responsible for these universal elements. A basic assumption which seems to be generally agreed upon is that all cultural groups for which we have historical records are essentially alike in their basic psychological equipment and mechanisms, regardless of their differences in time, geography and physique, and that the cultural differences among them reflect only the responses of essentially similar organisms to unlike conditions. With this basic premise in mind, it is interesting to search back into the ancient history of parks and recreation to get a glimpse of how the patterns developed and spread over time and geographic area.

Marie Luise Gothein in her monumental book *A History of Garden Art* credits the Asiatics with being the real inventors of parks. The particular Asiatics to whom she referred were the Sumerians, a people even more ancient than the Egyptians. As evidence of the park idea she cites the "Epic of Gilganesh," a story which was pieced together from inscribed tablets excavated in Mesopotamia. Gothein traces the western Asiatic parks from the vineyards and fish ponds of the Sumerian king, Gudea, about 2340 B.C. down through the hanging gardens of Babylon about the ninth or tenth century B.C., past the introduction of flowers in the parks in the seventh century B.C.[1]

Centuries later Greek writers told of the parks and gardens of Persia. Socrates tells how carefully the Persian kings guarded their gardens and parks. Gothein reported the following:

> We find from all accounts and from monuments also that these paradises were first and foremost hunting-parks, the fruit-trees grown for food, just as in the Babylonian-Assyrian sites. . . . The Persians were also familiar with the chase in the open country. A grand hunting-ground was given to the young Cyrus by his grandfather, in the hope that it would keep him at home, but he despised it, and, fired with longing, summoned his companions and went off, for in this park there were so many animals that he felt as though he was only shooting captive creatures.[1]

In ancient India there were not only parks for the kings but great recreation and park areas for communities as well. A description of a park in the twelfth century B.C. in the city of Polonnaruwa in Ceylon includes:

> . . . spouts of water, conveyed thither in pipes and machines, made the place appear as though clouds were incessantly pouring down drops of rain. There was a great array of different baths that delighted masters and men. We hear also of other parks and other baths, and even of gardens that the rich made for the recreation of the poor.[1]

In many respects the Greeks brought civilization to new heights, and one of their important areas of contribution was in parks and recreation.

> In Plato's time the gymnasium and the park were so closely connected that the philosopher wanted to have gymnasiums in such places only as were well-watered and specially favoured by Nature. In Rhegium such a zone was in existence in the Paradise of the elder Dionysius, and in Elis at an earlier date there was wild woodland round the gymnasium instead of garden. But we may be quite sure that gymnasiums were attached to hero sanctuaries, for the clear light of history gives us the origin of one that was set up in Syracuse: the town raised a tomb in the Agora to Timoleon the liberator, and founded a Heroon with annual games. Hence arose later on a magnificent gymnasium with halls, exercise grounds, garden grounds, and an Odeon for musical performances.[1]

Wealthy and influential Romans were noted for having one or more large villas, and many of them had features of parks with special emphasis on hunting.

> . . . Quintus Hortensius had already made a park of fifty yokes of land, and enclosed it with a wall, and on this estate he had set up on the higher ground a shooting-box where he entertained his friends in a peculiar way. He had a slave dressed like Orpheus who sang before them, and then sounded a horn, whereupon a whole crowd of stags and boars and other quadrupeds came up, so that to him who told the tale the spectacle seemed more delightful than the hunt itself.[1]

Generally speaking throughout the Roman Empire the villas were on the outskirts of the towns or in the countryside. In Rome itself they invaded the city, so that the city was spotted with gardens. Here was the first significant move to bring the country to the city. Further, the Romans seemed to be the first to invent the floral greenhouse, using mica for windowpanes.

As the Roman Empire in the first century of the Christian era expanded northward into what is now France and Germany, the great villas and hunting parks spread—some of them even as far north as Great Britain.

> Everything that the Romans did in these provinces, in the way of gardening and cultivation, was destined to perish when they were compelled to remove their troops under the German onslaughts. The open villas and gardens were the first victims and these Northern lands had to wait for hundreds of years before they could make a humble beginning with a new garden art. In the North the thread was broken, and only after wild, stormy years can we discover a new trace, again starting from the South.[1]

During the early Christian era prior to the fall of Rome, little was new in the historical development of parks and recreation. The thousand years following the fall of Rome, commonly know as the Middle Ages and sometimes called the Dark Ages, were truly dark from the standpoint of park and recreation development. The idea of parks was barely kept alive—largely in the monasteries, which frequently were the former villas of the nobility and later possessed by the church.

Gradually some of the barons began to acquire sizable estates, and the art of gardening grew from the simple chore of raising fruit and plants to planting gardens of interest and beauty. By the thirteenth and fourteenth centuries there were a number of such villas, and a popular feature of most of the gardens was the maze (a network of hedges) which was interesting and constructed as a puzzle in which to find one's way.

By the end of the thirteenth century in Italy and particularly in Florence, public grounds were established for the pleasure of common people. These took the form of walks and public squares, frequently decorated with statues.

During the early phase of the Renaissance in the 1500s the private grounds and estates of the noble and the wealthy developed in fabulous fashion. In the period between 1500 and the later part of the eighteenth century the central European and Scandinavian countries, and even to some extent Russia, made great progress toward the development of parks and gardens. Among the popular facilities were private fishing and hunting reserves, summerhouses, grottos and formal gardens. Water displays including canals, ponds and elaborate fountains (some with extravagant statues), all became part of the numerous parks and gardens. Outdoor theaters, much like those of the Greek and Roman eras, were reintroduced, as were facilities for certain games—tennis courts, archery ranges, race courses and lawn bowling greens. Music became part of the entertainment in many of the gardens. This was the period when several still famous parks were established—as the Tuileries and the Luxembourg in Paris, Versailles outside of Paris and the Parque de Madrid in Spain. This new movement, which had its origin in Italy and especially in Florence, crept northward into France and the Low Countries, then Germany, Scandinavia and England.

By the latter part of the eighteenth century England had developed a park and garden character of its own, which in turn influenced other countries of the continent. The English gardens assumed the appearance of informal walks and plantings. Rock walkways were developed and greens were provided for bowling. The bowling greens of England became the "boulingrins" of France. It was during the late part of this era that parks and gardens became more acceptable to the commoners, and it was also during this time that the true "people's park" came into existence. The trend toward parks inside communities and accessible to all spread to France and Germany, and then to other countries in both northern and southern Europe.

In America, as abroad, municipal parks were a late development. In the New England colonies the traditional common public ground known in England appeared again in a new setting. Boston set aside a common as early as 1634, and in 1640 took action to protect it from future encroachment. The lower green at Newburyport appears on the most ancient plat of the old town. All through Massachusetts, Connecticut and New Hampshire numerous examples still exist of more or less beautiful village greens of various origins and in various states of preservation.

It is natural that England exerted the strongest influence on the early phases of the American park and recreation movement. However, as our country developed it established a park and recreation character of its own, and in some respects the United States has now become the world leader in the provision of park and recreation areas and facilities. This is especially true concerning outdoor recreation. In some other aspects of park and recreation development, however, the United States has not equalled the accomplishments of certain European countries.

THE STRUGGLE FOR CITY PARKS

The rapid and somewhat chaotic expansion during the industrial revolution was damaging to urban life in countless ways. For European cities which had centuries to develop a base in humanistic values and logical order, the changes were distressing, but for new and rapidly developing cities, like many of those in America, the changes brought on by the industrial revolution were disastrous in many respects.

For one thing, European cities had parks. Most of these were the private estates of titled and wealthy European families. Nondemocratic at their inception, they nevertheless formed the basis of public park systems for Europe's older cities.

Moreover, many cities with classical histories possess street patterns and civil organization which are highly humanistic and livable. The streets were originally planned for pedestrians and slow-paced carts, and allowed for an intimacy that still exists today. The topography of the land was incorporated into the design of the cities rather than demolished by bulldozers in order to lay out a symmetrical pattern. Thus at the peak of development a typical European city possessed great open spaces combined with centrally located organic nuclei, and this combination resulted in convenience without congestion.

Amsterdam's traditional canals, which radiate from the city's center, offer both a means of civic structure and open space. Amsterdam's modern plan calls for linear development in three directions from the city's heart—like a three-fingered hand—thumb, index, and little finger. Replacing the ring and forefinger are narrow green spaces of agricultural and recreational development. This interlacing of rural and urban fingers gives structure to the city's growth patterns and maintains contact with nature as well. The superpark Amsterdamse Bos represent one such green finger and offers 2,500 acres of carefully planned watery wilderness to the nearby citizenry, easily within cycling distance. The middle finger, extending out from the city, is represented by the new town of Amstelveen. This model city from nearly every standpoint has been carefully planned to include a system of linking greenways and canals, while at the same time providing boundaries which are fixed permanently by adjacent parks and polders (land reclaimed from the sea). Although the corridor park was invented by an American, Frederick Law Olmstead, it is probably seeing its greatest development in the cities of northern Europe.

Paris' two superparks, the Bois de Boulogne and Vincennes, in conjunction with Vie de Triomphe and the Seine, create the framework for a highly stylized urban system. Based on existing urbanography, a far-reaching plan by Baron Haussmann, Paris emerged in the nineteenth century as the most exciting and urbane city of Europe. Her two green lungs help to separate the city proper from her inner suburbs, and are themselves connected across the heart of the city by the river and the Vie de Triomphe. In this manner Paris remains distinct from her surroundings in a way which was never accomplished in London. Inner-city green space is provided by medium-sized parks, such as the Luxembourg, Buttes-Chaumont, Jardin des Plantes, Montouris and Tuileries.

By European standards many large American cities are park poor, and getting worse. The growth in park acreage is not proportional to the growth in land area and population of many of our cities, particularly such fast-growing cities as Houston, Phoenix, Dallas and Los Angeles.

CONTRIBUTIONS FROM OTHER COUNTRIES

Numerous forms of recreation in America were transferred to this country from western Europe. The first colonists brought with them their old-world songs, games, folk dances, sports, and hobbies, and the continued migration of people from Europe have kept alive many of the folkways of the old countries, even though the language and many of the customs have been forgotten by the new generations. In many regions of the country strong evidence can still be found of folk songs, dances and games from England, Spain, Sweden, Denmark, Germany, France, Poland, Czechoslovakia, Israel, Greece, Italy and Switzerland. Also the influence of the European cultural arts upon the American way of life has certainly been significant. Further our city parks have been influenced strongly by the French, Germans, English and Danish, and most of the early park designers and architects in America were from those countries.

We are indebted to certain European countries for some of our athletic sports. American football had predecessors in ancient Greece and Rome, and in more recent times in England and other countries influenced by England, in the form of rugby. Even baseball, which is said to be as American as the Fourth of July, has many similarities to the much older game of cricket, which is still popular in England, South Africa, Australia and New Zealand. Basketball is the one American game which was almost entirely original, although some aspects of basketball can be related to more ancient games. Emigrants from other countries have also influenced such outdoor activities as snow skiing and mountain climbing.

OUR CONTRIBUTIONS TO OTHER COUNTRIES

The creation of national parks and the maintenance of a national park system were ideas of American origin. The first national park in the world was Yellowstone, established in 1872. Now the national park system of the U.S. includes almost 300 areas of different kinds, of which 38 are national parks. Over 1300 such areas have been established in nearly 100 other countries of the world. The first country to follow in the footsteps of the United States was Canada, which in 1885 set aside a small portion of what is now Banff National Park. Canada today has a national park system second only to that of the United States.

Certain countries of Africa have some of the most significant national parks in the world, including world-famous Kruger National Park in the Union of South Africa and Victoria Falls in Rhodesia. The Sabie Game Reserve, forerunner of the Kruger National Park, was established in 1898. Other countries in Africa that have national parks are Algeria, the Congo, Uganda, Kenya and Tanzania.

Sweden was the first European country to enter the national park scene when it passed a law relative to the establishment of such parks in 1909. Finland, France, Belgium, Great Britain, Greece, Italy, Poland, Spain, Russia, Switzerland, and Yugoslavia have since established national parks.

In Asian countries the movement to reserve national areas has been slow except in Japan, where in 1931 a national park law was adopted. Today Japan's park system is highly developed, and it includes areas for boating, camping, hiking, fishing, and skiing. Meager beginnings of park systems have occurred in Lebanon, Iran, India, Burma, Indonesia and other Asian countries.

New Zealand and Australia have set aside extensive national park areas, and national park systems have at least begun in Mexico, Brazil, Argentina, Chile, Peru and Venezuela.

The National Park Service of the United States, through its division of International Affairs, has assisted other countries in establishing national parks. With its highly successful park system the U.S. is in a position to make an even greater contribution to the remainder of the world in this form of recreational endeavor. The United Nations has also become involved in national park improvement.

The organized camping movement with planned programs and educational objectives became popular in the United States. This was greatly influenced by the romance of the American Indians and the drama of the western movement through the American frontiers. The widespread popularity to foreign countries of these dramatic phases of American life has undoubtedly influenced the appeal of organized camping in other countries. Also, the development of youth organizations such as the Boy Scouts, Girl Scouts, Campfire Girls, YMCA, YWCA, 4-H Clubs and those of several churches has contributed to the organized camping movement.

The American athletic games that have contributed the most to other countries are basketball and baseball. Basketball has become especially popular in many countries of the world, and baseball is gaining rapidly in popularity in such countries as Japan and Italy. Lacrosse, which is Canada's national sport, originated with the North American Indians. However, its popularity has not become widespread.

Publicly financed community centers and playgrounds with organized programs probably originated in the United States. Such centers and playgrounds do not exist in other countries in anywhere near the same number, and did not even appear in other countries until quite recently.

The recreation and park occupational field is larger and better developed in the United States than other countries, with the areas of the world that are next best developed in this regard being central and northern Europe, especially England, Germany, Switzerland, the Netherlands and Sweden.

INTERNATIONAL ORGANIZATIONS

The *World Leisure and Recreation Association*, previously known as the International Recreation Association, was originally established in 1956. It is a nonprofit world service agency which has accredited consultant status with the United Nations. It is supported by membership dues, contributions from individuals, foundation grants and income from service contracts. The WLRA services are organized into four general categories: education, research, information distribution and consultation. Some of the specific kinds of projects that it becomes involved in are: (1) the sponsorship of international conferences and congresses, (2) the conduct of study tours, (3) various kinds of research and information gathering procedures along with the dissemination of information, (4) a global directory of agencies and organizations providing services in the recreation and park field, (5) publication and distribution of a bimonthly bulletin for members of the organization, (6) consultation services to governments and private agencies, (7) assistance with the organization of national and regional agencies and associations in support of recreation and parks, (8) leadership training programs in countries where such help is needed.

The *International Youth Hostel Federation* has youth hostel associations in 34 countries including the United States. The youth hostel movement originated in Germany in 1910 when Richard Schirrmann, a German schoolteacher, began taking his students on long walking trips. The problem of finding overnight shelter led to the establishment of simple lodging. Schirrmann spent the rest of his life in the expansion of the hostel movement. Early in the movement the hostels were used primarily by school children, and they are still popular with this group, but older youth and young adults on vacation make up the majority of the present membership.

A youth hostel provides low-cost dormitory and cooking accommodations primarily for those who do not use mechanized means of travel, but rather walk, cycle or canoe from place to place. The hostels are meant to be centers not only for overnight stays but for making friends, exchanging experiences and learning about the customs, history and attractions of a particular country. Youth hostels are a significant force for the development of international understanding as people from many countries mingle and exchange information. Youth hostel systems are most highly developed in the countries of central Europe, but the movement has gained much popularity in northern European countries and a limited system of hostels has developed in the eastern part of the United States and Canada.

Other organizations of international significance with strong impact on leisure time activities are the Boy Scouts World Bureau, The World Association of Girl Guides and Girl Scouts. The YMCA, the Girl Alliance of YMCAs, the World YWCA, and the International Federation of Settlements. There are also international organizations for several specific sports and special interest groups—archery, basketball, bowling, canoeing, golf, tennis, skating, skiing, yacht racing, chess, stamp and coin collecting and many others. Concern over the conservation of national resources and outdoor recreation has led to the formation of such worldwide organizations as the World Wildlife Organization, the International Commission of National Parks, and the International Union for Conservation of Nature and National Resources.

Many other organizations could be discussed, but those that have been mentioned are the more prominent ones, and they give substance to the idea that much is going on by way of international exchange and coordination relative to leisure pursuits.

EUROPEAN COUNTRIES

Typically the better developed countries of Europe have achieved a higher level of sports participation among the masses, and have promoted the arts and folk culture, more successfully than we have in the United States. Soccer, team handball, cycling, motor racing, sailing, yachting and horsemanship are among Europe's more popular sports. Private clubs are numerous in European countries, particularly in the central and northern countries.

Interest in the cultural arts is inherent in the history and tradition of European countries. Many opportunities in the performing arts are provided by private individuals and semipublic organizations, but in most countries of Europe opera, ballet, and symphony receive substantial support from both municipal and national government agencies. For the most part the theaters, opera houses and museums are owned and operated by local governments.

Folk culture, particularly in the form of dance and music, is more prominent in Europe than in any other area of the world. The history and the cultural traditions of European countries are unusually rich. During the last several centuries, Europe, more than any other area of the world, has been the focal point for the development of civilization. Other cultures of the world have been influenced more by European standards than by those set in any other region. Because of their long history, strong traditions and relatively long-term stability, European nations have developed a base for folk culture that is unequalled. Dance, music and folk customs are prominent in the educational systems, and are important aspects of the social life. Major folk festivals,

where the folkways of the people are colorfully demonstrated and perpetuated, are common.

Some of the older and well-established cities such as Paris, London,
Madrid and Vienna have some of the finest municipal parks in the
world, and comprehensive systems have been effectively developed
throughout European countries. The origins of many European municipal parks, which have been in existence for many decades, can be
traced to the gardens and hunting grounds owned by royalty, as previously discussed.

Europeans in certain regions have traditionally been vigorous outdoorsmen, especially those who live in the northern countries and in
the Alpine regions. Hiking, camping, skiing, and mountain climbing
have long been popular forms of outdoor recreation. Bicycling is more
popular in Europe than any place else in the world, and it serves an
excellent purpose in terms of transportation, recreation and fitness
development.

The typical modern European lives in an environment that is less
mechanized and less industrialized than the United States. For this
reason the pace of living is somewhat slower and has undergone less
change than in America. All forms of daily, weekend, vacation and
retirement leisure have changed less rapidly in Europe than here. In
this respect, and in most of the social and economic developments that
influence recreation and leisure, the European countries are generally
two to three decades behind the United States.

Following are specific points of information about leisure and recreation patterns in a few of the European countries. It is not necessary to
discuss each country because in many cases the information about
them is similar. The discussions here include countries where the leisure and recreation trends are the most prominent.

England

Being separated by water from the European mainland, England has
developed along a pattern somewhat different from that of other European countries, even though it still has much in common with the
others. English people are heavily influenced by tradition, and among
their favorite sports are cricket, rugby, soccer, tennis, badminton, golf,
horsemanship and boat racing. Auto racing and cycling have gained in
popularity during recent times. The English have traditionally been
interested in the development of their youth and have numerous and
well-structured youth programs. England has also long demonstrated
significant leadership in the cultural arts and literature, and has possibly been the most literary nation of people in the world.

Within the last few years London has completed a superb multipurpose complex known as the Crystal Palace, with a century-old Victo-

rian background, having modern recreational facilities for the whole family and advanced training facilities for experts in a variety of sports. A unique feature of its Olympic-sized swimming pool is a glass side where coaches and other interested spectators can watch the action of the swimmers and divers from below water surface. This complex has led to decisions in other parts of England to abandon the building of single-purpose recreation facilities in favor of multipurpose complexes. Numerous municipalities either have recreation complexes under construction or in planning, and in this respect are far ahead of most other European countries.

Germany

Germany has been known for its aggressive and rugged people. This has carried over into staunch discipline of youth and well-organized youth programs. The high society of Germany has customarily been well schooled in the performing arts, and Germany has been prominent in the furtherance of these activities. The common people of Germany are enthusiastic about their folk art and customs, and the practice and perpetuation of these are integrated extensively into the social life of the people. Soccer, cycling and water sports are popular. In the Bavarian region (southern Germany) skiing, hiking and mountain climbing are very popular.

Switzerland

Switzerland is sometimes called the world's most advanced nation in the field of health, welfare and recreation concepts and facilities. During recent times the Swiss have made great advances in the development of all-inclusive year-round multistory recreation complexes which go up instead of sprawling out. They have completed a dozen and a half such complexes in Zurich alone. Their aim is to have one of these complexes within a 15-minute walk of every home in the large suburban areas, and one in each smaller community with a large enough population to support it. Back of this is the philosophy of what they call "togetherness"—the idea of holding communities and families together in common interests. Being one of the richest nations per capita in the world (often heralded as the richest), the leaders there claim that the ability of the Swiss to finance complexes of this kind and other worthwhile community projects is because they have been able to avoid the expense of war over a period of several decades, a claim that no other major European country can make. Their social and economic stability is closely interwoven with their leisure time activities, and their leisure activities are purposely designed to add to their social stability. The Swiss are also proud to claim the world's lowest divorce rate, its lowest juvenile delinquency rate and its lowest hospital occupancy rate.

France

Even though France has traditionally been a world leader in the cultural arts, its reputation is based primarily on earlier times than the present. From the standpoint of wholesome and desirable living patterns, particularly during leisure time, France has never recovered very well from the devastating setback it experienced during World War II. Even though France has gained a considerable amount of political and economic prestige since the war, it has not gained a position of leadership in any form of social affairs. The French people are known for the "gay life," but they are sadly lacking in substantial leisure time opportunities of the kind that result in positive development of the participants.

In terms of sports, soccer and cycling are the only two that are really prominent, while skiing, hiking and mountain climbing are popular in the Alpine region of France. The cultural arts are gaining in prominence, but their status is not what it was prior to World War II. France lives much more on its past reputation in the arts than on its present productivity.

In recent years the European physical fitness test administered by the Minister of Youth Sports has gained in popularity, and family camping has undergone a substantial expansion in France. The support of youth hostels enables thousands of French youth to vacation independently or in groups or to take tours which include bicycling and hiking.

Spain, Italy and Greece

These countries are old European nations the great days of which were in the past. In a sense it is unfair to each of them to be grouped together, and yet for the purpose of this discussion their similarities are great enough to justify it. At different times in history, these nations have been the great ones of the world, but during recent times political and economic strife have kept the living standards to a relatively low level. The great majority of the people in these countries are hard pressed to maintain an acceptable living, and the masses do not have a substantial amount of leisure time or the means to do much with the leisure thay have. These countries attract many tourists because of the historical and cultural significance of their many sites of interest.

From the standpoint of leisure time opportunities, *Spain* is more advanced than the other two. Soccer and tennis are prominent sports there, and vacation resorts along Spain's southern coast are popular attractions for both the Spanish people and those from other European countries. The larger cities such as Madrid and Barcelona have several multipurpose sport complexes, but these are not adequate to meet the needs of the population. One point of encouragement is the National

Institutes for Sports, headquartered in Madrid, which provides leadership in the ''Sports for All'' campaign. Young married couples and families are encouraged to take part in sports programs with the motto ''Start together and grow together.'' Spain is rich in folk customs, and Spanish dance and music are still relatively popular activities among the masses. Soccer and bullfighting are the two most popular spectator activities.

In *Italy* soccer is by far the most prominent sports activity, while American baseball is increasing rapidly in popularity. Italian folk culture is still relatively popular but is not performed at a very high level. In the northern sector, hiking, climbing, and skiing are popular activities.

Greek folk culture is the most popular leisure time pursuit in that country, and soccer is the only sport that receives much emphasis. Unfortunately Greek history is the most prominent aspect of life in that country today.

Netherlands

The Netherlands is one of the more progressive nations at the present time in terms of community planning and the provision of adequate leisure time opportunities for both youth and adults. Popular activities there include cycling, soccer, ice skating, team handball and aquatic sports. The Dutch Sport Federation operates a TRIM ''Sports for All'' program, and urges each person to take up two activities. Many of the sports clubs have joined the program, and they have contributed much impetus to the national movement. (Also refer to ''Amsterdam'' in the earlier section entitled ''The Struggle for City Parks.'')

Sweden, Norway, Finland and Denmark

These countries are among the more sports minded of Europe, and their living conditions and philosophies toward life are conducive to the development of wholesome leisure time programs.

Sweden has one of the highest standards of living of any country in the world, and it maintains a society which is well structured and demonstrates high quality in many aspects. Sweden has an abundance of attractive outdoor resources and the people there are generally hearty outdoorsmen. Summer hiking and winter ski touring are very popular, as are team handball, soccer, track and field, and cycling. Swedish gymnastics, including rhythmic gymnastic activities for girls, has maintained a high level of interest. The cities of Sweden are well laid out and noncongested, and they generally contain a good balance of well-planned parks and waterways. Sweden has maintained an appealing ''recreation environment'' by careful planning and adequate protection of its beautiful landscape.

The Swedish Sports Federation is a union of special associations and groups or clubs. The aim of the Federation is to increase the fitness and strength of Swedish citizens by recreation and sports competition. The Federation is trying to spread the idea of sports and physical activity to as many people as possible through its TRIM "Sports for All" program similar to that of the Netherlands.

Sweden has never been prominent in the cultural arts, although these activities do play a fairly significant role in the lives of contemporary Swedish people. The folk culture of Sweden is less interesting and receives less emphasis than in some of the other European countries, but here again does provide important leisure time outlets for many of the people.

Life in *Norway, Denmark* and *Finland* is very similar in many respects to that of Sweden and the recreational activities of the people are generally the same. In Norway a little more emphasis is placed on fishing and hunting and less emphasis on organized sports. In Denmark, soccer, cycling and ice skating are more popular than in the more northern countries, while cross-country skiing and track and field

Figure 33. In the Scandinavian and mountain regions of Europe ski touring is one of the most enjoyable winter activities. This is another of the European sports to become popular in the United States. (Swiss National Tourist Office photo.)

receive less emphasis. The folk culture is quite similar in all of the northern countries, and it receives about the same amount of emphasis in each country. The same is true about the relative importance and level of participation in the cultural arts.

Countries of Eastern Europe

Included in this block of countries are Poland, Czechoslovakia, Rumania and Yugoslavia. The living standards and living patterns are quite similar among these countries. They have been slow in recovering from the effects of World War II and their social and economic development has been further retarded by the domination of Communism. However, despite these conditions there are some bright spots in leisure time trends in these countries. Considerable emphasis has been placed, and is being placed, on the elevation of performing arts and of folk culture, and youth organizations, primarily controlled by government agencies, are enjoying success. Emphasis is placed on sports for youth and young adults, especially sports included in the world Olympics, and the favorable results of these efforts are becoming more apparent at each Olympiad.

Soviet Union

Increased recreation services have been developed in the Soviet Union during the last several decades. Even though leisure was enjoyed by only a small percentage of people for centuries, today the majority of Russians enjoy leisure time activities.

Every aspect of Soviet life is regarded as part of a collective scheme to build the national morale, improve health and increase national productivity. The concept of leisure within the Soviet Union has been closely linked to the promotion of socialist discipline and the development of communal solidarity. Economic expansion in Russia has required stringent controls over all aspects of living, including the use of leisure time.

Parks and play centers have been traditionally located very sparsely throughout the country, but during the past two decades there has been a boom in parks and sports facilities. The government has been active in establishing vacation centers for families, and for many of the Soviet people vacations away from home are becoming a reality. Vacation resorts offer downhill and cross country skiing, ice skating and other such activities in the winter, and in the summer fishing, hunting, hiking and aquatic activities.

An extensive youth movement is under state direction, the primary purpose of which is political indoctrination and the development of excellence. Russia has thousands of camps for children and youth, and there are over 3,000 pioneer youth houses or centers. When the Soviet youth reach their teens they join the Konsonol, which is a unit of the party.

Characteristically the Soviet Union is known for its cultural activities. State-sponsored groups in the performing arts—opera, ballet, concerts, legitimate theater and circus—are numerous and highly developed. The extremely popular Bolshoi Ballet receives a large annual grant from the government.

The primary emphasis of the Soviet government regarding leisure and recreation is in the field of sports and physical culture. Russians view physical education and sport as a necessity "in developing national strength for unity, and prestige." When the work day is over, industrial and office workers by the thousands join students, engineers, farmers and other sport lovers in crowding the country's gymnasiums, stadiums, and water sports areas.

THE ORIENT

In central and northern Asia (except for the Asian portion of the U.S.S.R.) so many of the countries are underdeveloped and economically poor that leisure time pursuits of the kinds that we know and are interested in are almost nonexistent for the masses of the population. Most of the people of such countries as Mongolia, India, Iran, Afghanistan and Arabia are able to concern themselves only with the bare necessities of survival, while their opportunities for leisure time pursuits are extremely meager. Governmental and private leadership in the field of parks and recreation is almost nonexistent. Japan, Taiwan and Thailand are able to concern themselves more with leisure than any of the other countries on the Asian continent.

Japan

The Japanese have done a remarkable job of recovering from the devastating effects of World War II. A strong economy and a high standard of living, with a reduction in working hours, have resulted in a recreation boom in Japan.

There has been a phenomenal increase in baseball and golf, relatively new sports in Asia. Baseball has grown to the extent that the Japanese are now providing strong competition with major league teams in America. The 530 golf courses in Japan cause it to rank fifth in the world in this activity, even though a small percentage of the courses are for public use. Gymnastics, volleyball, combative sports, fencing and skiing are also popular. Aside from baseball, judo, boxing, and sumo (a form of wrestling involving heavyweight athletes) are the most popular spectator sports.

The cultural arts—music, drama, sculptoring, painting, ivory carving and metal work—are popular, and Japanese music and dance have increased significantly in popularity during the past decade. Japanese gardens (garden parks) are popular in both large and small sizes and these add much to the "recreation environment."

Tokyo possesses the world's largest and most diversified multipurpose recreation facility, the Korakuen Center. It is located in the heart of Tokyo, where land is said to be scarcer and higher priced than in any city in the world. The center serves 11 million visitors per year on a self-sustaining fee basis.

Republic of China (Taiwan)

The major responsibility for recreation in this country rests with the Recreation Activities Society of the Republic of China. The organizations through which most of the recreational activities are organized are the Chinese Youth Anti-Communist Corps and the National Salvation Corps. These prominent youth organizations organize activity and sports clubs and plan youth group vacations. Several multipurpose recreation complexes have been planned and some have been constructed in recent years. The larger cities, particularly Taipei, the capital city, have beautiful parks and fountains. Many of these feature statues and shelters of striking oriental design.

Thailand

Sports such as Thai boxing, unorthodox forms of fencing, badminton, table tennis and kite flying are popular in Thailand. American bowling and certain forms of aquatic sports have gained in popularity during the past decades. Track and field competition is often sponsored through community and school agencies. Thailand music, dance, and arts and crafts are still popular in their traditional forms, but American music and dance have also become popular, mostly because of the long-term presence of American military personnel.

People's Republic of China (Mainland China)

The major sports in Mainland China include table tennis, swimming, soccer, track and field, speed skating and weight lifting. As is that of the Soviet Union, Communist China's approach to leisure is that all forms of recreation should contribute to national goals and be under direct control of the Republic.

The government has subsidized extensive vacation and sports projects, spending billions of dollars for multipurpose facilities and stadiums, playgrounds and equipment. Huge crowds jam the new large arenas for athletic events and fitness and cultural demonstrations. Spontaneous leisure pursuits are sparse because the people are under heavy government control and their activities are closely monitored.

AUSTRALIA AND NEW ZEALAND

Australia and New Zealand still have an abundance of open spaces and natural resources which offer a variety of outdoor recreation opportunities. In recent years numerous national parks and reserves have been set aside and appropriate conservation measures have been taken for the protection of resources for recreation and other uses.

The *Australian* Institute of Parks and Recreation has been instrumental in promoting the development of municipal parks and community recreation centers, and the public use of outdoor recreation resources. The Institute has also been influential in promoting the use of school facilities for recreational purposes by youth and adults alike. The popular athletic sports in Australia are rugby, soccer, basketball, track and field and cricket. The English sporting heritage still exerts a strong influence in both Australia and New Zealand.

In *New Zealand*, the government has encouraged the expansion of numerous volunteer agencies by assisting them with financial support. Among the agencies are the National YMCA, YWCA, National Youth Council, and National Council of Churches. In New Zealand the schools have a direct responsibility for preparing people for the wise use of leisure. The charge to the schools there is much the same as in the United States.

SOUTH AMERICA

It is not feasible to discuss all of the countries of South America and neither is it necessary, because from the recreation point of view the situation in the different countries is quite similar. Thus only Brazil and Argentina are discussed here.

Brazil

Brazil is the largest country in South America both in terms of land area and population, and probably it is the most prominent in terms of world recognition and influence. The standard of living in Brazil and other South American countries is relatively low, although there is a portion of the population near the top of the social structure which lives rather well.

Soccer is by far the most popular sport and Brazil has developed some of the best teams on the international scene. They have been highly competitive in World Cup competition during recent years. Basketball is the second most popular sport while other popular activities include tennis, swimming and track and field. Aside from the playing of soccer on the playgrounds and in the streets, most of the sports activities are centered in the sports clubs which are numerous in Brazil.

There are many attractive seashore resorts on Brazil's beautiful coastline. Fishing, swimming and surfing are popular activities among those who go to the seashore for recreation.

The cultural arts are not well developed in Brazil and are generally participated in by only a few at the top of the social scale. Being a relatively young country, Brazil is not blessed with a rich and interesting folk culture.

There are no strong efforts by the government or influential non-government agencies to afford the people substantial and high-quality leisure time opportunities. For the common people of Brazil most of their leisure time is used in playing cards and other table games, listening to the radio (some have television) and attending fairs and carnivals which are quite numerous. The children participate extensively in playground and street games, and there are some who are enthusiastically involved in Latin American dance and music. In Brazil there is a strong distinction between the life-styles of those who are well off and can afford servants and club memberships and the masses who can afford very little.

Argentina

Argentina, with its Andes Mountains, includes the "Alps" of South America. It also has more coastline than any other South American country. These two factors offer abundant outdoor recreation opportunities, including extensive hunting, fishing, skiing and other activities related to alpine and seacoast regions. The environment of plentiful outdoor beauty has seemingly influenced the plans of cities in that country. Buenos Aires for example has more than 150 parks spread throughout its geographic limits, giving it one of the most spacious feelings of any city its size.

Argentina has a relative rugged frontier personality which naturally relates to its outdoor environment and sparse population. In this respect it somewhat parallels the present situation in Canada and Australia and the frontier days of western America some time ago. Because it is a relatively youthful nation, it has not developed strong traditions or a strong folk cultural; however, it is by no means totally lacking in this regard. The cultural arts in Argentina are quite limited, and the same can be said of a high-level social environment. In other words highly traditional and sophisticated leisure time opportunities are not very prevalent.

Argentinians are typically better off economically than other South Americans and their environment and living conditions are generally more desirable, yet they are not blessed with a wide variety of wholesome leisure time outlets; neither do they enjoy the benefits of well-organized municipal and state programs or youth service agencies. Hopefully these forms of service will grow as the country develops. Otherwise the recreational opportunities in that country will probably fall into the same limited pattern as those of the other countries in South America that are more densely populated.

CANADA AND MEXICO

On the two sides of the United States, Canada and Mexico are quite opposite in most respects. The characteristics of the land of the two countries, as well as their histories and the backgrounds of those who settled them, are distinct and different.

Canada

Canada is at about the same stage of development as the United States was approximately three decades ago. There is still an abundance of open space, much of which is highly desirable for recreational use. The country has adequate natural resources of various kinds and there are no overpopulation problems. The educational system is quite similar to that of the United States and so is the social structure. The popular Canadian sports include ice hockey, lacrosse, skiing, rugby, ice skating, track and field, American football and soccer. Hunting, fishing, hiking, mountain climbing, and other forms of outdoor recreation are prevalent. Rodeos, frontier carnivals and winter carnivals are common festivities.

One of the unique features of Canada is its split between English- and French-speaking people. This results in the perpetuation of two major cultural backgrounds, and the folk cultures associated with these two backgrounds are important to the people. Also there are small but strong concentrations of people from Germany, the Ukraine and the Scandinavian countries, and each of these groups perpetuates its own folk cultures.

Canadian cities ordinarily include a rather abundant supply of large and small parks, and often there are rivers and natural lakes within the city limits which greatly enhance the recreational environment. The amount and kind of youth organizations parallel those in the United States. Municipal recreation and park systems in Canadian cities are similar to those in the United States, and they are in about the same stage of development. The Canadian national park system is second only to that of the United States.

The Canadian Park and Recreation Association has been a major force toward encouraging and stimulating dialogue and communication. The Association sponsors conferences and seminars, encourages the development of research programs and acts as an information center for data and studies related to parks and recreation. Its bimonthly publication is *Recreation Canada*.

Mexico

Actually the people and culture of Mexico resemble those of South American countries more than the United States. The most popular sports in Mexico are soccer, baseball, basketball and jai alai, a court game somewhat similar to handball. Bullfights, horse races, and dog races are popular spectator events.

Leather craft and jewelry making are popular Mexican crafts that are valuable both for recreation and commercial products. Mexican folk music and dance are popular and relate closely to those of Spain.

For the most part youth organizations are not well structured in Mexico, and municipally sponsored recreation and park systems are sparse. However, in the larger cities, especially Mexico City, there are some elaborate and beautiful parks, fountains and decorative gardens. Festivals, including Mardi Gras parades and fireworks displays, are not uncommon in Mexico.

REFERENCES

1. Gothein, M. L.: *A History of Garden Art*, 2 vols. (Wright, W. P., Ed.). J. M. Dent & Sons, London, 1913.

11

Areas of Recreation Services and Leadership

Recreation services for the various segments of the population have expanded in numerous directions, and the services have been categorized into general areas. The purpose of this chapter is to give an overview, along with some rather specific information, about the different kinds of recreational services and the kinds of agencies through which the services are provided. This will also give quite a clear picture of the areas of specialization and the broad categories of employment opportunities available in this field.

COMMUNITY RECREATION

From the standpoint of the number of participants and amount of total expenditure, community sponsored recreation programs constitute by far the largest phase of the total recreation field. Chapter 9 gives a considerable amount of information about community sponsored recreation, including some alternative plans of organization and sponsoring authorities. Additional insight into community recreation can be gained by analyzing the different kinds of leadership positions that are typically found at the community level. These positions can be divided into four general categories: *administrators* (executives), *supervisors, center or special facility directors*, and *direct leaders*.

The responsibilities of a leader in an *administrative position* includes planning, organizing, and administering a recreation and/or park program to meet the needs and interest of those being served. The title might be *manager, director, superintendent* or *executive*. Most administrators are responsible for both recreation programming and park management; however, sometimes these two major responsibilities are placed under separate heads. Typically the responsibilities of the administrator include the following:

1. Recruit, select, assign, supervise and evaluate the departmental staff
2. Provide administrative guidance to supervisors and center directors to be sure that their phases of the program are managed effectively

3. Oversee the acquisition, planning, construction, improvement, and maintenance of various facilities

4. Prepare the proposed budget, administer the budget, and account for all revenue and expenditures

5. Give leadership to the public relations efforts of the department

6. Arrange and encourage in-service training to improve the performances of staff members

7. Instigate, support and evaluate research relating to the departmental operation

8. Motivate and inspire departmental personnel

9. Give leadership in the use of effective procedures of evaluating both personnel and programs, and consistently utilize the results for personnel and program improvements

10. Administer all other work of the department in accordance with the prescribed policies and basic procedures established by the governing body (usually a board or commission)

The necessary training and experience of an administrator vary considerably with the size and complexity of the department. Usually they involve graduation from a recognized college or university with at least a bachelor's degree in recreation and park management or some closely related field, plus successful experience over a period of several years. A graduate degree is often helpful and sometimes required. Substantial evidence of a sound philosophy and superior management ability outweighs most other considerations.

Supervisory positions represent a secondary level of administration. Typically a supervisor would be responsible for all the activities and/or facilities within a specific geographic district (general supervisor) or a specialized area of the program (special supervisor). A *supervisor of a geographic district* would be responsible for the administration of all portions of the recreation program and facilities within the district. His responsibilities would be similar to those of the department administrator, except the supervisor's responsibilities would pertain to only a portion of the total community. A *special supervisor* would be responsible for a specialized phase of the program for the whole community, such as athletics, aquatics or social activities. Usually a department would not have both kinds of supervisors but one or the other, depending on the preferred administrative organization; however, in some large departments there are supervisors of both kinds. Normally the qualifications for a supervisor include a bachelor's degree in recreation or a closely related field along with a considerable amount of successful experience.

A *director of a center* should be effective in promotion, programming and working with people, particularly the kind of people in the vicinity of the center. The director is in charge of the center's staff and facilities and is charged with the responsibility of utilizing these effectively to accomplish the purposes of the center. Ordinarily the center director reports to an area supervisor or to the department administrator.

Another kind of director is the one placed in charge of a special facility, such as a botantical garden, a zoo, a waterfront area, a museum, or a cultural center. The person holding one of these positions is usually a specialist in the particular area of interest for which the center was designed. Here again the director would be responsible for utilizing his staff, facilities and other resources as effectively as possible to accomplish the purposes of the special facility.

Direct leaders are those who furnish face-to-face leadership. They have responsibilities such as organizing and directing athletic contests, directing aquatic programs, teaching dance, preparing concerts and recitals, promoting and directing dramatic productions, leading children in playground activities, etc. Direct leadership positions are often held by people who work on a seasonal basis, or by full-time employees who have earned an associate degree or equivalent.

OUTDOOR RECREATION

Outdoor recreation is a commonly used term meaning essentially the same as resource-oriented recreation. It is defined as those recreational activities which occur in an outdoor (natural) environment and which relate directly to that environment. In recent years there has been increasing concern from several quarters over the diminishment of outdoor recreation opportunities. This has been prompted by the awakening of the American people to the fact that the natural environment is being destroyed, and unless appropriate protective measures are effectively applied outdoor recreation opportunities will be seriously diluted and even reduced to an unacceptable level. Nongovernment agencies concerned about preservation and conservation of natural resources for the good of man, as well as other species, have been active in bringing about this movement. Such organizations as the Nature Conservancy, the Audubon Society, the National Wildlife Federation and the Sierra Club have had penetrating effects upon people's thoughts and actions toward the protection and use of natural resources. Government agencies have also been active in this movement, and during the past two decades have caused a great deal to be accomplished toward the protection and proper use of natural resources with high recreational value. The agencies of the federal government that have been the most active in this regard are the Bureau of Outdoor Recreation, the National Park Service, the U.S. Forest Service, the Corps of Engineers, and the Bureau of Reclamation. In addition, other agencies that manage significant amounts of natural resources have each made their contributions by setting and enforcing guidelines and standards relative to the use of outdoor recreational resources. Corresponding state agencies have also been active in this movement; these include state park departments, state forestry departments, divisions of water resources and fish and wildlife agencies. There has been much cooperation in connection with this movement between state and federal government agencies and government and nongovernment agencies at the local levels.

Many agencies and organizations have had to reevaluate their roles and actions relative to outdoor recreation, and some changes have occurred in the philosophies of both conservationist and preservationist.

Figure 34. Recreation in the great outdoors is part of the American heritage. (National Park Service photo.)

Prior to a few years ago most agencies involved in outdoor recreation conducted their business by yielding to pressures of the public with little long-range planning. Prior to 1960 only a few agencies had taken aggressive and positive approaches to planning in advance of public demand. This was probably largely caused by the fact that most resource management agencies have outdoor recreation as only one of their functions, and often it is secondary to the primary purpose for which the agency was established. As the great rush of the American population to the out-of-doors developed, as it has at a steady rate since World War II, the prominence of outdoor recreation gained on some of the more traditional uses of natural resources. Now outdoor recreation is often given consideration equal to the more traditional uses of land and water.

The major part of the leadership for outdoor recreation is provided through government agencies, because these agencies control most of the outdoor recreation resources available for public use. The involvement of branches of the federal government is described in Chapter 7 and the involvement of state agencies in Chapter 8.

In the selection of outdoor recreation employees, most agencies in the past have given primary attention to college graduates whose educational emphasis was in the biological sciences, especially forestry. However, personnel with majors in recreation, social science, landscape architecture and engineering have been hired on occasion. The present philosophy of government administrators seems to favor personnel with dual talents who can effectively relate to both people and resources. They want professionals who are competent in working with all kinds of natural and man-made areas, and who know how to make the best of the aesthetic, functional and economic potentials of the areas. More importantly, however, the professionals must always be aware that the areas are for people.

Among the federal agencies with staff members who are specialists in some form of outdoor recreation are the Bureau of Outdoor Recreation, the National Park Service, the U.S. Forest Service, the U.S. Fish and Wildlife Service, the Bureau of Reclamation, the U.S. Army Corps of Engineers, the Bureau of Land Management and the Tennessee Valley Authority. All of these are large resource management agencies with areas receiving extensive recreational use by the public. Therefore, recreation planning and management have become important responsibilities.

Each state government is organized differently, but there are close similarities relative to the kinds of functions that the state government performs and there is considerable consistency as to the kinds of state divisions involved in outdoor recreation. Typically outdoor recreation personnel are hired in the state departments that manage the state park system, the state forest system, the wildlife resources and the water resources. Despite the fact that these jobs are not the exclusive domain of the recreation professionals, every state government has some need for outdoor recreation specialists.

THERAPEUTIC RECREATION

Originally termed hospital recreation, the therapeutic recreation movement has expanded its scope considerably. Initially the field was geared primarily to the needs of psychiatric or long-term patients in federal and large state hospitals. Today, however, the movement provides rehabilitation-oriented recreation services to the physically disabled, the mentally retarded, psychiatric patients, the socially disabled and dependent aging persons.

Working with hospital patients is unusually satisfying to some people, while others cannot adapt to it. Programs are based on the philosophy that people confined to hospitals for long periods of time need and benefit from participation in wholesome and interesting leisure time activities. The programs are designed to encourage positive attitudes and high morale among the patients, while at the same time developing their personalities.

Many of the hospitals that employ recreation specialists are owned either by the state or federal government, e.g. state mental hospitals and federal veterans hospitals. In such cases the employment conditions of recreation therapists are defined by civil service specifications. Those seeking recreation therapy positions need to prepare themselves

Figure 35. Special balance arm enables this handicapped youngster to participate in bowling. (M. Tachdjian photo.)

by completing a specialized program in this field at a four-year college or university. (A few positions are available for people who have completed an associate or two-year college program.) For those who want training beyond a bachelor's degree, several institutions offer specialized preparation at the master's degree level.

Leading psychiatrists have given strong support to recreation therapy as a form of rehabilitation. The late Dr. William C. Menninger, former director of the famed Menninger Clinic in Topeka, stated, "It has been the privilege of many of us practicing medicine in psychiatry to have had some very rewarding experiences in the use of recreation as an adjunctive method of treatment."[1]

Dr. Menninger outlined three basic psychological needs that can be met through recreation:

1. Competitive games as an outlet for instinctive aggressive drive
2. Creative activities in art, music or literature as a release
3. Entertainment activities as a means of providing relaxation and vicarious involvement

According to Weiskopf, "in serving the patient, therapeutic recreation services have the following specific objectives: (1) instill morale, (2) encourage the formation of proper habits and attitudes, (3) channel aggressive drives into constructive outlets, and (4) encourage desire to overcome physical and mental barriers and stimulate new or dormant interests and talents."[2]

It is important for us to keep in mind that recreation has not only played an important part in the treatment program of many illnesses

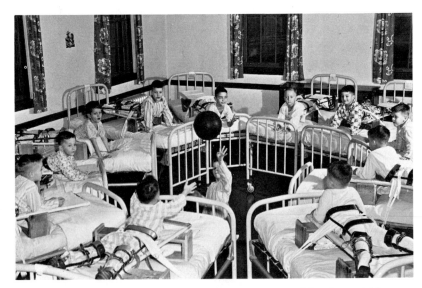

Figure 36. Even bedridden children have a strong need for play activities.

but that it has been a contributing factor in enabling former patients to remain well.

A recreation leader should understand that the handicapped:

1. Are first and foremost people . . . who have the same basic needs, desires and interests as the nonhandicapped . . . that the handicapped are more like others than they are different from them
2. Need to participate as regular members of the community through recreation interests . . . not through isolated groups of persons who happen to have the same type of handicap
3. Have the same right as others to choose and to share in the planning of their own recreation activities, and to participate voluntarily
4. Can participate in a wide variety of activities in the community, particularly if they have the encouragement and guidance of good leadership

Data presented by the National Therapeutic Recreation Society, a branch of the National Recreation and Park Association, include a number of interesting facts about employment of therapists:

1. The record of employment is quite stable, with more than 55% of those presently employed having been in this professional field for six years or more
2. The ages of the employees are rather evenly distributed between ages 21 and 65
3. The field of employees is about 55% female and 45% male
4. State owned and private hospitals employ almost 70% of the recreation therapists on hospital staffs. Federal hospitals employ 13% and the others work in local hospitals or other local agencies
5. Of all of the employed therapists about 65% work in hospitals, while the other 35% are employed in special schools, community agencies, etc.

RECREATION IN CORRECTIONAL INSTITUTIONS

Professionally adapted and applied recreation can aid in the rehabilitation of those in correctional institutions. The inmates can be exposed to programs and activities in which they experience success and socially acceptable satisfaction—both of which are too often foreign to their past experiences. In essence a well-planned recreation program gives institutionalized individuals the opportunity to acquire skills, knowledge and interests. This is necessary if they are not only to return to community life but also to benefit from other therapeutic efforts during their stay in the correctional institution.

The objectives of an institutional recreation program include:

1. Assisting in the total treatment and rehabilitative process
2. Providing a setting that will aid social adjustment and effective functioning within the social system
3. Developing skills that can be carried over into the home, the community and the work environment
4. Furnishing experiences to help individuals accept themselves and their limitations while encouraging them to utilize their capacities, to increase their feelings of self-worth and to focus on the positive aspects of their interests

Unfortunately recreation programs in correctional institutions are very sparse, and little attention has been given to this approach to rehabilitation. A few recreation specialists conduct activities in correctional institutions, but the job opportunities are not numerous by any means. Hopefully this avenue of service and employment will open up significantly in the future.

EMPLOYEE RECREATION PROGRAMS

Quite a large number of companies and industrial plants that employ large work forces provide recreation opportunities for their employees and dependents as part of their benefit programs. Employee recreation programs often involve the ownership of specialized facilities such as private parks, golf courses and shooting clubs. They can foster leagues and tournaments designed to furnish participation opportunities to employees and family members in a variety of interesting and developmental activities.

These programs deviate considerably from one another because circumstances are different with different companies. The geographic locality, the size of the employee force, other recreation opportunities available in the vicinity, and the policies of the company all influence the extent and nature of the employee recreation program. Usually such a program is under the leadership of a recreation specialist.

The National Industrial Recreation Association is the specialized professional organization for employees and companies in this field. The fact that it has a membership of 8,000 companies indicates that the size of this branch of recreational service is larger than most people would tend to think.

PRIVATE CLUB RECREATION

The programs of private clubs vary considerably depending upon the specialized nature of the clubs, their size and their financial means. Golf or country clubs are probably the most numerous of the private clubs. A country club might employ a golf professional who is primarily an instructor, while the same club might have an aquatics specialist to oversee a swimming program and a clubhouse manager to oversee the activities for which the clubhouse was designed. Other private clubs providing recreational opportunities are tennis clubs, swim clubs, sailing and yacht clubs, and health clubs (or health spas).

Anyone employed in these jobs must have specialized knowledge and skill in the particular activity involved, along with an appealing personality that attracts and holds clientele over an extended period of time. For example, a tennis or a golf pro must have a reputation as a performer which will give him entry into a pro position, and cause people to want to sustain him in that position. Of course, over the long term the success of the program and of the leader depends on the effectiveness with which the pro performs all aspects of his duties.

COMMERCIAL RECREATION

As in other profit-making businesses, commercial recreation is based upon the free enterprise concept, where the individual or company prepares and distributes services and products in an effort to make a profit. This fact of business life (operating at a profit) forces the successful entrepreneur to remain sensitive and responsive to the public that is being served.

It is becoming ever more apparent that the increasing recreation needs of Americans will not be met effectively in the future by the combined efforts of local, state and federal government agencies, and there is no reason that these agencies should even attempt to provide all of the opportunities. As a result there will be a significant growth in commercial recreation programs in the future. However, commercial operations will include only those activities for which the public will pay, and which the commerical organization can convert into a profit. Examples of kinds of commercial recreation operations are: boys' and girls' ranches, guide services for wilderness tours and expeditions, travel agencies, bowling alleys, amusement parks, outdoor recreation resorts, commercial waterfront areas, swimming pools, ski resorts, skating rinks, golf courses and minature golf courses, tennis clubs, and marinas. Professional sports and other "gate receipt" entertainment activities are unique forms of commercial recreation.

The success of commercial recreation enterprises and the personnel involved with them varies, just as in other kinds of businesses. Those going into commercial recreation need to be somewhat cautious and plan very carefully with respect to amount of investment compared to potential return. Certain management characteristics and abilities are vital to success, such as ability to meet and deal with the public effectively, efficient personnel and financial management, ingenuity and creativity in programming, and effective promotion. Proper business management and business procedures are basic to a commercial recreation operation, as they are to any other business endeavor.

Commercial recreation firms that qualify under the stated criteria can obtain federal financial assistance (low interest loans) and planning assistance through the Small Business Administration or the Federal Housing Administration. Also, some states offer assistance programs for the purpose of stimulating recreation and tourism enterprises, with the understanding that the success of these enterprises has a bolstering effect on the local economy.

How does a person become qualified for a career in commercial recreation? Fortunately Langeman and Rockwood have provided some meaningful answers to this question as a result of a research study to learn which attributes commercial recreation executives looked for in beginning level personnel. These attributes are organized into three categories—*technical, human/behavioral*, and *conceptual*.[3]

Technical

Beginning-level personnel in commercial recreation should be able to:

1. Understand the values and limitations (philosophy) of commercial recreation.
2. Understand government regulations as they apply to commercial recreation, i.e. boating, camping, horseback riding, swimming, and snowmobiling.
3. Evaluate the money-producing potential of commercial recreation programs, facilities, and areas.
4. Verbally express themselves.
5. Plan and organize their own work.
6. Write effective letters and memoranda.
7. Place people in a company according to their abilities.
8. Screen and select new employees through interviews and other appropriate means.
9. Plan and conduct effective orientation and training programs for company personnel.
10. Analyze a financial statement.
11. Understand recreation land value.
12. Understand economic aspects of business as they pertain to commerical recreation—supply and demand, trade and growth, and income and profit.
13. Understand company policy and practices.
14. Understand the liability laws concerning commercial recreation.
15. Understand contracts, insurance, franchising, and leasing.
16. Understand master planning and zoning.
17. Understand the requirements and limitations of the physical factors of land as they relate to commercial recreation, i.e. vegetation, sewer, water, soil, and terrain.
18. Understand tourist trends and patterns.
19. Understand the mobility patterns as they affect commercial recreation, i.e. roads, highways, and traffic centers.
20. Understand and evaluate a feasibility study.
21. Understand the techniques of advertising, promotion, and publicity which create a demand for commercial recreation.

Human/Behavioral

Beginning-level personnel in commercial recreation should be able to:

1. Know why people buy services in commercial recreation.
2. Enjoy the work of helping people have fun.
3. Promote goodwill for the field of commercial recreation.
4. Sense morale problems and analyze their source so as to take corrective measures.
5. Recognize in employees ability which will attract customers.
6. Attract competent people around them and their company.
7. Communicate and interpret company policy to employees.
8. Anticipate and correctly predict the actual and potential needs of customers.
9. Follow through on details in implementing decisions made by the policymakers.
10. Perceive unethical business practices.
11. Sell themselves and their ideas to groups and individuals.
12. Have a competitive attitude.

13. Practice a positive attitude.
14. Demonstrate self-discipline.
15. Demonstrate persistence in working towards goals.
16. Motivate and inspire others to work without the use of formal authority.
17. Convey the best possible image of the company.
18. Empathize with and be sensitive to others' needs.
19. Show willingness to improve themselves.
20. Accept responsibility.

Conceptual

Beginning-level personnel in commercial recreation should be able to:

1. Draw logical conclusions based upon available facts (ability to reason).
2. Allocate time and effort to bring the greatest return.
3. Perceive a need for changes and improvements within the company.
4. Understand that each decision affects later decisions.
5. Understand that many details need to be taken care of efficiently for clients in commercial recreation so that they will have a pleasurable experience.
6. Understand the local politics and culture of the community.
7. Recognize abilities of personnel that would qualify them for promotion to a higher position.
8 Understand the potential problems in commercial recreation and the possible ways of preventing and solving them.
9. Build an effective organizational structure, with proper channels of responsibility and authority that are fixed to proper individuals.
10. Understand that problems must be handled in light of the total situation and in such a way as to improve the overall position of the company.

It should be obvious that a college degree cannot guarantee entry into the commercial recreation field. Some attributes can be developed only through experience and observation. But choosing the right curriculum can give aspiring practitioners a head start.

OUTDOOR EDUCATION

This field is closely related to outdoor recreation, but it is separate in the sense that it has educational objectives and is often associated with the school system. Those interested in this field ordinarily would qualify by pursuing a program in outdoor education, which would typically be offered through a college of education. However, only a few such programs exist, and full-time outdoor education jobs in the schools are sparse.

There are less formal approaches to outdoor education; a few cities and federal agencies manage outdoor education or interpretative centers for the purpose of teaching people who come there more about nature and natural processes.

Since 1952 the American Alliance for Health, Physical Education and Recreation has sponsored an outdoor education project. This project, along with other efforts in outdoor education, has made a significant contribution toward people's understanding of nature and its importance in many respects, including outdoor recreation.

RECREATION TEACHING

One of the important aspects of the total recreation field is the teaching. There are two aspects to this: (1) the educational preparation of people to use leisure time beneficially, and (2) the professional preparation of park and recreation leaders. A large number of people are involved in the first category, but in most cases they are not labelled as recreation teachers. They are primarily teachers in the public schools who instruct in the subjects which have high carry-over value into leisure time—photography, fine arts, physical education, etc. There are no accurate figures of the number of people involved in this kind of supporting effort to the recreation field.

In the second category, about 2,600 college and university faculty members are presently involved in the 360 college recreation curricula (including junior colleges). These college curricula emphasize the professional preparation of recreation and park leaders, but some of them also include general education courses for the college student body.

TOURISM

Tourism for pleasure is a very significant part of the total travel industry and therefore it should be identified as a field of recreational opportunity. Of the 50 states, 46 have ranked tourism as one of the top three industries. About 20% of tourist travel takes place on airplanes, buses, trains, and cruisers, much of it involving organized tours. Practically all of the remaining 80% is by private automobile.

Travel for pleasure has a significant overall impact on the economy because it results in a large number of dollars spent for transportation costs, food, lodging and entertainment. Further, the employment market is bolstered considerably because of the goods and services required by tourists.

According to information from Discover America Travel Organizations, Inc., about $75 billion is spent in the U.S. each year for tourism—5.1% of the total gross national product. Traveler spending directly generates more than 3.5 million jobs, representing 3.4% of the total civilian employment force. The total payroll for these jobs exceeds $20 billion per year.

It is hard to know just how to interpret these figures in terms of their relationship to recreation, but certainly tourism must be considered a leisure time activity and thus related to the recreation field.

ARMED FORCES RECREATION

Ever since World War II the armed forces have been committed to providing recreational opportunities for military personnel and their dependents. The recreation leadership positions are filled by a combination of military personnel and civil service employees, with certain of the positions being clearly identified as civil service jobs. Most of the positions are within the United States, but there are some opportunities at U. S. military stations in foreign countries. These jobs include management of a program or a phase of the program which ordinarily includes the following;

1. Sports, including self-directed, competitive, instructional, and spectator contests
2. Motion pictures
3. Service clubs and entertainment including dramatic, dance and musical activities
4. Crafts and hobbies
5. Youth activities for children of military families
6. Special interest groups such as automotive, motorcycle and power boat clubs, or hiking, skydiving and rod and gun clubs
7. Management of cultural and special events
8. Management of recreational facilities such as picnic areas, swimming pools, gymnasiums and golf courses
9. Management of libraries

The mission of the program can be best described by an excerpt from the Air Force Sports Program Manual. The mission of the programs in the Navy, Army and Marine Corps would be essentially the same as described here:

> The special Services program fulfills the recreation needs and interests of Air Force personnel and their families by providing maximum opportunities for them to participate in leisure-time activities that help to stimulate, develop and maintain their mental, physical, and social well-being. Recreation is a fundamental part of the American way of life; and Air Force military personnel and their families need and deserve self-rewarding creative recreation programs and opportunities equal in variety and quality to the best offered in the most progressive civilian communities. Proper recreation activities improve the individual's mental state, character growth, and job performance. Moreover, military personnel and their families who participate in recreation activities are more likely to have favorable attitudes toward an Air Force career.[4]

The following inventory summary of all Department of Defense recreation facilities is indicative of program magnitude:

Bowling centers	555
Recreation auto shops	752
Crafts shops	1382
Entertainment workshops	93
Field houses	35
Gymnasiums	730
Branch libraries	605
Main libraries	547
Youth centers	587
Enlisted men's service clubs	684
Tennis courts	2338
Softball fields	1471
Outdoor swimming pools	748

EMPLOYMENT OPPORTUNITIES FOR WOMEN

The National Recreation and Park Association conducted a study in 1970 and another in 1973 to determine the status of women in the park and recreation profession. The 1970 study showed that only 23% of the full-time professional positions were occupied by women, whereas by 1973 33% were so occupied. Other data show that the trend toward increased numbers of women employees in other professions has remained intact since 1973. It seems safe to assume that the same has occurred in the park and recreation profession.

Studies in law, science, sociology, medicine and engineering have showed that salaries for women range from $1,000 to $3,500 per year less than for their male counterparts with similar education and experience. However, there has been a consistent trend toward closing the salary gap. The NRPA 1973 study showed that women's salaries in parks and recreations fell below those of men by $1,717 per year. In the administrative positions, men earned an average of $4,000 per year more than women in comparable positions. The difference between men and women at the supervisory level was $920 per year, and in the lower employment categories the difference was only $458.

It was found that there was a closer proportion of men and women employees in the lower positions and that men dominated the higher positions. A relatively small percentage of the administrative positions were filled by women.

It was also found that, on the average, women employees had one year less formal education than their male counterparts. Further women had one year less professional experience than the men who occupied comparable positions.

There are fewer women than men available for employment in the park and recreation field. This is indicated by the fact that of those majoring in this field fewer than half are women. Further, the proportion of women majors who are graduated is lower than the proportion of men, because many of the women get married along the way and drop out of school. Additionally, fewer women graduates seek employment because of marriage. Actually, therefore, employment opportunities for women—in view of the number of women available—are as good if not better than for men. Many positions in the field of recreation and parks can be filled by women just as well as men and employers often actively seek women employees. A woman who is well qualified and has desirable personality characteristics for this field of work will find opportunity for gainful employment if she is free and willing to locate herself in areas where opportunities exist.

OPPORTUNITIES FOR MINORITIES

In the past, employment of minorities in the field of recreation and parks has been fairly restricted to recreation programs in large cities. Minority employees are especially valuable in districts occupied by their own ethnic groups. Recreation administrators have learned that members of minority groups often respond more readily to a program if the leaders working in the geographic area are of the same background as the residents. For this reason, there are good employment opportunities in metropolitan areas for well-trained members of minority groups.

Federal and state agencies are bound by law to give equal opportunity to members of minority groups and women. The recreation occupations reflect the trend toward equal employment opportunities for persons of commensurate abilities, and salaries for women and members of minority groups are steadily becoming more equalized with the salaries of other employees in comparable positions.

OPPORTUNITIES FOR THE DISADVANTAGED

In addition to planning programs and services for the population as a whole, substantial efforts must be directed toward special population groups whose needs are related to economic inadequacies and environmental deficiencies. Very often the culturally, educationally, and economically disadvantaged are the same individuals who are recreationally disadvantaged. Therefore, to some degree, they lack opportunities for preparing themselves to become effective leaders in recreation and park programs. However, there are many exceptions to this. Further, some program administrators arrange workshops and clinics to help disadvantaged prospective employees to overcome their deficiencies. More of this needs to be done.

Employment of the disadvantaged is especially relevant to the park and recreation field because the recreation leader must be able to understand the problems of the neighborhood and community and communicate with the residents. Ethnic and racial balance in personnel greatly enhances the effectiveness of local park and recreation systems.

The NRPA and AAHPER conducted a joint survey of 980 agencies throughout the United States to determine the number of disadvantaged workers in local public park and recreation agencies. Twenty-one distinct job classifications were listed. The survey revealed that disadvantaged workers held approximately 13% of the full-time jobs and 25% of the part-time positions, most of which were seasonal. More than half of the disadvantaged workers were in occupational categories of semi- or nonskilled personnel—facilities supervisors, semiskilled park personnel, attendants and aides and certain clerical positions. Of those occupying part-time and seasonal positions the majority were attendants and aides. When the information from this recent study was compared to information from an earlier study (1967), the comparison showed a substantial employment increase in the categories of recreation leaders, attendants and aides, activity specialists, facility supervisors and park rangers.

In the same study, it was found that a little more than 1% of park and recreation employees are from among the handicapped. Of these, about 3 of 10 were professionals while the other 7 were in nonprofessional jobs.

REFERENCES

1. Menninger, W. C.: Recreation and mental health. Recreation Magazine, November 1948, p. 340.
2. Weiskopf, D. C.: *A Guide to Recreation and Leisure*. Allyn and Bacon, Boston, 1975, p. 191.
3. Langeman, R. B. and Rockwood, L. R.: Be prepared . . . for a career in commercial recreation. Parks and Recreation, July 1975, pp. 30-31.
4. Air Force Sports Program Manual. Air Force Publication No. 215-1, Washington, 1966, p. 1.

12

Leadership Characteristics And Requirements

A stage has been set which will require more and better recreational leadership in the future than at any time in the past. Professional opportunities within the broad spectrum of parks, recreation, and conservation will involve many critical issues ranging from the inner-city ghettos to the wilderness of the great outdoors, and from face-to-face interaction with people to the less personal but equally meaningful elements of rivers and forests. In every instance, regardless of the special interest area pursued, people will be the ultimate beneficiaries.

The leaders who give direction and impetus to this vast effort will come from many walks of life, and they will be involved in a variety of ways. Some will be highly specialized technicans who are skilled in certain areas of leisure pursuits, while others will need to be generalists in the sense that they have broad insight and understanding of the total field and its related fields. Some will need to be facility planners, designers and managers, others will emphasize direct program leadership, while still others will concentrate on education for leisure.

There will also have to be an adequate number of sensitive and skillful connoisseurs who create and mold tastes, communicate purposes and appreciations, encourage the planning and installation of adequate areas and facilities, and accept the responsibility for cultural initiative and the development of cultural traditions. In other words, at the top of the profession must be those with insight into the good life, who know the needs of individuals and society, and who are able to help large numbers of people achieve enrichment and happiness.

In the future the people of America will become even more liberated from the utilitarian process that for ages has improverished cultural and creative development, and they will find themselves in an environment of new opportunity for personal enrichment and service. They will be more free to think, feel, and exercise their own desires without keeping too sharp an eye on the bare necessities. Whether this condition turns out to be desirable and beneficial will depend largely upon the success of educators in instilling high values and a sense of real purpose, and the amount and quality of leadership available to provide leisure time opportunities which are appealing, satisfying and truly developmental.

MEANING OF LEADERSHIP

Leadership is a commonly used word which most people correctly interpret, but still it is worthwhile to analyze its meaning in some detail.

A typical dictionary definition of leadership would include the following descriptions: one who leads others, such as a person who goes before to guide or to show the way; or one who presides or directs a group or a program or a movement; or one who conducts; or one who has authority to preside and direct. The emphasis in these phrases is on guiding and directing. However, many of the authorities on the subject of leadership choose to stress the role of the leaders as a *persuader* or an *enabler* rather than as a director. For example, Davis describes leadership as, . . . "the ability to persuade others to seek defined objectives enthusiastically. It is the human factor which binds a group together and motivates it toward goals."[1] Pfiffner described leadership in a similar manner, . . . "the art of coordinating and motivating the individuals and groups to achieve desired ends."[2] Leadership has also been described as interpersonal influence toward the attainment of specified goals, and the capacity to help others express their desires constructively and progressively.

If it is accepted that leadership is the act of influencing people toward desired goals or objectives, then it is apparent that leadership can be both *direct* and *indirect*, with direct leadership resulting from direct contact between the leader and those being led, and indirect leadership resulting from the leader purposely influencing people without having contact with them. An obvious example of *direct* leadership is that of a person administering a program where, through the administrative process, he influences how other employees perform their responsibilities, and how effectively they are able to carry out their own leadership roles. From such a position the leader can influence the total program. Another example of direct leadership is that of a person who gives public speeches, and thereby changes people's knowledge, concepts and feelings about certain matters. A teacher is a direct leader who regularly influences people's lives along a set pattern leading toward certain educational objectives.

An example of an *indirect* leader is one who writes materials that influence those who read the materials, or one who speaks over radio or television, or one who indirectly communicates to a large number of people by communicating directly with only a small number who might be referred to as his "disciples."

To be more specific, a leader in this field can be defined as one who exerts influence on people's use of leisure time by persuading them and providing opportunities for them. His influence might have the affect of providing more and better facilities, or providing a better program of activities from which people can choose, or motivating and guiding people toward better choices and more participation in more worthwhile activities.

It is apparent that leadership is a complexity with numerous aspects. This is fortunate, because a large number of people who have different leadership abilities can fit different leadership patterns, and thereby make important leadership contributions. Practically all of the professionals employed in the recreation and park field are in leadership positions of one kind or another. The leadership role might be direct or indirect, and it might have to do with facility planning, or with programming, or with motivating and guiding people, but whatever the position it will have the potential of influencing the lives of people. The extent to which that influence is properly accomplished determines the success and value of the leader.

IMPORTANT LEADERSHIP CHARACTERISTICS

While highly specialized jobs require specific forms of preparation there are some personal characteristics which are essential for almost all leadership positions in the recreation field. Although the following list is certainly not all inclusive, it does include the more important leadership traits.

1. A cooperative attitude and the ability to create congenial relationships among individuals and agencies
2. A sincere interest in public service and in the positive development of individuals and society as a whole
3. Personality traits which are appealing to members of the public, along with strong character traits which induce respect
4. A variety of skills, interests, and appreciations which will serve as worthy models for other people and cause them to devote their leisure time to developing themselves along the same lines
5. Good judgment, a strong sense of personal responsibility, and high moral standards in all areas of human relationships
6. A keen insight into the kinds of leisure time opportunities people need in order to round out their lives and achieve enrichment and fulfillment
7. An ability to work effectively with people of various ages, beliefs and backgrounds without interferences because of differences of race, sex, origin, or religious affiliation
8. The specific knowledge, skills and insights necessary for the particular job to be done. An administrator of a recreation program must possess basically the same administrative skills as a school administrator or a business manager, while a designer of recreation facilities must possess basically the same kinds of competencies as other designers, and a teacher of leisure time activities must be competent by standards comparable to other teachers
9. The ability to see the bright side of life and to enjoy all aspects of it, and cause others to do the same

10. A basic conviction that all human beings have worth and dignity, and a determination to help them improve the quality of their lives

11. A sincere belief in the importance of leisure and the benefits that can be gained from it

12. The ability to work effectively with others, drawing forth their best efforts as a catalyst or enabler, rather than as an authoritarian director

13. The ability to think clearly and logically, to understand and analyze problem situations, and to arrive at intelligent conclusions

14. Skill in communicating effectively with others, both verbally and in written form

15. Such personal qualities as warmth, patience, empathy for the needs and feelings of others, and a sense of humor—all of which contribute to the ability to get along well with others

16. Emotional and psychological maturity. The successful leader should understand himself and others, should be as free from irrational prejudice as possible, and able to manage disagreement or opposition constructively

17. The quality of being a "self-starter"—being able to clearly identify goals and move forcefully and directly toward them

18. Integrity, honesty, and loyalty to the organization one works for, and to its goals and philosophy

19. The capacity for making difficult decisions and then standing by them, without stalling or equivocating

20. The ability to be both visionary and practical—having high ideals and visions of what might be possible in the future, and at the same time maintaining a realistic sense of practical problems that must be overcome in the present

21. Flexibility in the sense that the individual is ready to grow and change over a period of time, rather than cling to outmoded views or attitudes

22. A point of view that sees cooperation, rather than competition and jealousy, as a way of life

A leader's behavioral style may either contribute to or detract from his effectiveness. Certain behavioral approaches can be identified and clearly linked to successful performance with participants or co-workers. For example, a recreation leader, in addition to such *technical* acts as filling out reports, preparing schedules, or assigning personnel to job stations, must also engage in a set of *interpersonal* behaviors. These involve such interactions as communicating, assisting, rebuking, clarifying, giving support, praising, criticizing, guiding, inspiring, and motivating group members. Such behaviors should be as positive, constructive, and consistent as possible.

In general, "democratic" leadership behavior is believed to be more effective than "autocratic" or "laissez-faire" leadership. Similarly, "participative" supervisors, who display consideration for the attitudes, feelings and needs of those working under their direction, and who strive to improve their sense of autonomy and responsibility and strengthen their degree of motivation, are believed to be more successful than other types of supervisors.

PRINCIPLES OF RECREATION LEADERSHIP

Richard Kraus prepared ten principles of recreation leadership which should be meaningful to all prospective professionals in this field. With permission of the author the principles are presented here.[3]

1. The leader must operate on the basis of a sound philosophy of recreation and leisure. He must regard recreation as a significant aspect of human life, with a high potential for enhancing human growth and development and improving the total quality of community life.

2. The leader must have a sound knowledge of the basic theories of play, both past and present. He should also have a basic understanding of human development and of psychological principles that will help him work constructively with various individuals in improving motivation, dealing with individual or group behavior problems, and promoting healthy values.

3. The leader should be sensitive to the process of group dynamics, and should make use of whatever approach is likely to be most effective within a given situation or with a particular group—such as "democratic," "authoritarian," or "permissive" approaches. At the same time, he should move in the direction of democratic involvement, attempting to involve participants as fully as possible in the processes of active participation in group decision-making and self-management.

4. The leader should respect the needs of individuals within the groups he serves and must clearly recognize the differences among individuals in these groups. At the same time, he must balance these concerns with an awareness of the needs or rights of the groups themselves, of the agencies that sponsor them, or of the larger community.

5. The leader must regard recreation, not as an end in itself, but rather as a means to an end. Thus, a successful carnival, a tournament victory, or a high level of playground attendance are worthwhile only if they have helped to achieve the important purposes of community recreation.

6. The leader should strive for a reasonable balance between competition and cooperation, recognizing both as important forms of group activity. He must also strike a balance between other potentially conflicting goals or emphases in program development, with the "greatest good for the greatest number" being his basic objective.

7. The leader should attempt to create an effective organization for planning and carrying out programs in order to realize as large a return as possible on all facilities, activities, and staff services.

8. The concerned leader should constantly evaluate the effectiveness and the specific outcomes of his programs as well as the quality of his own functioning. In so doing, he must measure outcomes against the stated goals of his agency or department, the expressed wishes of participants, and his own personal goals.

9. Leadership must constantly seek to promote desirable social values. The leader should consistently make his views or moral position known, and should set a constructive example for participants.

10. Successful leaders must be prepared to accept responsibilities and risks, to experiment and explore, to initiate, to pioneer. They cannot be satisfied with programs that just "get by," or with repeating the status quo. "Tired blood" is bad enough in an individual, but in a program concerned with promoting exciting and creative human involvement it is fatal. Therefore, the effective leader must constantly seek to innovate, to build his program, and to promote more meaningful services.

In applying these principles, the leader must recognize that there may be three different sets of values or expectations—those of the *sponsoring agency*, the *participants*, and *his own*.

The goals of *sponsoring agencies* may vary widely. For example, recreation programs for the *retarded* are likely to give heavy emphasis to helping individuals learn to live independently in the community and to reducing inappropriate behavior or appearance. Recreation in a *correctional* institution would be geared to promoting favorable morale in the penal setting, developing constructive social values, and introducing leisure interests and attitudes which will be helpful to residents after their return to the community. Recreation programs sponsored by *religious* organizations are likely to give emphasis to promoting special moral or spiritual values, to strengthening family-centered recreation activities, and to reinforcing the tie between young people and the religion itself. It is essential that the leader be able to accept and work constructively with the agency goals if he is to be an effective staff member.

Similarly, he must be able to understand and accept the needs and wishes of the *participants* he serves. However, this does not mean that he accepts these wishes in a completely noncritical way. Instead, it is his responsibility to interpose his own views and judgment, and to balance their desires—which may not be altogether desirable or constructive—with his more mature or justifiable purposes.

Finally, the recreation leader must balance both agency and participant goals with *his own* personal objectives, philosophy of recreation, and judgment of appropriate program goals and priorities.

The Oakland, California, Recreation Department Handbook points out to employees in the department that each one is:

> among the ten most wanted people
> an artist—with people instead of paint
> a friend—to everyone, big or little
> a builder—of health and character
> a pioneer—in trying out new ideas
> a reformer—of bad habits or poor sportsmanship
> a believer—in the best of everyone

The purpose of this list and other associated materials in the handbook is to emphasize the social role of the recreation leader, particularly in terms of working constructively with young people on playgrounds and in community centers.

In the Stockton, California, Recreation and Park Department Manual it points out that the playground and recreation center leader is expected to function in the following ways:

> *As an Organizer.* Make a survey of your playground and neighborhood to find out what it has and what it needs. Organize and develop such activities as will . . . produce the best physical, mental and moral results

As a Leader. Teach games, both old and new; direct club organizations and promote indoor and outdoor activities as outlined by the supervisors and in accordance with the policies of the Department

As a Host. Encourage all persons attending the playground or center to enter into the various activities . . .

As a Coach. Develop teams and competitive events of all kinds, giving instructions when necessary . . .

As a Teacher. Promote literature and study clubs, dramatics, hand work, and nature lore . . .

As an Advertiser. Provide a bulletin board. Plan a program at least one day ahead. See that all announcements are attractively displayed . . .

As a Clerk. See that all reports are submitted *on time* to the main office . . .

As a First-Aider. Apply first aid *only* in emergency. Know the accident procedure completely and thoroughly

As an Authority. Supervise carefully lavatories and *out-of-the-way* places. Do not permit marking on walls of buildings or fences. Eliminate all smoking, swearing, rowdyism and gambling, etc. . . .

As a Friend. One of your most important jobs as a leader is to be a friend to all who participate on your playground or in your center.

LEADERSHIP IN PUBLIC RELATIONS

The recreation leader plays an important role in promoting effective public and community relations. In any recreation department or agency public relations are essential for the following reasons:

1. To create a favorable public image of the department and to encourage positive official or legislative support
2. To encourage maximum attendance at regular programs and special events
3. To enlist volunteers to help in the program
4. To overcome public misconceptions or distortions about the program
5. To develop a strong core of support from the public for requests relative to budget, areas and facility, staff, etc.

Public relations must not be left to chance alone. Individuals skilled in this field should be given the responsibility for arranging major public relations events such as interviews, tours, radio or television programs, and for preparing newspaper releases, magazine articles, reports, brochures and other publicity materials. However, all public relations cannot be carried on effectively by central office specialists. Instead public relations must be the direct responsibility of recreation leaders on the grassroots level who meet and deal with the public at swimming pools, community centers, playgrounds, athletic fields, waterfront areas, museums, cultural events, camps or wherever the program reaches the public.

In terms of face-to-face public relations Kraus has listed three important procedures that all recreation leaders should follow:[4]

1. Acquaint themselves with the neighborhood as fully as possible—its streets, buildings, businesses, churches, and other organizations. Whenever possible, chat with parents and program participants. Special efforts should be made to help each participant feel that he or she is wanted in the program, and that

there is a helpful, friendly, and courteous attitude on the part of all staff members.

2. When there are requests or problems, treat them with sincere interest and respect. Each problem should be given prompt attention and handling. Policies should be explained fully and tactfully when they are challenged. Use all available information or resources to solve problems or meet requests of residents.

3. Set a positive image for the public. Neat appearance and responsible conduct on the part of recreation and park employees will help give neighborhood residents a favorable view of the department. Facilities and equipment should also be maintained in the best possible condition. If department morale is high and recreation workers project a strong, optimistic view of their program, public attitudes will reflect this.

In addition to the favorable impressions that should be developed through face-to-face contact between the recreation leaders and the public, the leaders must also be concerned about effectively using the mass media. They should submit through regular departmental channels suggestions for news releases or photographs which would make good publicity. They should keep the central office accurately advised of athletic contests, tournaments and special events with emphasis on good "human interest" stories. Each leader should also watch for opportunities to gather photographs and bits of information that can add to the effectiveness of brochures and reports. It is a fact that the more favorable exposure the activities and personnel of the program can receive the higher will be the level of participation and the more support the department will have from the public in general and from the officials who make decisions that affect the department.

IN-SERVICE PROFESSIONAL PREPARATION

Unfortunately some individuals in this and other fields assume that, once they have gotten a college degree and accepted full-time employment, the need for additional professional preparation has ended. Nothing could be further from the truth, especially in this day and age. The term "commencement" as it is used in connection with college graduation is truly representative of an important fact of life. It is a time to commence the pursuit of one's larger and more permanent goals, and to commence additional preparation and improvement on a continuing basis. Additional preparation of full-time professionals in this field can involve several approaches: regular reading of professional literature, attendance at professional conferences, workshops and clinics, completion of college short courses or evening courses in graduate programs, or completion of programs offered by professional consulting firms.

By referring to Chapter 15 and the appendix a good overview can be obtained of the literature available in this field. Chapter 15 includes all of the recreation and park related organizations, and lists the periodicals prepared and circulated by each organization. The bibliography lists the recently published textbooks in the field. Knowledge about the availability of new books can best be obtained through book review sections of the major periodicals dealing with this field. All new books pertinent to the field are reviewed in those sources.

Opportunities to attend and participate in national, regional, state and local conventions, conferences, clinics and workshops vary with each individual, depending on his location, his particular responsibilities and his financial condition. It can be safely said, however, that some such opportunities are reasonably available to all members of the profession. Each person should capitalize as best he can on the opportunities available in his particular situation. Those who establish themselves as recognized professional leaders, and particularly those who are successful with new and innovative approaches, will find ample opportunity for leadership roles in

Figure 37. A "summer in the park" is often used to stimulate interest. (National Capital Parks photo.)

in-service training programs. This in itself is a great benefit, because it improves the image of the department which the person represents, and often the one in the leadership role learns more and benefits more than anyone else.

The feasibility of completing college short courses and evening school graduate courses is somewhat dependent upon one's location and his working conditions, but many professionals are within convenient distance of a college or university program where valuable courses of this kind are offered.

A number of consulting firms have moved into this field, particularly the area of commercial recreation, by carrying out research, assisting in planning, and consulting on management problems. These firms offer a series of management seminars geared to the needs of executive personnel in recreation, tourism and related fields. Also they are available on a contract basis to prepare and present workshops and clinics to the personnel of a department.

CHARACTERISTICS OF A PROFESSIONAL

All of those who are employed in professional leadership positions in the recreation and park field have some obligation to contribute toward the professional status of the field. In order to do this they should be aware that certain characteristic features are used by the public as criteria to help identify whether an occupational group constitutes a profession. Some of these features are as follows:

1. The work calls for specialized preparation over a considerable period of time and must be based on a good background of general education and cultural development
2. The members of the group strive, through the use of selective admission procedures, to maintain a high level of performance of duties
3. The work consists of the practice of an art, based upon the application of sound principles
4. The members of the group formulate and abide by a code of ethics
5. There are varied specialized services within the occupation
6. The members of the group intend to make the occupation their life work
7. The members of the occupational group are characterized, in spite of their specialized differences, by a high degree of unity of purpose, spirit, ideals and organization
8. The members of the group involve themselves continually in in-service preparation

In addition to the criteria for a professional field, certain individual characteristics contribute to a member's true professionalism. By demonstrating these characteristics an individual will elevate the image of his occupational field and contribute toward its acceptance as a legitimate profession. By not demonstrating these characteristics the leader will have an opposite effect.

1. Professionals do not require close and constant supervision
2. They do not regard themselves as employees who need a "boss"
3. They do not perform their work only by the hour, basing salary on hourly rates
4. They take full responsibility for the results of their efforts and acts
5. They continually seek ways in which to improve themselves
6. They contribute to the skills and insights of their profession
7. They respect the confidences of others by not violating them
8. They demonstrate loyalty to their colleagues by refraining from gossiping with or about others
9. They refrain from passing on significant and confidential information received through the grapevine
10. They handle their grievances through proper channels
11. They refrain from complaining habitually and grumbling
12. They meet their obligations both legal and moral
13. They are sensitive to the problems of their fellow workers and strive to be helpful to each other
14. They do not attempt to advance themselves at the cost of their colleagues
15. They are proud of their profession and are desirous of rendering the highest quality of service they can perform
16. They present a personal image in all aspects that will contribute not only to their own well-being but to the improvement of the profession

STYLES OF LEADERSHIP

David Gray[5] has pointed out two contrasting styles of community recreation leadership. One he refers to as the "chain-link philosophy," which holds that the primary concern of the leaders is to operate the playgrounds, the centers, and the other facilities. It identifies their tasks as surveillance of grounds to assure compliance with rules, safety, proper use of facilities and control of equipment; development of a schedule for use of the facility; planning and execution of a program of activities with the staff in face-to-face leadership roles; coordination of maintenance activities to ensure the readiness and sanitary condition of the premises. Such a philosophy rewards facility managers and holds that what happens in the center is what counts.

In contrast to this view, there is a concept of professional recreation personnel which perceives them as community figures. This concept identifies as central the development of people, community interaction, improvement of the community, preservation of the virtues of urban life, and concern for the social problems of our time.

A really good recreator working within this concept can operate in a community without elaborate facilities and earn his salary. He can become a person of stature for the contributions he can make to community living and the growth of people, without ever throwing a light switch, handling a ball, taking in a flag, or locking a gate. His job can be to generate events that look for a place to happen, not to fill up a facility that he is hired to manage. This vision of the recreator as a community organizer raises serious questions about the way we recruit, educate and deploy staff, and about the nature of professional work. There is no doubt that most "professional" recreators do much work that is subprofessional.

The really difficult professional task in these times is the role of community catalyst. In this role, the recreator assumes the tasks of organizer, moderator, mediator, stimulator, interpreter, adviser and teacher. Using recreation content and method, such a figure seeks to improve the social climate of the community. There is no precise model for this kind of professional. The task may be accomplished in one community by an outstanding minister, in another by a particularly able school principal or an effective YMCA employee, but most communities lack such a person; they are the poorer for it.

Under the direction of an individual performing well in this community role, our recreation centers could become true community centers. This would require abandonment of the chain-link fence philosophy, broadening of the concept of what constitutes recreation involvement in community affairs, reeducation and redeployment of the staff, and a new interpretation of the mission of the center.

The key concepts in the community role are *engagement* and *participation*—engagement in the problems and issues of our time and participation in the lives of our communities. The recreation program cannot be withdrawn and uninvolved and still perform its potential community role. The program cannot serve a small, clean orderly segment of the community while there is violence in the streets and expect the populace to support it. Community centers should be "commons" where diverse elements can meet and interact.

REFERENCES

1. Davis, K: *Human Relations at Work.* Mc Graw Hill, New York, 1967, p.96.
2. Pfiffner, J. N. and Presthus, R.: *Public Administration.* Ronald Press, New York, 1968, p. 92.
3. Kraus, R.: *Recreation Leadership and Supervision.* W. B. Saunders, Philadelphia, 1975, p. 39.
4. *Ibid.*, p. 240.
5. Gray, D.: Tyranny of the chain-link fence. California Parks and Recreation, August 1968.

13

The Economics of Recreation and Leisure

It is difficult to accurately determine the economic value of leisure time activities. There are few exact figures with which to deal and the scope of the leisure time market is extensive. Further, there is no clear-cut definition of what should and should not be included under the label of leisure time activities.

Another complication is the problem of knowing the portion of leisure time spending which should be classified as recreational spending, because not all leisure time pursuits can truly be called recreation. As explained earlier in this book, some forms of leisure activities are only amusers and time wasters and some activities even cause negative (decreative) results.

In spite of the unavailability of complete and accurate financial figures there are some meaningful facts and estimates available from reputable agencies and economic specialists which can add considerably to our understanding of the leisure time market and its economic significance.

As early as 1968 the brokerage firm of Merrill, Lynch, one of America's largest, announced that the annual leisure time market was approaching the $150 billion mark. The firm estimated that by 1980 the leisure market might reach $250 billion annually. Merrill, Lynch also stated that in terms of stock values the leisure time market would outperform the improvement of the economy in general.[1]

In 1969 *U.S. News & World Report* described the leisure market as the fastest growing phase of business in America. It was stated in the article that "Affluent Americans, with more time on their hands and money to spend than ever before, have boomed leisure into one of America's biggest businesses. The figure tops the current annual outlay for national defense."[2]

In 1972 the same magazine said this about the leisure time market: "It is more than the outlay for construction of new homes, it surpasses the total of corporate profits, it is far larger than the aggregate income of the country's exports, and estimates are that the dollar value of leisure time expenditures will more than double during the decade of the 1970's."[3] In 1972 Peter Henle provided information which generally substantiates the claims made by Merrill, Lynch and *U.S. News & World Report.*[4]

This large sum of money is spent on a great variety of leisure activities including travel, sports equipment, campers, boats, summer homes, snowmobiles, hunting and fishing supplies, cultural events, athletic tickets and a multitude of other items. Also included is the cost of capital improvements for recreational purposes. This by itself involves a tremendous outlay of cash each year, as indicated by the

Figure 38. The ultramodern Bahia Mar Hotel and Yachting Center as seen from the air over Fort Lauderdale beach. (Photo courtesy of Bahia Mar Hotel & Yachting Center.)

following facts. During the last quarter century outdoor playgrounds have increased in number almost threefold; the number of tennis courts has almost doubled; swimming pools have more than doubled; and indoor recreation centers have tripled in number. The annual expenditure of tax-supported recreation and park programs has increased about fourfold during that period.

People cannot spend money on leisure time pursuits unless they have it. Fortunately many Americans have a relatively large amount of money, much more than they have had in the past. In a general way this is indicated by the gross national product. Few aspects of life in America are more impressive than the tremendous amount of goods and services produced. The total annual market value of these goods and services is referred to as the gross national product (GNP), and is a general but reliable indicator of the economic well-being of the nation. In 1930 the GNP was approximately $105 billion. By 1970 it had increased to $970 billion, and it now exceeds $1200 billion per year.

For these figures to have comparative meaning we must take into account the increase of population during that same period and the inflationary effects of our economy, but even when these important factors are applied to the GNP increase the result is that Americans have more buying power today than ever before. Although the increase in buying power has not been dramatic, it has been fairly constant, and on the average Americans now have about 25% more purchasing power than they had in the mid-1950s.

To view the economic trend in a different way let us consider the per capita income. In 1965 the average income for every man, woman and child in America was about $2300. By 1970 it had reached $3200, and now it is over $5400. Here again these figures cannot be viewed as directly comparable because the costs of goods and services have become considerably inflated since 1965. Still, income has increased slightly faster than inflation, thus resulting in increased per capita purchasing power.

A certain percentage of income is consistently spent on leisure time interests, and that percentage tends to go up as purchasing power increases. With increased purchasing power people are inclined to spend a smaller percentage on the "essentials" and a larger portion on the "extras" that give them enjoyment and pleasure.

THE EFFECTS OF LEISURE TIME ON EMPLOYMENT

Leisure time activities provide direct full-time and part-time employment to several hundred thousand people in the United States, and indirect employment to a much larger number. Included are (1) those in the general categories of producers and distributers of leisure time products and services, (2) planners, designers, builders and maintenance workers of leisure time facilities, and (3) those employed in the various kinds of recreation leadership positions.

Henle stated that in 1970 there were approximately 26 million full-time and part-time workers in leisure time occupations in the United States.[4] This seems like an overstatement, and its accuracy would depend on the definition of leisure time occupations. It is a fact that a very large number of people are employed directly and indirectly in providing lesiure services. Only a portion of the total number of employees are recreation and park professionals, while many others provide a multitude of services to people who engage in a great assortment of leisure activities.

According to the National Recreation and Park Association, as long ago as 1968 there were more than 150,000 people employed full-time and part-time in the local public park and recreation sector alone. The NRPA estimated that over 500,000 individuals worked in commercial recreation jobs. There has not been a more recent study to furnish updated information, but based on other related trends it would seem safe to predict that the number of employees has increased by 30 to 40% since 1968.

Millions of people are employed in numerous industries that produce equipment, materials and services designed to meet our leisure needs. As the recreation movement expands it will provide many additional jobs—from laborers and clerks to skilled technicians and professional leaders. The leisure time field has the potential to create considerably more employment wealth in the future than it has to this point.

EFFECTS OF PARKS AND RECREATION ON PROPERTY VALUES

The fact that a land area has recreational features, either natural or constructed, which are attractive to people causes the land to increase in value. Generally people like to live close to interesting recreational opportunities. Also people often want to build vacation homes near recreation attractions; others want to build commercial establishments in order to profit from the increased number of people who come there; and still others want to own land for speculative purposes. At any rate the simple law of supply and demand causes property values to escalate and the real estate business to boom.

The rate of the escalation depends mostly upon the ratio of the supply of property to the demand created for it. In some cases the property near recreation developments skyrockets while in other cases the escalation is gradual, but in any case those who own property near significant recreation attractions stand to gain as a result.

Effects of Outdoor Recreation Developments

An interesting analysis was developed by the National Park Service where it explained that often communities in the vicinity of proposed national park and recreation areas fear the loss of tax revenue because of the land being stricken from the tax rolls. Experience shows that new enterprises develop adjacent to the parks, and property values increase significantly. In some cases the value of the land remaining on the tax rolls has increased 50-fold over an extended period of time, and in the long run the tax revenue has been significantly greater because of the park then it would have been otherwise.

One of the best case studies of property escalation is provided in a Bureau of Outdoor Recreation publication.[5] It describes a well-documented situation in the Pearl River Reservoir area near Jackson, Mississippi. A detailed analysis was made of 304 sales involving over 25,000 acres of land adjacent to or within close access to the planned reservoir project. An analysis was also made for the same period of 101 sales transactions covering more than 11,000 acres in a comparable area not influenced by the project, and which served as a control (a

Figure 39. Apostle Islands National Lakeshore in Wisconsin. This had a significant escalative effect on surrounding land values. (National Park Service photo.)

standard for comparison) for the study. The average price paid per acre of land adjacent to the project showed an average annual increase of slightly less than 9% prior to announcement of the project. After the announcement prices increased 165% the first year, 191% the second year, 216% the third year, 236% the fourth year and 258% the fifth year. The price per acre of the control area for the same period of time continued to increase between 8 and 10% per year, as it had during the few previous years.

Another interesting example was given in a study conducted by the Bureau of Outdoor Recreation to determine the extent to which occupants of vacation homes in northern New England (including Maine and parts of Vermont and New Hampshire) participated in outdoor recreation, and the amounts they spent in connection with their vacation homes. The BOR calculated that 28,410 vacation homes in the northern New England areas were included in the study. It was computed that on the average each home owner spent $2,425 each year locally and $180 elsewhere within the region. If these calculations are correct, then approximately $425 million is spent each year in connection with owners' use of vacation homes.

Further, it has been estimated by economists that $1,000 of direct expenditure by out-of-the-region vacation visitors adds 1.55 times that amount to the region's total economy. This would mean that the total economic impact of the vacation homes in northern New England is about $658 million annually (1.55 times $425 million).

The scenic and recreational features of the northern New England region added value to the land. Then the use to which the land was put because of these features, and the large expenditure that has resulted, have created jobs which have attracted other people to the vicinity. All of this has caused the price of the land to escalate; land prices in that region are now exorbitant compared to what they were before the recreational potential of the region was recognized and developed.

Recreation is also used as a means of upgrading economically disadvantaged rural areas throughout the United States. With assistance from government, many rural landowners have converted their properties into recreational resources, thus attracting increased numbers of visitors to their regions and adding generally to the local economy.

One of the ways in which Indian tribes have improved their economies is through the development of recreation attractions. As an example, when the $110-million Kinzua dam and reservoir was planned for western Pennsylvania, the Bureau of Indian Affairs assisted the Seneca tribe, which was forced to give up much of its property, in developing a huge new tourist program, including shops, lodges, museums, an Indian village, a motel, a 100-boat marina, an outdoor amphitheater and an indoor theater for Indian ceremonials and folklore festivals. It was estimated that this new development would draw several hundred thousand tourists each year. Numerous other such projects have been developed or are presently being developed by other Indian tribes.

City Parks and the Value of Real Estate

Five years after New York's Central Park was first acquired it was found desirable to enlarge it by the addition of 65 acres to the north. The appraised value of this 65 acres at the time of the original park acquisition was $183,850, but six years later the park commission had to pay the new appraised value of $1,179,590, more than six times the original appraisal. This was due to a number of factors, the most prominent of which was the placement of the original park.

A long list of similar examples could be described. In fact, almost every major city in the country would have its own stories to tell about the positive effects that parks have had on the surrounding property values. Certainly it would be a rare case that the opposite occurred.

Because of the consistently positive effect on property values when a significant park site is selected, some government officials have advocated the theory of "excess condemnation" as a method of helping to pay for park land. This theory, simply stated, means that more land would be acquired either by condemnation or other procedures than would be included in the park. After the park boundaries were determined the excess property on the fringe areas of the park would be sold off at a much higher price than originally paid. The principle is sound but its implementation by a public agency is difficult and often impossible, because condemning private property for public use and then reselling part of the property at an escalated market value is generally an unacceptable practice.

However, this procedure is commonly followed in certain kinds of nonpublic projects. For example, private golf courses, marinas and other such areas are often partially paid for by purchasing more property than will actually be developed; after the development the excess property is sold to private individuals at significantly more than the original rate of purchase. This practice is especially common with golf courses, where the property that borders a course can be subdivided into prime residential lots.

A rise in real estate values of a complete neighborhood can readily take place when a park acquisition or development occurs just before the surrounding property is built upon. The park can have a marked influence toward improving the general character of the neighborhood, causing a higher type of development and higher land values. It is generally agreed by land economists that, in a proposed one-square-mile neighborhood developed privately, a fully completed 10-acre park could be justified as a gift to the public, because the presence of the park would increase the value of the remainder of the property enough to offset the cost. However, in a developed area a new park would have a smaller influence on the escalation of land prices, because the essential character of the neighborhood would have already been determined. From the economic point of view, the best time to acquire land and develop parks in a neighborhood is either prior to or at the time the neighborhood originally develops.

Estimating the Direct Economic Value of a Park

Placing values on parks in economic terms was for a long time purely an academic exercise. For the most part there has been no practical need for establishing a price, because parks are not sold at the marketplace. City parks have traditionally been public holdings that symbolized the city's character, that imparted dignity and charm to the city's appearance, that permitted breathing room within the city, and that would last forever.

Now, however, with practically all else in today's world, parks have lost their "eternal permanence" and there are many attempts to evaluate them on the basis of economics. Therefore, it is of practical necessity to try to find some economic measures by which to justify the existence of at least some of the parks, state and federal as well as municipal parks.

Clawson and Knetsch[6] explained that the immediate value of a park can be roughly measured by surveying the users of the park and finding out how much each would be willing to pay per use. As an example they indicated that certain users of a state park would be willing to pay $5.00, others $4.00 and others lesser amounts. By determining the number of users that would pay each amount and the total number of users, it is easy to calculate how much the users would be willing to pay if payment were necessary. In other words, this indicates the revenue the park would probably produce if fees were charged. In one sense this could be interpreted as the immediate financial value of the park to the public. However, this procedure does not take into account related values, such as the escalation of the value of adjacent property and the influence that the park has on land even half a mile or a mile away. Neither does it take into account the general positive feeling that parks give to members of a community, even those who never use them. The fact that the parks are available and part of the total community plan seems to be a source of social satisfaction.

Another approach sometimes used in the case of state or national parks is to attempt to calculate the approximate amount of money spent within and close around the park by those who come to visit—in other words, the effect that the park has on local commerce. This again deals with only one aspect of the value of the park, but it is important information.

Certain government resource management agencies, including the Corps of Engineers and the Bureau of Reclamation, have placed estimated values on visits by fisherman, boaters, campers, etc., to calculate the economic value of the recreational characteristics of a project. This procedure provides substantial economic information, but still is not indicative of the total economic value that accrues from recreational areas.

Because of the difficulty of arriving at accurate economic estimates, such estimates are seldom used in the settlement of priorities between parks and highways, river developments, power plants, airports and other such economically measurable installations.

In the final analysis it seems that the value of a park is what the governing agency thinks it is, and is willing and able to pay for it. This is essentially the same as saying that a rare work of art is worth whatever a buyer is willing to pay. It is not a precise method of pricing, but in most cases the most meaningful one and the one that prevails. However, it is true that some of the procedures of making economic estimates described here might influence the amount that the governing agency is willing to pay, and the persistence with which the agency might try to acquire or hold the park in the face of pressures to do otherwise.

PURCHASE OF GOODS AND SERVICES

In order to get a more detailed view of how leisure time activities affect the economy, let us analyze some of the specific areas of recreation in terms of the purchase of goods and services. These expenditures have both a direct and indirect effect on the economy. The direct effect is obviously the immediate exchange of money in the purchase of goods and services. The indirect effect is in the form of the second- and third-level transactions that result from the direct expenditures. For example, if a person buys a pair of snow skis for $150 that represents a direct expenditure. The distributor in turn purchased the skis from a manufacturer, who in turn purchased materials and parts from subcontractors or parts manufacturers, who in turn purchased raw materials. This chain reaction has a filtering effect through the economy causing the direct purchase to have a farther-reaching effect than the mere purchase itself.

Winter Sports

Downhill skiing has mushroomed in recent years into one of our most interesting and spectacular activities. Not only is it vigorous and fun, but there has developed with it a colorful and appealing social atmosphere. The old adage that "it ain't what it used to be" is certainly true with skiing, because it is much better then it used to be in almost every aspect. The greatly improved skiing equipment and the speedy and comfortable lifts have revolutionized skiing in terms of both enjoyment and popularity. During recent years the number of skiers has increased at a rate of more than 15% annually.

At major ski resorts daily lift passes now range between $7 and $13 per day. Popular brands of skis of quality construction range in price from $100 to $250 per pair, and the remainder of the ski outfit also carries a substantial price tag. This is not to imply that a person cannot participate enjoyably in this activity with relatively inexpensive equipment and clothing. It is a fact, however, that most skiers buy medium- or high-priced equipment, and when all of the costs are considered a tremendous amount of money is spent each year by the six million skiers in America. Added to the costs of lift passes and equipment and clothing are the costs of travel, lodging and food.

In addition to downhill skiing, which is the king of winter sports from the standpoint of financial outlay, significant contributions are made to the economy through ice skating, cross-country skiing and snowshoe touring, winter camping and snowmobiling.

Snowmobiling deserves special attention in this discussion. Being relatively new, it has increased in popularity even faster than skiing, and it has now become so popular in some areas that it is causing difficult problems relative to ecology, especially in terms of disturbing wildlife habitat, and accidental injuries. It is estimated that there are now more than 2.5 million snowmobiles in the snow belt covering the northern United States and southern Canada, and this number increases significantly each year. The price of one of these machines ranges from several hundred to $2000. It is apparent that the initial cost plus the operating expenses of snowmobiles makes a prominent economic contribution.

Water Sports

Only during the last couple of decades has recreational power boating become popular with large numbers of people. This is probably primarily the result of the increased buying power of Americans combined with the development of appealing equipment. Also, the development of water skiing has added greatly to the interest in power boating, because many people own power boats primarily for water skiing. Further, many middle-aged and older people find travel in the out-of-doors more pleasant on board a motorcraft than by most other methods, and it is true that much beautiful scenery can be appreciated by boat travel.

The Power Boat Association of America estimates a total of about four million power boats presently in use, and most of them used for recreation. The average cost of these boats is between $3,000 and $4,000. In addition to the tremendous initial outlay for purchase, the operating costs are significant, and these costs make ongoing contributions to the economy.

In addition to motorcraft, there are less but still significant expenditures associated with sailing, canoeing, kayaking and other recreational water crafts. Surfing and skin and scuba diving, with the more elaborate forms of recreational underwater exploration, also make a large economic contribution.

Beach activities, largely sunbathing and swimming in the surf, are relatively inexpensive in themselves, but they make a sizeable contribution to the economy through expensive beach house ownership and rental, and through food and concession services.

Swimming (of the nonbeach type) involves a different kind of economic outlay, largely in the form of capital improvements. Practically every community of any size in the entire nation has at least one swimming pool and in addition there are many privately owned pools for commercial use by the public. Further, there are residential pools in the backyards of hundreds of thousands of American homes. It is not unusual for a large community pool to have a construction cost of a million dollars or more, and most private family pools cost upward of $3,000. The salaries of supervisors, instructors, lifeguards and maintenance employees constitute a huge payroll on the national scale.

Hunting and Fishing

It is estimated that in the U.S. 20 million hunters go into the field each year. In most cases each hunter has an expensive firearm, a good supply of ammunition and a long list of hunting accessories. For many hunters, the gun and accessories are owned more for personal pride and enjoyment than for practical use. Whatever the case, they serve a recreational or special interest need. In certain western states where hunting is a prominent activity the few days associated with the major hunts involve more financial expenditure than any other equal period of time during the year, including preparation for Christmas. Most of the expenditures are associated with travel and camping. Many hunters invest a great amount of money in equipment used in support of hunting activities. Trail motorbikes, four-wheel-drive vehicles, trailer houses and campers, and horse outfits all head for the hills in spectacular numbers.

Fishing is no less prominent in its contribution to the economy. Fishing is somewhat related to boating, which has already been discussed, and it also involves an extensive amount of travelling, the purchase of food, lodging, and equipment, and the use of off-road vehicles in much the same way and to about the same extent as does hunting. It is estimated that almost one-third of the 219 million people in America become involved to some degree in this recreational activity. Some do it almost every day in season while others participate only on rare occasions.

Outdoor Athletic Sports

From the participation point of view, golf and tennis are the most popular outdoor sports, with tennis being the fastest growing sport in the country. It is needless to emphasize that golf is an expensive activity, and many Americans still consider it too rich for their blood. Fortunately however, with the construction of many municipal golf courses in the last three decades, golf is now within the financial reach of most middle-class Americans; it has always been within the reach of those in the upper-income brackets. For many who belong to private country clubs, the nongolf activities sponsored by the club are just as appealing as the golf itself, and add much to its economic contribution. The American Golf Foundation estimates that there are over 20 million golfers in the United States, almost one-tenth of the population.

With the national and international TV exposure given to tennis in the last few years, it has emerged as one of America's truly popular outdoor sports; its participation rate is still increasing rapidly.

With golf and tennis, the major expenditure is in capital outlay, because golf courses and tennis courts are expensive items. In addition, a significant amount of money is spent on a daily basis for equipment and accessories.

Soccer is the second fastest growing outdoor sport in America, and it is a truly excellent participation activity. Youth soccer leagues are springing up all over the country, and the game is now popular in the public schools at every level. The attention being given to professional team franchises and increased exposure in the news media has contributed much to its popularity. Soccer is the most popular sport in the world, though never in the United States, but the internationalization of sports is contributing to its increased popularity here.

Other popular outdoor sports which involve a large number of participants and make significant economic contributions are baseball, softball, cycling and jogging. Athletic fields and cycling and jogging paths involve an extensive amount of capital outlay and maintenance costs, in addition to the purchase of equipment and supplies.

Tourism

Travel for pleasure is America's primary recreational activity, in terms both of number of participants and money spent. According to the U.S. Travel Council, almost half of the American people participate in some form of travel vacation each year, and many people take several pleasure trips annually. It is not uncommon for some people to go on a trip almost every weekend, and to take many shorter drives to close-by points of interest. Travel for pleasure is a boon to resorts, hotels, motels, eating establishments, auto service stations, the automobile industry, airlines, and numerous other commercial enterprises. Subtract the economic impact of this major leisure time activity and a big step would be taken toward economic collapse. Just the direct employment segment of tourism makes a major contribution to the economy.

According to the American Automobile Association (AAA), Americans spend $60 billion annually on vacation and pleasure trips. Further, the AAA estimates that Americans drive over 225 billion miles each year just getting to and from vacation areas. Seventy-five percent of all domestic pleasure travel involves the automobile. It is estimated by the U.S. Council on Tourism that, for every day a tourist spends in a particular geographic area, $29 is added to the economy of that area.

Each year foreign travel becomes a bigger item in the leisure time budget. The Department of Commerce estimates that 5 million Americans go abroad each year, and they spend $5 billion. Unfortunately much of this expenditure benefits the economy of foreign countries more than that of the United States, but there is some reciprocation by foreigners who travel to the U.S.

Camping

Here the term camping includes the use of traditional camping equipment, camp trailers, campers, trailer houses, and mobile homes. Some camping is done in connection with hunting and fishing excursions, as explained in the section on those activities, but most camping is done either for the pleasure of camping itself or in connection with sightseeing vacations. Taking into consideration the luxury units and motorized vehicles involved in camping today, this activity has increased in total financial outlay more in recent years than almost any other phase of recreation. Visualize for example the amount of money spent on campers alone. It is estimated that there are almost 5 million of these units in the United States.

As to traditional camping equipment, think of the large number of sleeping bags that are purchased each year, in addition to tents, mattresses, stoves, backpacks, prepared camping foods, etc. Backpacking itself has become a popular activity associated with camping.

Vacation Homes

Owning a second home primarily for vacation purposes has become the rage among the affluent and semiaffluent in the American society.

Tens of thousands of second and third family homes are located on beaches, in mountain areas, in the deserts and other areas that have scenic and special interest attractions. Many of these second homes are condominiums, and the condominium movement is still gaining momentum. All of this construction and maintenance of nonresident homes and cottages adds immensely to the economy.

Flying

Hobby flying has become quite popular among the affluent. It is an unusually expensive activity that most people cannot afford. However, many more people can afford it today than ever before, partly because of the increase in average annual income and partly because of the pool ownership programs that have become popular in recent years. Pool ownership makes it possible for a person to buy a share, e.g. one-tenth of an airplane, and be able to use it a certain number of hours per month or per year.

Other interesting aspects of flying for pleasure are glider flying, parachuting, skydiving, and hang-gliding. Obviously the economics of all of these flying activities combined have a measurable impact.

Spectator Activities

The king of spectator activities is television, with a per capita average of more than two hours per day spent in front of the set. This in itself is not necessarily good or bad. If the programs are of high quality so that they actually add in some respect to the person's life, and if the viewer gets sufficient activity and other involvement so that his life has desirable balance, then there is no strong argument against two hours of television per day—but this is often not the case. The usual argument against television is that those who watch it need physical activity and other involvement to maintain their health and keep their lives in balance, and often what they watch on television makes no positive contribution to their lives. It simply uses up time or has a negative influence. In terms of economics, however, it is a fact that the great majority of the 52 million homes in America have at least one television set, and many homes have two or more sets.

Spectator sports occupy a prominent position in the use of leisure time. The leader of these from the standpoint of attendance is baseball. Football is a close second, followed by basketball. Billions of spectator hours are spent each year watching professional, college, high school, and even junior high school and youth teams participate in sports. More than a billion dollars are spent annually for the purchase of athletic tickets and in support of concessions.

Racing activities represent another large contribution to the economy—horse races, dog races, auto races, and motorcycle races.

Some of these events are among the most profitable in the world from the standpoint of single-event expenditures.

Indoor Sports

Recreational participation in handball, indoor tennis, basketball, volleyball, weight training, and the like is possible only because of an extensive amount of capital outlay. The construction of multipurpose gymnasiums and other indoor facilities is very expensive, and it represents a strong commitment by those who finance the facilities (usually the public). Even though many of these facilities are built as part of educational plants, they are used extensively for recreational purposes, and some of the facilities are built almost exclusively for leisure time use. Community centers, sports clubs and health spas are good examples.

Cultural Arts Activities

This group of activities includes plays and dramatic productions, music participation and entertainment, and art, photography, and dance. There is no reliable estimate of the numbers of people who attend these activities or who participate in them, but it is certain that they are very large, probably about comparable to the numbers involved in spectator sports. It is estimated that the economic effect of these activities is about equal to that of spectator sports.

The capital outlay for concert halls, studios, and outdoor theaters is in itself a significant item in the economy. The purchase of tickets and the current expenses of production and travel are added to this.

Hobbies and Do-It-Yourself Projects

Millions of Americans spend billions of dollars each year on hobbies of different kinds. Gardening of one kind or another, for example, is done by a high percentage of the population. Gem polishing, ceramics, amateur photography, collecting, art, playing of musical instruments and many other personal interest pursuits fall under the definition of hobbies. This multitude of activities performed by practically all members of the population accounts for a very large total expenditure each year.

The do-it-yourself movement has become big business, with estimated annual expenditures running into the billions of dollars. Although these activities are often motivated in part by the desire to avoid the high costs of hiring, they are also forms of recreation. Minor home construction projects, furniture building, home repairs, rebuilding of automobiles and motorcycles and other such activities fall into the do-it-yourself category. Certainly some of the motivation to become involved in these projects is recreational in nature.

Reading

Reading for pleasure is one of the greatest occupiers of leisure time, and it is a good use of time to the extent that the reading material is properly selected. A danger is that one might read so much that his life lacks the desirable amount of participation in physically and socially active pursuits. Even though most books and magazines are inexpensive, the total effect of the tremendously large numbers purchased each year results in a sizable expenditure and an important economic contribution.

Other Activities

Several kinds of leisure time activities not already mentioned are important to the economy. Among these are resorts and entertainment complexes such as Disneyland, Sea World, and Coney Island; zoos, museums and galleries; scenic gardens and garden parks; and amusement parks.

EFFECTS OF ECONOMIC INSTABILITY

During the past few years a number of the larger cities in the nation have been caught in a traumatic financial squeeze by declining tax bases and the need to provide ever more costly welfare, education, law enforcement, low cost housing, transportation and environmental control. In such cities recreation and parks have been placed in a precarious position on the budgetary totem pole.

Generally park and recreation administrators have responded to such financial problems by moving in the direction of "pay-as-you-go" facility and program developments. More and more certain kinds of new facilities are being developed in municipal and county programs with the expectation that their costs will be substantially offset by fees and charges. If all citizens could afford to pay a reasonable fee for the use of such facilities and programs, this would certainly be a logical solution to the problem.

However, even in today's affluent society, about 26 million people or roughly 12% of our population belong to families whose incomes are below the "minimum subsistence level." Such families live at the bare edge of necessity. With less than $5,000 per year, an urban family of four cannot possibly afford to use facilities or participate in programs where fees are charged. They are essentially dependent upon recreation and park opportunities provided and paid for by public agencies.

The problems of poverty, unemployment, and inflation in our society today have direct effects upon our use of leisure time and our selection of recreational activities.

Poverty

In Larabee and Meyersohn's book, *Mass Leisure*, people in different social classes are shown with varied selections of leisure activities. The authors state:

> It is clear that the tendency to choose leisure activities on the grounds of membership in a particular social class begins in adolescence and becomes more pronounced in maturity. As people get older and settle into the ways of the class to which they belong, they choose leisure activities which are congenial to their class. The growing divergence between the uses of leisure by the middle class and lower class is clear.[7]

To more fairly distribute recreational opportunities among the people, those in the lower class socially and economically must have some means of equality with the better-off citizens. Donald E. Hawkins, in an article published in *Parks and Recreation*, treats an idea to alleviate the poverty-stricken people from their economic slump, and place them in a more equal level with the better-off people. Hawkins said,

> To overcome these problems, some social scientists are proposing that the Federal Government could wipe out poverty by providing a "guaranteed income" for all American families. Under this plan, the Government would set a median income level that is necessary for each family.[8]

However, many people, probably the great majority, feel that a guaranteed income is an immoral proposition, claiming that no citizen of the United States who works should be required to pay a guaranteed income to a person who does not work.

Whatever the case, to allow impoverished people to participate with the rest of society, some aid or special consideration must be given. As will be pointed out later, when people have no money, or money becomes tight, one of the areas of involvement cut back first is that of recreational activities.

Unemployment

The problem of unemployment is also a plague in terms of recreation participation. The person who is without work is not only materially hampered in terms of participation but he is also mentally in a bind. Again when money is not to be found, the pleasures of leisure activities are among the first to feel the pinch. A real problem with unemployment and recreation is the quality of recreation selected by an unemployed person during his increased amount of unoccupied time. Jay B. Nash, in his book *Philosophy of Recreation and Leisure*,[9] points out that man has essentially three choices of how to spend his leisure time:

1. Going to sleep mentally in some "looking on" process
2. Wasting time in delinquency and dissipation
3. Engaging in some qualitative phase of creative participating activity

In many cases of unemployment, the person finds himself depressed or unexcited and consequently falls into the state of either sleeping mentally or wasting time delinquently. Such has been the case with many workers laid off because of the energy crisis. Unless the unemployed can receive some direction and purpose, they will probably not be motivated to find the third category listed by Nash, that of creative involvement in qualitative activities.

Inflation

In a survey conducted by *Changing Times,* [10] this question was placed before 25,000 people: "Where has inflation hit the hardest and what have you done about it?" Categories were developed in which the responses to that question could be listed. Below are the categories and percentage of responses of how people cut back:

Recreation	59%
Food—eating out	52%
Appliances	48%
Clothing	—
Purchase of auto	—
Food at home	—
Rent	3%

When cutbacks were made, recreation was the first place that most people selected to reduce their spending.

The problem of maintaining a stable economy while expanding is a matter of prime importance with many aspects, with recreation and leisure being one of them. When the economy is not at full swing there is no possibility of a recreational boom. With inflation, unemployment and poverty hampering segments of the American population, both the quality and quantity of recreational activities are reduced.

REFERENCES

1. Leisure Investment Opportunity in a $150 Billion Market. Securities Research Division, Merrill, Lynch, Pierce, Fenner and Smith, New York, 1968, p. 4.
2. U.S. News & World Report, September 15, 1969, p. 36.
3. U.S. News & World Report, April 17, 1972, p. 42.
4. Henle, P.: Recent growth of paid leisure for U.S. workers. Monthly Labor Review, March 1972, p. 256.
5. Recreation Land Price Escalation. Bureau of Outdoor Recreation, Washington, 1972, pp. 10-11.
6. Clawson, M. and Knetsch, J. L.: *Economics of Outdoor Recreation.* The Johns Hopkins Press, Baltimore, 1966.
7. Larabee, E. and Meyersohn, R.: *Mass Leisure.* Free Press, Glencoe, 1958, p. 178.
8. Hawkins, D. E.: *Parks and Recreation,* May 1971, pp. 36-39.
9. Nash, J. B.: *Philosophy of Recreation and Leisure.* William C. Brown Co., Dubuque, 1960, p. 163.
10. *Changing Times,* April 1974, p. 16.

14

Issues Relating To The Recreation And Park Field

In connection with every discipline, profession, academic field or topic of discussion there are related issues. By its very nature an issue has two sides: the argument in favor and the argument against. Some issues are resolvable, but many issues are continuous in the sense that they are never completely resolved, but are only debated, struggled with, and sometimes partially solved. The nature and prominence of an issue change with changing circumstances, and over a long period of time an issue may lose its significance and fade away to the point that it is no longer worthy of serious concern.

An issue may be defined as an identified problem which must be confronted and which has arguments both pro and con, but which is not immediately solvable. There are broad issues which relate to the whole field of recreation and parks, and there are specific issues which relate to phases of the total field or to specific localities. The content of this chapter has to do with selected broad issues that relate to the field in general. Not all of the major issues are included here, but a good sampling is presented.

IS THE RECREATION AND PARK FIELD A PROFESSION OR A DISCIPLINE OR BOTH?

(This first issue is discussed under a format different from the others because of the nature of the question.)

A *discipline* is defined as a field of knowledge or branch of learning. A *profession* is an occupational field which requires a high level of educational preparation, depends primarily upon the effective use of the mental and communicative processes as opposed to manual skills, is based on a substantial and carefully organized body of knowledge, and is perpetuated by unified objectives and professional commitments by its members. Richard Kraus lists the following criteria of a profession:[1]

1. General acceptance of the field by the public
2. A specific body of knowledge
3. The existence of basic research in the field
4. Certification of programs and employees in the field
5. Well-defined personnel standards
6. An effective recruitment program
7. Professional organizations
8. A code of ethics
9. Members of a profession generally expected to provide an important service to humanity

It is clear that the recreation and park field fills the criteria of a *discipline*, and it is not likely that anyone would argue this fact. However, the question of whether the field clearly qualifies as a *profession* is more in doubt. There are many who claim that it cannot logically be called a profession because the field is relatively new, the positions of employment are not well standardized, and there are no standardized procedures for certifying individuals or accrediting the preparatory curricula. On the other hand there are those who argue that it has strong characteristics of a profession, including professional preparation curricula at a large number of reputable colleges and universities, well-established professional organizations, increasing amounts of research and a worthy and valuable service to perform for humanity.

The following additional points relate to this question.

1. Many people are employed in this field on only a part-time or seasonal basis, e.g. school teachers who work in recreation positions during summer months.
2. There are many people who, because of their personality characteristics, can be very successful in certain kinds of recreation positions without undergoing a particular kind of formal preparation and without aligning themselves with the professional organizations. However, these are exceptions, and the rule is that those who furnish the most substantial leadership in the field fit the criteria of professionals.
3. Among the different kinds of jobs in the field, there is lack of consistency with respect to the characteristics and preparation that a person must have in order to qualify as a candidate. On the one side of the ledger it is claimed that progress is being made toward the solution of this problem even though the progress is slow and spotty. On the other side it is claimed that there has been plenty of time for the leaders of this occupation to develop and enforce more standardization relative to employee qualifications.

IS THERE A CLEAR NEED FOR ACCREDITATION OF PROFESSIONAL PREPARATION CURRICULA IN THE FIELD OF RECREATION AND PARKS, AND, IF YES, WHO SHOULD BE THE ACCREDITING AUTHORITY?

The number of colleges and universities offering professional curricula in the recreation and park field has increased from several dozen during the World War II years to well over 300. This enormous growth in curricula and the corresponding growth in the number of students majoring in the field have caused great concern about the lack of standard content in the curricula and the lack of curricula accrediting procedures. This topic has been the center of many discussions during the past decade and, even though there has been some progress toward standardization of curricula, there has been very limited progress toward formal accreditation procedures.

The Case for Accreditation

1. Because so many institutions have become involved in the preparation of recreation and park leaders, it has become impossible for all of the leaders of these curricula to actively exchange ideas, and it is not feasible for any professional organization to informally exercise the standardizing influence that is needed. As a result, for the most part, each institution determines its own criteria for placing courses in the curriculum and its own content of each course. An effective accrediting procedure would help greatly to achieve standardization among the different curricula, and it would help ensure standardized course content and a minimal level of preparation of the graduates.

2. Accrediting is needed to give employers confidence that a person who has graduated from an accredited program is well prepared to enter the job market.

3. Clearly stated accreditation requirements would be an effective method of communicating to the leaders of the recreation and park curricula the procedures, courses, and subject matter content that are important in the preparation of those entering the profession.

4. Accreditation would contribute toward protection of the public from malpractice in the area of recreation and park leadership.

5. Accreditation of the curricula would contribute toward the general acceptance of this occupational field as a recognized profession.

6. Graduating students would have an increased feeling of security and confidence because of having been graduated from an accredited program.

7. In many areas civil service examinations are used in the selection of people for recreation and park positions. Standardization of curricula which would result from accreditation would help form a better basis for the preparation of fair civil service examinations.

The Case against Accreditation

1. Professional preparation in the recreation and park field is relatively young and accreditation standards would restrict desirable experimentation in the programs. In this dynamic field, time and flexibility for experimentation are still needed.

2. There are a great variety of job opportunities in this occupational field, and it would be difficult if not impossible to establish accreditation standards that would have a meaningful relationship to many of the jobs.

3. There is no agency qualified and ready to administer an accreditation program. It would be inappropriate to have such a program administered by a government agency, and there are no nongovernment agencies prepared to handle it.

4. Where accreditation procedures have been experimented with there has been little success.

5. Because of the increasing use of civil service examinations for recreation positions, the time will soon come when the influence of the civil service examinations will have a standardizing effect on curricula, and this will cause accreditation to be less important.

IS THERE AN APPARENT NEED FOR CERTIFICATION OF INDIVIDUALS IN THE PARK AND RECREATION FIELD SIMILAR TO THE CERTIFICATION OF TEACHERS?

The question here is whether individuals within the profession should be required to be certified for the particular level and kind of employment for which they are supposedly prepared.

The Case for Certification of Individuals

1. Certification of individuals would guarantee a minimal level of competence among the certified members of the profession.
2. By hiring individuals who are certified employers would have increased assurance that their employees are well prepared.
3. The certification of individuals would have an uplifting effect on the quality of professional preparation programs, because students would naturally migrate toward the more excellent programs to be assured of certification after graduation.
4. Certification of individuals would add pride to those who become certified, and it would contribute toward increased stature of the occupational field and better recognition of the field as a profession.

The Case against Certification of Individuals

1. Because of the great variety of positions in this occupational field and the lack of standardization of the preparation needed for the different jobs, it would be impractical to try to administer meaningful and useful certification procedures.
2. A certification program ought to be administered by a state agency and this would result in another unnecessary responsibility of government, increased government costs, and undesirable government control.

IS IT TRUE THAT THOSE WHO HAVE THE MOST LEISURE ARE THE LEAST EQUIPPED TO USE IT BENEFICIALLY?

Today, as in the past, those who possess the most leisure are the very rich and the very poor, the old and the young. Are these, and others who for one reason or another have an abundance of leisure, ill prepared to use it?

The Case in Favor of the Claim that Those with the Most Leisure Are the Least Equipped To Use It

1. The very poor are among those with the largest amount of leisure, because of the high rate of unemployment among this group. Unemployment among those who want to work is a special kind of leisure which is "forced." This group generally has a low level of formal education, low social status, and very little financial means to pursue special interests. Also this group, because of lack of education and restricted cultural experiences, lacks ideas and insights on how to use leisure time beneficially.

2. Children and youth have a relatively large amount of leisure time. Some claim that their use of it is frivolous and nonessential in terms of contribution to their own development and to society. (However, many people would strongly disagree with this claim.)

3. Those belonging to the older age group often have physical limitations that seriously restrict the kinds of leisure activities they can do. Also many of them lack the energy to want to do anything except passive activities, and many older people lack the means to involve themselves in activities that are very expensive.

Those who are forced to retire when they really want to continue working are psychologically unprepared to accept leisure and use it beneficially. They have lived by the work ethic and now they are forced to endure its antithesis. For many this adjustment is extremely difficult, and it is generally believed by the medical profession that this is a contributing factor to the unusually high death rate during the first two or three years following retirement.

The Case against the Claim that Those
with the Most Leisure Are the
Least Equipped To Use It

1. The very rich are among those with a relatively large amount of leisure. However, many of them choose to not take leisure but rather to use their time and energy in money-making projects. This inclination partially explains why they are rich. However, aside from this fact, it is evident that the very rich are better prepared to use leisure than the population in general. Generally they have a broad spectrum of interests and the background and skills to become interestingly involved.

2. Some people reject the claim that unemployment is a condition of leisure. They say that it is a forced situation which is unwanted and which is not conducive to a leisure mode, and that this form of free time should not be considered when evaluating the use of leisure.

IS THE TREND TOWARD THE USE OF LEISURE IN AMERICA GENERALLY POSITIVE OR NEGATIVE?

The real question here is whether leisure time, in view of the way we use it, tends toward being a blessing or a curse. Obviously it has great potential for either, but there are no guarantees of the outcome. This is dependent directly upon the cumulative effect of individual choices.

The Case in Favor of a Positive Influence

1. It is claimed by some that a constructive attitude is developing toward the acceptance of leisure as an important part of life, which can add to both one's development and enjoyment.

2. Our educational system is doing a better job than in the past of preparing people for beneficial use of leisure by broadening their base of information, and thereby affording them more options. Further, people today are being taught more useful skills and appreciations that contribute to beneficial uses of leisure time.

3. There is evidence of increased sophistication among the population relative to their selection of leisure time activities. There are booms in the fields of cul-

tural arts, personal fitness, the more sophisticated sports, wholesome outdoor activities and travel to places of scenic and historical significance.

4. There has been a rebirth of craftsmanship—a premium on creative hands as well as on creative minds.

5. There has been an increase in emphasis among community agencies toward the provision of community-centered activities which develop a feeling of community pride and solidarity.

6. A great amount of interest has developed and much has been accomplished toward the preservation of the natural environment, the improvement of deteriorating cities, and other aspects of the total environment. All of this contributes toward the maintenance of what some call a *recreational environment*—one which contributes toward the enjoyment of life.

7. There has been some success in the upgrading of television programs, causing them to have a more constructive influence on the personality.

8. Community recreation programs have been broadened to include a much greater variety of worthy activities which appeal to a larger segment of the population, instead of concentrating only on children and youth.

9. There seems to be a growing understanding of the concept that an abundant amount of leisure is here to stay, and that this leisure offers an unequalled opportunity for people in all segments of the population to live better balanced and more enriched lives. People seem anxious to grasp this opportunity.

The Case in Favor of a Negative Influence

1. It is a dismal fact that crime among both adults and juveniles is at the highest rate in American history, and is still increasing. For the most part, crime is a leisure time activity, and some claim that its causes are related directly to the increase of leisure.

2. There is evidence that increased affluence and increased leisure (or decreased work) have caused young people to lack commitment, and that many of them neglect their responsibilities as citizens.

3. Some claim that increased leisure, with more sedentary forms of work, has contributed to the lack of physical fitness.

4. There is a belief among some that leisure has provided an opportunity for almost all members of the population to become active participants in the cultural arts when many of them lack the background and preparation to perpetuate the more desirable aspects of the arts, and that because of this leisure has had a degenerating effect on the cultural arts.

5. There is evidence that the additional freedom of which leisure is a part has had a negative influence on proper self-discipline, particularly among young people.

6. The rapid change in the amount of available leisure combined with other rapid changes in society has caused a split in the generations. People of different generations simply do not understand each other or each other's living patterns and attitudes, and this contributes to generation gaps.

7. Much of the increased leisure is spent in spectator activities which are primarily amusers and crowd pleasers, and which often really do not contribute to the constructive development of the watchers.

SHOULD OR SHOULD NOT RECREATION PROGRAMS HAVE ANY RESPONSIBILITY FOR PREPARING PEOPLE FOR DEMOCRATIC LIVING?

Some people argue that leisure should be a time free of commitment toward any kind of accomplishment except immediate individual enjoyment, while others argue that people have an obligation to use leisure in a way that will improve themselves and strengthen the fibers of society.

The Case in Favor of Responsibility toward Democratic Living

1. At the foundation of democracy is freedom, and one of the most fundamental aspects of freedom is the freedom of choice. Leisure time has been defined as "choosing time," and the choices that people make determine the quality or lack of quality of their involvement during leisure hours. More specifically, it can be said that the recreational activities in which one chooses to participate have a strong influence on his life-style and development. In this sense recreational activities become directly dependent upon the freedom aspect of democracy. Some would claim that this causes a built-in responsibility for recreation programs to perpetuate democratic ideals and help prepare people for democratic living.

2. According to Brightbill, "Freedom in a democratic society makes demands and imposes responsibilities and duties, just as it provides privileges and opportunities."[2] He implies that one of these responsibilities is the perpetuation of democracy through recreation programs.

3. One of the goals of recreation as stated by the Commission on Goals for American Recreation is "living in a democratic society."

4. As stated by Sherwood Gates, "In a society dedicated to the fullest possible growth of all of its people, free time and recreation activities have an incomparably important place."[3] He continues by saying, "These activities should be both the breeding ground and the practicing and improving ground of democracy as a way of life." Howard Dandford stated, "The goals of personal fulfillment and democratic human relationships must be among our deepest concerns, our professional pre-occupation. . . ."[4]

5. Numerous authors and philosophers have pointed out many similarities between our own society and earlier democracies which declined, and some of the similarities relate to increased leisure and negative influences related to leisure time.

The Case against Responsibility toward Democratic Living

1. If leisure time is really free time with which one should be able to choose, then why should there be obligations toward democratic living or any other such obligations?

2. Some claim that it is the responsibility of the family and the educational system, and not of recreation leaders or recreation programs, to see that social, moral and ethical values are taught and practiced, and that democratic ideals should fit into this same pattern.

SHOULD PUBLIC RECREATION BE INVOLVED IN THE COLLECTION OF FEES AND CHARGES FROM PARTICIPANTS, OR DOES THIS DISCRIMINATE UNFAIRLY AGAINST THOSE WITH LESS FINANCIAL MEANS?

The argument has long existed as to whether public sponsored programs should include only those activities that can be financed from public funds or whether an attempt should be made to expand the programs by supplementing public funds with money from fees and charges. A great variety of examples could be used and each one would have its own pros and cons. The question here has to do with the general concept and not with any specific situation.

The Case in Favor of Fees and Charges

1. It is believed by many that participants appreciate some activities more when they have to pay a fee.
2. No government agency or combination of agencies can afford to provide the recreational needs of all of the people by use of public funds alone. By supplementing with fees and charges the program can be expanded beyond the minimal level.
3. Fees and charges sometimes help to solve discipline problems, because only those who are committed to participation pay the fees.
4. Those who want to participate in activities that are unusually expensive or which appeal only to a small segment of the population should pay a special fee because these can be included only if the program is expanded beyond the level that should be financed by public funds.
5. Those living outside the geographic area who therefore do not contribute to the tax base that supports the program should pay an out-of-area fee in fairness to those who contribute through taxes.
6. Willingness to pay is a useful indicator of the importance that people attach to special interest activities.

The Case against Fees and Charges

1. The charging of fees restricts the participation by those unable to pay for the privilege, and this is unfair.
2. There is a danger that the administrator will lose sight of the program's objectives and become obsessed by the production of revenue. This could result in overemphasis of income-producing activities at the expense of a well-balanced public program.
3. Some believe that the charging of fees turns the program too much toward a business operation instead of a public service program, and revenue from a public operation is distasteful to some people.
4. In one sense charging of fees in a public sponsored program is comparable to double taxation.
5. There is a danger that if too much revenue is earned through the program the tax support base may be reduced.
6. In many cases the overhead for the collection of fees is too high for the amount collected and the net revenue is too small to justify the collection.

There is no blueprint on this policy. Each community must deal with the matter of fees and charges according to its own particular problems. However, in all cases it is important that the inclusion or exclusion of recreation services be based as much as possible on public need and not on revenue. Basically most people agree with the idea that children's activities should be exempt from fees and charges and that all other activities which are popular and relatively inexpensive should be provided without fees. It is also generally agreed that special interest activities that involve a lot of promotion and administration for the number of participants, such as rock polishing, and those which require expensive facilities, such as golf and skiing, should have charges associated with them; otherwise the general public would underwrite expensive special interest activities of small segments of the public.

IS IT ADVISABLE FOR PUBLIC PROGRAMS TO COMPETE WITH COMMERCIAL ENTERPRISE IN THE PROVISION OF RECREATIONAL SERVICES AND OPPORTUNITIES?

Recreation for profit provided through commercial agencies has developed into a multibillion dollar per year enterprise. Likewise, recreation provided without charge by public agencies involves the expenditure of billions of dollars each year. These gigantic expenditures testify to the demand for recreation of the kind provided both by commercial enterprise and by public agencies. There are no clear distinctions between the activities which should be publicly sponsored and those which should be commercially sponsored. As a result competition often exists.

The Case in Favor of Competition between Public and Commercial Recreation

1. It would be an impossible burden upon the taxpayers and philanthropists to offer all recreational services that are needed. On the other hand many members of the population cannot afford to pay the price of certain forms of commercial recreation, and they have the same needs for participation as those with more means. In view of this circumstance, some argue that public agencies should provide at least minimal opportunities in a variety of recreation so that those with little means will have ample opportunities. Those with greater means will naturally migrate toward commercially provided activities to supplement the opportunities provided by public agencies. A prime example of this line of thinking is that of golf, where there are public golf courses with relatively low fees and commercial and private courses where participation is much more expensive but which offer some extras, such as clubhouse privileges, swimming, etc. Also there are public tennis facilities as opposed to private and commercial tennis operations.

2. There is a belief that public sponsorship of recreation opportunities up to a certain level neutralizes the opportunity for commercial enterprise to exploit the public by charging exorbitant fees.

The Case against Competition between Public and Commercial Recreation

1. Some people believe that in a society such as ours, which is based on the free enterprise system, demand as indicated by the willingness to pay ought to determine the services provided, and public services have no right to influence that balance by providing services at a lower cost or competing with commercial agencies.

2. Commercial recreation enterprises dare not be dull or they will lose their appeal and their profit-making edge. On the other hand, a public agency can provide similar activities at a less interesting level and with less promotion because the need for profit is not present.

3. Some claim that it is unfair for a public agency to become involved in any way that would detract from the profit-making potential of commercial enterprise because in doing so the owner of the enterprise is being directly competed against by a public agency which he helps to support through taxation.

It seems to be generally agreed by park and recreation leaders that public agencies should encourage and help foster desirable commercial recreation enterprises because (1) morally this seems to be the right thing to do in a free enterprise system, and (2) it results in a more complete overall offering since public agencies cannot fill all of the recreational needs of all of the people. There are certain forms of recreation that are financially prohibitive for public agencies, but which can be successfully sponsored through commercial enterprise for those who can afford them. A proper balance, involving the correct amount of cooperation and also the correct amount of competition between public and commercial agencies, would seem desirable for doing justice both to the public and to those attempting to make a living as commercial operators.

However, there is another element to this: public programs which are designed to cause positive results ought to compete head-on with commercial enterprises which exploit the public and are undesirable.

SHOULD OR SHOULD NOT SCHOOL AND COLLEGE PROGRAMS BE CONCERNED ABOUT PREPARING STUDENTS FOR THE PROPER USE OF LEISURE TIME BOTH AT THE PRESENT AND IN LATER LIFE?

Those who accept the proposition that the healthy personality is one who plays and takes his play seriously believe that schools and colleges should help prepare students for the constructive use of leisure. Others feel that the schools should be almost entirely occupation oriented, and that the "extras" in life should be learned through private initiative and nonschool agencies.

The Case for School and College Concern with Preparation for Proper Use of Leisure Time

1. The schools and colleges already have many of the physical facilities necessary for a wide range of recreational activities. It would be an economic waste to use them only for instructional purposes a few hours each day and deny the public who pay for the facilities additional use for pleasure and education for leisure.

2. The purpose of the educational system is to prepare people to live effectively and happily in their society and to perpetuate and improve it. Contemporary Americans enjoy a liberal amount of leisure time, and are confronted with the real prospect of more leisure in the future. In view of this the preparation for the worthy use of leisure time is within the basic purpose of education.

3. One of the seven cardinal principles by the U.S. Commission on Education in 1917 was "the worthy use of leisure time." Other important and influential

bodies or organizations who have stated objectives of education during the past 50 years have consistently stated or at least implied preparation for the worthy use of leisure as one of the objectives.

4. It has been claimed that the *educated person* is one who is not only prepared to work but also to "live," to live fully and completely during his discretionary as well as his obligated time.

5. A person who has a balanced education is not only informed about economic and business matters but also about social graces, cultural arts, literature and physical culture. The knowledge and appreciation gained through instruction in these areas carry over into the use of leisure time.

6. The question has been asked, "If the educational system does not accept the prime responsibility for preparing people to use leisure time beneficially, then who will accept it?" If such education is not accomplished it will contribute to the destruction of the very society that is sponsoring the educational system. We must either educate for the worthy use of leisure or be willing to accept severe consequences.

7. It is well established that we learn more efficiently during our youth; therefore we should be taught early in life how to live effectively in society. Learning meaningful recreational skills and appreciations late in life is a poor substitute for learning them early.

Figure 40.   Pottery making can be an interesting creative outlet.

8. It is a fact that we generally enjoy doing those things we do well and avoid doing what we do poorly. Therefore, if we learn to do well the things that are developmental and wholesome we will be inclined to participate in those activities.

9. The cost of learning in school is much less than through private instruction; private instruction is financially prohibitive to many. This means that if the masses are to become educated for leisure it must be done through the schools; otherwise major segments of the population will be deprived of this benefit.

10. As long ago as the time of World War I John Dewey, the most prominent educator of his era, stated, "Education has no more serious responsibility than making adequate provisions for enjoyment of recreative leisure; not only for the sake of immediate help, but . . . for the sake of its lasting effect upon habits of the mind."[5]

The Case against School and College Concern with Preparation for the Proper Use of Leisure

1. It has often been stated that the schools should stick to the three R's, and that learning about other matters should be the responsibilities of individuals and outside agencies.

2. Some would support the idea that because of the increased costs of education all or most of the "nonessentials" should be trimmed out in order to lessen the tax burden.

3. Many of the strongly academically oriented people feel that too much space and too many facilities are devoted to such nonacademic activities as sports, music and drama. This is exemplified by one educational administrator who remarked as he drove past a tennis class, "Look at those kids. They ought to be in school."

4. It is sometimes claimed that the offering of the less academic subjects results in these subjects being partially substituted for some of the more solid subjects that every student should take.

5. It is claimed that by handling the traditional responsibilities well the schools already have more to do than they can accomplish effectively. Adding to this the responsibility of educating for leisure has a diluting effect on the traditional subjects.

IN EDUCATIONAL PROGRAMS SHOULD THE SO-CALLED RECREATIONAL OR LIFETIME SPORTS RECEIVE GREATER OR LESSER EMPHASIS THAN AT PRESENT?

Those who believe that the main purpose of education is preparation for life think that those sports with an abundance of useful carry-over to later life should receive greater emphasis, while sports that are mostly suitable only for school curricula should receive less. The characteristics that determine whether a sport fits into the "lifetime" category are (1) whether it is useful for a variety of age groups, (2) whether facilities and participation opportunities are generally available, and (3) whether the sport has proved to be interesting enough so that people usually want to continue participating in it.

The Case in Favor of Greater Emphasis
on Lifetime Sports in the
School Curricula

1. If we believe that the educational system should prepare students for wise use of leisure time in adulthood as well as during their school years, then greater emphasis than at present should be placed on lifetime sports.

2. Most students will have limited opportunities to learn new sports after their school years are over. Therefore, the sports skills that people need for lifetime enjoyment should be learned as part of their formal education.

Figure 41. Learning useful lifetime skills is a need that every person has. (Los Angeles Youth Services photo.)

The Case against Additional Emphasis
on Lifetime Sports

1. Many of the so-called lifetime sports are not vigorous enough to contribute to an acceptable level of physiological fitness among youth, even though these sports can serve a worthwhile purpose in the maintenance of fitness during adult life.

2. The cost of supplying space, facilities and equipment for the teaching and participation of such lifetime sports as golf, tennis and archery is in many cases prohibitive.

3. Some people believe that if we place additional emphasis on lifetime sports we will be teaching our young people to be old before their time from the standpoint of sports participation.

SHOULD RECREATION ACTIVITIES BE BASED ON INDIVIDUAL NEEDS OR ON THE SOCIAL NEEDS OF THE COMMUNITY, STATE AND NATION?

Arguments pro and con about this issue are much the same as arguments on whether education in our society should be centered on the individual or on the development of a strong state and nation.

The Case in Favor of Basing Recreation
Programs on Individual Needs

1. In a democracy the individual is the focal point. Therefore it should be accepted that recreation programs be based primarily on the needs of individuals.

2. In a democracy it is generally accepted that the community, state or nation is no better in any respect than the accumulation of the individuals who compose it. By placing emphasis on the needs and interests of individuals, the community, state and nation can best be served.

3. Some claim it is not possible to base a recreation program on anything except the needs of individuals. The idea of gearing the program toward the needs of the community, state or nation is strictly philosophical and has little practical application.

The Case in Favor of Basing Recreation
Programs on the Needs of the Community,
State and Nation

1. Additional physical fitness is a national need; thus leisure time activities which improve fitness should be promoted through recreation programs. It is the responsibility of recreation leadership to do this in order to strengthen the nation.

2. Inappropriate use of leisure time, particularly on a mass scale, can have a strong deteriorating effect on society. It is one of the fundamental responsibilities of recreation leaders and educators to teach people the importance of proper use of leisure and provide them with ample opportunities in worthy activities. By not doing this they will neglect their responsibilites to the community, state and nation.

From the points presented on the two sides, it is obvious that recreation programs should be concerned with both individual needs and the needs of the community, state and nation. It is largely true that if the needs of the individual are truly met, then the basic needs of society will also be met rather well. However, if only the selfish interests of individuals are served, then there is certainly a possibility that the needs of the community, state and nation will not be met. The key to success is to properly serve individuals in a way that causes them to be improved individuals and improved citizens, and at the same time to capture opportunities to foster and perpetuate the principles of democracy.

SHOULD RECREATION ACTIVITIES BE PURPOSELY DESIGNED TO DEVELOP THE PERSONALITIES OF THE PARTICIPANTS OR ONLY FOR ENTERTAINMENT?

The very nature of recreation indicates that it should be *entertaining,* that is, enjoyable to the participant. If it is not enjoyable the person probably will not participate of his own free will for the satisfaction derived therefrom. But when the participation is made possible through public funded, community, state or federal agencies, then should it simply be entertainment or should there be some *developmental objectives* and some expected beneficial outcomes?

The Case in Favor of Recreation Purposely Designed to Develop the Personality

1. Many people believe that recreation activities that are purely entertainment should be sponsored commercially and paid for by the participants, and that the expenditure of public funds for such activities cannot be justified.

2. The leaders of society have always strived to conduct programs and activities which would improve the citizens. Improvement of individuals has seemingly always been a worthy endeavor. If this is to be accomplished in the future it will need to be partially accomplished through the use of leisure, because there will be more leisure and less time spent in other aspects of life.

3. It could be argued that there are a sufficient number of recreation pursuits that are both entertaining and developmental to make it unjustifiable to spend any significant amount of public resources on activities that are not developmental.

4. Some believe that participation that is purely entertaining does not really recreate a person, but simply amuses him, and that true recreation depends upon something happening to the individual which causes change in a positive direction—physical development, emotional excitement or the thrill of creative accomplishment.

The Case in Favor of Recreation as Entertainment Only

1. It could be argued that people enter into recreation during leisure time which has been earned with labor, and that the activities they choose are those which they find entertaining. Attempting to accomplish purposes beyond entertainment is a violation of what the participants expect from their recreation.

2. Some claim that there are ample side benefits from recreational entertainment which add to the intrinsic value of the entertainment itself, such as the economic impact and the prevention of delinquency and crime. Further, participating in entertaining recreation which is socially acceptable serves as an antidote to physical and emotional stress.

SHOULD OR SHOULD NOT PUBLIC RECREATION PROGRAMS INCLUDE INSTRUCTIONAL COURSES IN ACTIVITIES THAT ARE VALUABLE AS LEISURE TIME PURSUITS, OR SHOULD INSTRUCTION BE LEFT TO THE EDUCATIONAL SYSTEM AND PRIVATE INITIATIVE?

The question here is whether recreation departments should sponsor clinics, workshops, and short courses in activities such as skiing, swimming, surfing, scuba diving, dance, music, drama, etc., or whether this is competitive with the educational system and really not the role of a recreation department.

The Case in Favor of Instructional Courses through Recreation Programs

1. Some claim that the schools have placed too little emphasis on the teaching of recreational skills and have generally done a poor job of educating people for leisure; therefore recreation programs must include instruction.

2. It is not feasible for the schools to do much teaching away from the school site, and many recreation skills require facilities not included in school plants. Most schools do not have swimming pools; some do not have tennis courts, staging and props for dramatic productions or equipment and areas for teaching photography. Ski areas, skating rinks and beaches are often too far away for the schools to use.

3. The schools cannot be expected to do all of the teaching that needs to be done. Many other agencies need to be involved and the recreation department should be one of those. The educating done by other agencies should be viewed as supplemental to the school program and not in competition with it.

4. It is well established that people tend to participate in those things which they do well. Therefore, it is important to teach recreation skills and appreciations that are wholesome and valuable, and part of this must be done through the department that is logically the most concerned, the recreation department.

The Case against Instructional Courses through Recreation Programs

1. Recreation programs supported by public funds are charged with the responsibility of providing recreation facilities and programs, and it is part of their charge to carry on educational courses.

2. Funds and facilities used for instruction are taken away from other uses in the program.

3. Some recreation departments promote instructional courses so vigorously that they make people feel obligated to learn new activities when they really want to participate in the activities they already know.

IS THERE A CLEAR CASE TO SUPPORT THE IDEA THAT A STANDARD FORM OF SPONSORSHIP (GOVERNING AUTHORITY) IS PREFERABLE IN PRACTICALLY ALL LOCALITIES, OR DOES THIS DEPEND LARGELY UPON LOCAL CIRCUMSTANCES?

The question here is whether a combined department of recreation and parks, separate departments, school district control, county control, or special district control is best. This is important, and it can correctly be labeled an issue, but there are so many aspects to the question that it is not practical to deal with them in this section; further, they have already been discussed rather completely in Chapter 9, to which the reader should refer.

REFERENCES

1. Kraus, R.: *Recreation Leadership and Supervision.* W. B. Saunders, Philadelphia, 1975, p. 216.
2. Brightbill, C. K.: *Man and Leisure.* Prentice-Hall, Englewood Cliffs, 1961, p. 13.
3. Butler, G. D.: *Introduction to Community Recreation,* 5th ed. McGraw-Hill, New York, 1976, p. 47.
4. Danford, H.: *Creative Leadership in Recreation.* Allyn and Bacon, Boston, 1970, p. 66.
5. Weiskopf, D. C.: *A Guide to Recreation and Leisure.* Allyn and Bacon, Boston, 1975, p. 118.

15

Professional and Service Organizations

In addition to government agencies and private enterprise, a large number of professional and service organizations are involved in the recreation and park field. Some of these are concerned with the broad overview of the field, others only with specific phases of it. Some of the organizations have major interests in addition to their recreational function. It is not feasible to list all of the national, regional, and state organizations that are involved, but most of the national organizations are listed, and many of these have district and state affiliates. There are some regional and state organizations separate from any of the national organizations, but none of these is included here.

Descriptions are given of the organizations concerned with the broad aspects of this field, while the organizations with more specialized recreation interests are only listed, with their current addresses and the periodicals which they publish.

American Alliance for Health,
Physical Education, and Recreation (AAHPER)

The Alliance is concerned with four major professional areas: health and safety, physical education, recreation and parks, and competitive athletics. Many of the Alliance members (more than 55,000) are teachers who are directly involved or vitally interested in the field of recreation, but many nonteaching members of the profession also belong. The Alliance contributes to the recreation profession through its various publications, through the sponsorship of workshops, clinics, and institutes related to professional improvement, and by the establishment of guidelines and criteria for certain aspects of the profession. Its monthly magazine is the *Journal of Physical Education and Recreation*. It also publishes numerous books and pamphlets. AAHPER's mailing address is 1201 16th Street N.W., Washington, D.C. 20036. It is an affiliate of the National Education Association.

National Industrial Recreation Association

Incorporated in 1941 in the State of Illinois, it currently serves as a national clearing house for the dissemination of information and ideas on employee recreation for 800 member companies in the United States and Canada. Its official publication is *Recreation Management*, which reaches 8,000 subscribers ten times a year. NIRA holds annual national and regional conferences and exhibits, and sponsors eight national tournaments. The national office is at 20 North Wacker Drive, Chicago, Illinois 60606.

National Recreation and Park Association (NRPA)

A nonprofit organization dedicated to the improvement of people in the profession and the advancement of the profession itself, it sponsors

Figure 42. Touring the back country in wintertime can be a fascinating activity. (Bureau of Reclamation photo.)

various publications, workshops, and institutes. Further, it provides direct consultation and technical assistance for the improvement of programs, leadership, and facilities. The Association also is dedicated to the building of public understanding of the recreation field.

NRPA was formed in 1966 by the merger of five pioneer organizations in the park and recreation field: The American Association of Zoological Parks and Aquariums, the American Institute of Park Executives, the American Recreation Society, the National Conference on State Parks, and the National Recreation Association. The NRPA is presently subdivided into the: American Park and Recreation Society, Armed Forces Recreation Society, Commissioners-Board Members, National Student Recreation and Park Society, National Therapeutic Recreation Society, and Society of Park and Recreation Educators. The NRPA publishes *Parks and Recreation* (monthly), *Leisure Research* (quarterly), and several books and pamphlets. The mailing address is 1601 North Kent Street, Arlington, Virginia 22209.

World Leisure and Recreation Association

A nonprofit international service agency dedicated to improving individual and community life through the constructive use of leisure and recreation, the WLRA conducts service programs in research, education, information and consultation. It offers these services globally through cooperation with other international associations, regional associations and national organizations in more than 100 countries. The association publishes the *WLRA Bulletin* (monthly). The address is 345 East 46 Street, New York, New York 10017.

Amateur Athletic Union of the United States, Inc.

3400 West 86th Street, Indianapolis, Indiana 46268.

Amateur Fencers League of America

249 Eton Place, Westfield, New Jersey 07090. Publishes: *American Fencing* (bimonthly).

Amateur Hockey Association of the United States

7901 Cedar Avenue South, Bloomington, Minnesota 55420. Publishes: monthly bulletin, plus an annual publication titled *Hockey/Arena Bix magazine*

Amateur Softball Association of America

P.O. Box 11437, Oklahoma City, Oklahoma 73111. Publishes: *Balls & Strikes* newsletter (monthly), *ASB Official Guide* (annually).

Amateur Trapshooting Association of America
601 West National Road, Vandalia, Ohio 45377.

American Alpine Club
113 East 90th Street, New York, New York 10028.

American Association of Botanical Gardens and Arboreta, Inc.
New Mexico State Department of Horticulture, Las Cruces, New Mexico 88003. Publishes: *AABGA Newsletter* (monthly), *The Bulletin of the AABGA* (bimonthly).

American Association of Museums
2233 Wisconsin Avenue N.W., Washington, D.C., 20007. Publishes: *Museum News* (bimonthly), *Aviso Newsletter* (monthly).

American Association of Zoological Parks and Aquariums
Oglebay Park, Wheeling, West Virginia 26003. Publishes: *AAZPA Newsletter* (monthly), *Zoos and Aquariums in the U.S.* (biannually).

American Badminton Association, Inc.
1330 Alexandria Drive, San Diego, California 92107. Publishes: *Badminton USA* (bimonthly).

American Bowling Congress
5301 South 76th Street, Greendale, Wisconsin 53129. Publishes: *Bowling Magazine* (monthly) and *ABC Newsletter* (monthly).

American Camping Association
Bradford Woods, Martinsville, Indiana 46151. Publishes: *Camping Magazine* (monthly), plus several books and pamphlets.

American Casting Association
P.O. Box 51, Nashville, Tennessee 37202.

American Federation of Arts
41 East 65th Street, New York, New York 10021.

American Folklore Society
Folklore Center, University of Texas, Austin, Texas 78712. Publishes: *Journal of American Folklore* (quarterly).

American Forest Institute

1619 Massachusetts Ave. N.W., Washington, D.C. 20036. Publishes: *Green America* (quarterly).

American Forestry Association

1319 - 18th Street N.W., Washington, D.C. 20036. Publishes: *American Forests* (monthly).

American Horse Shows Association

527 Madison Avenue, New York, New York 10022.

American Lawn Bowling Association

10337 Cheryl Drive, Sun City, Arizona 85351. Publishes: *A.L.B.A. Bowls* (quarterly), plus several booklets and brochures.

American Motorcycle Association

P.O. Box 141, Westerville, Ohio 53081.

American Nature Association

1214 - 16th Street, N.W., Washington, D.C. 20000.

American Platform Tennis Association

c/o Fox Meadow Tennis Club, Wayside Lane, Scarsdale, New York 10583.

American Snowmobile Association

13104 Crooked Lake Boulevard, Anoka, Minnesota 55303.

American Society of Landscape Architects

1750 Old Meadow Road, McLean, Virginia 22101.

American Water Ski Association

P.O. Box 191, Winter Haven, Florida 33880. Publishes: *The Water Skier* (bimonthly).

American Youth Foundation

3460 Hampton Street, St. Louis, Missouri 63100.

American Youth Hostels, Inc.

National Campus, Delaplane, Virginia 22025. Publishes: *AYH Guide and Handbook* (annually).

Antique Automobile Club of America, Inc.

501 West Governor Road, Hershey, Pennsylvania 17033. Publishes: *Antique Automobile* (bimonthly).

Association of College Unions

Willard Straight Hall, Cornell University, Ithaca, New York 14850.

Association of Interpretive Naturalists, Inc.

6700 Needwood Road, Derwood, Maryland 20855.

Athletic Institute

705 Merchandise Mart, Chicago, Illinois 60654. Publishes: numerous books and pamphlets.

Babe Ruth Baseball, Inc.

1770 Brunswick Avenue, P.O. Box 5000, Trenton, New Jersey 08638.

Bicycle Institute of America

122 East 42nd Street, New York, New York 10017. Publishes: *Boom in Bikeways* (3 times a year).

Boy Scouts of America

North Brunswick, New Jersey. Publishes: *Scouting Magazine* (monthly) plus several other publications on scouting.

Boys Baseball Inc.

P.O. Box 225, Washington, Pennsylvania 15301.

Boys' Clubs of America

771 First Avenue, New York 17, New York 10000.

Camp Fire Girls, Inc.

1740 Broadway, New York, New York 10019.

Conservation Education Association

1250 Connecticut Ave. N.W., Washington, D.C. 20036.

Conservation Foundation

1717 Massachusetts Ave. N.W., Washington, D.C., 20036. Publishes: *Environmental Issues* (monthly).

Discover America Travel Organizations, Inc.

Suite #920, 1100 Connecticut Ave. N.W., Washington, D.C. 20036. Publishes: *Discover America* (monthly) plus numerous pamphlets.

Garden Clubs of America

598 Madison Avenue, New York, New York 10022.

Girl Scouts of the United States of America

830 Third Avenue, New York, New York 10022.

Girls Clubs of America, Inc.

133 East 62nd Street, New York, New York 10021.

Hobby Industry Association of America, Inc.

200 Fifth Avenue, New York, New York 10010.

Ice Skating Institute of America

1000 Skokie Boulevard, Wilmette, Illinois 60091. Publishes: *ISIA Newsletter* (monthly) plus numerous pamphlets and brochures.

International Association of Amusement Parks and Attractions

1125 Lake Street Building, Suite 204-206, Oak Park, Illinois 60301. Publishes: *Actionews* (monthly).

International Bicycle Touring Society

846 Prospect Street, La Jolla, California 92037.

International Racquetball Association

P.O. Box 1016, Stillwater, Oklahoma 74074. Publishes: *Racquetball Magazine* (bimonthly).

International Softball Congress, Inc.

2523 West 14th Street Road, Greeley, Colorado 80631.

International Spin Fishing Association

P.O. Box 81, Downey, California. Publishes: *ISFA Newsletter* (bimonthly).

Izaak Walton League of America

1800 North Kent Street, Arlington, Virginia 22209.

League of American Wheelmen, Inc.

19 South Bothwell, Palatine, Illinois 60067. Publishes: *American Wheelman* (monthly).

Little League Baseball, Inc.

P.O. Box 1127, Williamsport, Pennsylvania 17701.

National Amateur Baseball Federation

Route No. 1, Box 280B, Rose City, Michigan 48654.

National Archery Association of the United States

1951 Geraldson Drive, Lancaster, Pennsylvania 17601.

National Association of County Park and Recreation Officials

1735 New York Avenue N.W., Washington, D.C. 20006.

National Association of Engine and Boat Manufacturers

Box 583, Greenwich, Cincinnati 06830.

National Audubon Society

950 Third Avenue, New York, New York 10022.

National Baseball Congress of America, Inc.

338 South Sycamore, Wichita, Kansas 67201.

National Campers and Hikers Association, Inc.

7172 Transit Road, Buffalo, New York 14221. Publishes: *Tent and Trail* (4 times a year).

National Council of State Garden Clubs, Inc.

4401 Magnolia Avenue, St. Louis, Missouri 63110. Publishes: *National Gardener* (bimonthly).

National Council on the Aging

315 Park Avenue S., New York, New York 10010.

National Duckpin Bowling Congress

711 - 14th Street N.W., Washington, D.C. 20005.

National Field Archery Association

Route 2, Box 514, Redlands, California 92372. Publishes: *Archery Magazine* (monthly) *Archery World* (bimonthly), *Bow and Arrow* (bimonthly), *Bowhunter Magazine* (bimonthly), plus numerous books and pamphlets.

National Forest Recreation Association

22841-A Medina Lane, Cupertino, California 95014.

National Golf Foundation, Inc.

707 Merchandise Mart, Chicago, Illinois 60654.

National Jogging Association

1910 N.W., Suite 202, Washington, D.C. 20006. Publishes: *N.J.A. Newsletter* (8 times a year).

National Parks and Conservation Association

1701 - 18th Street N.W., Washington, D.C. 20009.

National Public Park Tennis Association

155 West Washington Boulevard, Los Angeles, California 90015.

National Rifle Association

1600 Rhode Island Ave. N.W., Washington, D.C. 20036. Publishes: *American Rifleman* (monthly), *American Hunter* (monthly), *American Marksman* (monthly), plus several booklets.

National Shuffleboard Association, Inc.

10418 N.E. 2nd Avenue, Miami, Florida 33138.

National Skeet Shooting Association

212 Linwood Building, 2608 Inwood Road, Dallas, Texas 75235.

National Swimming Pool Institute

2000 K Street N.W., Washington, D.C. 20006.

National Trust for Historic Preservation

740-749 Jackson Place N.W., Washington, D.C. 20006.

National Wildlife Federation

1412 - 16th Street, N.W., Washington, D.C. 20036.

Nature Conservancy

1522 K Street, N.W., Washington, D.C. 20006.

North American Yacht Racing Union

37 West 44th Street, New York, New York 10036.

Outboard Boating Clubs of America

401 North Michigan Avenue, Chicago, Illinois 60611.

Photographic Society of America

2005 Walnut Street, Philadelphia, Pennsylvania 19103. Publishes: *PAS Journal* (monthly) plus numerous pamphlets.

Pop Warner Jr. League Football

1041 Western Savings Bank Building, Philadelphia, Pennsylvania 19107.

Rodeo Cowboys Association

2529 West 19th Avenue, Denver, Colorado 80204. Publishes: *Rodeo Sports News* (bimonthly), *Rodeo Reference Book* (annually).

Sierra Club

1050 Mills Tower, San Francisco, California 94104. Publishes: *Sierra Club Bulletin* (monthly) plus a large number of books and pamphlets.

Society of American Foresters

1010 - 16th Street N.W., Washington, D.C. 20036. Publishes: *Journal of Forestry* (monthly), *Forest Science* (quarterly).

Society of State Directors of Health, Physical Education, and Recreation

1201 - 16th Street, N.W., Washington, D.C. 20036.

U.S. Chess Federation

479 Broadway, Newburgh, New York 12550.

U.S. Field Hockey Association, Inc.

107 School House Lane, Philadelphia, Pennsylvania 19144. Publishes: *The Eagle* (8 times a year).

U.S. Figure Skating Association

Sears-Crescent Building, Suite # 500, City Hall Plaza, Boston, Massachusetts 02108. Publishes: *Figure Skating Magazine* (monthly).

U.S. Golf Association

Golf House, Far Hills, New Jersey 07931. Publishes: *The Golf Journal* (8 times a year), plus numerous pamphlets and booklets.

U.S. Gymnastics Federation

1225 North 10th Avenue, P.O. Box 4699, Tucson, Arizona 85703. Publishes: *USA Gymnastics News* (bimonthly), plus several booklets on gymnastics.

U.S. Handball Association

4101 Dempster Street, Skokie, Illinois 60076. Publishes: *Handball Magazine* (bimonthly), *National Racquetball Magazine* (bimonthly).

U.S. Judo Federation

Box 519, Terre Haute, Indiana 47802. Publishes: *Judo-USA* (monthly), *USJF Handbook* (biannually).

U.S. Lawn Tennis Association

71 University Place, Princeton, New Jersey 08540. Publishes: *Tennis USA Magazine* (monthly), *USTA Official Yearbook* (annually), plus numerous booklets and brochures.

U.S. Parachute Association

P.O. Box 109, Monterey, California 93940. Publishes: *Parachutist Magazine* (monthly).

U.S. Polo Association

1301 West 22nd Street, Suite 706, Oak Brook, Illinois 60521. Publishes: *Polo News* (monthly), *USPA Bluebook* (annually).

U.S. Ski Association

1726 Champa Street, Suite #300, Denver, Colorado 80201.

U.S. Squash Racquets Association, Inc.

211 Ford Road, Bala Cynwyd, Pennsylvania 19004.

U.S. Table Tennis Association

12 Lake Avenue, Merrick, New York 11566. Publishes: *Table Tennis Topics* (bimonthly).

U.S. Volleyball Association

557 Fourth Street, San Francisco, California 94107. Publishes: *USA Volleyball Review* (bimonthly).

Wilderness Society

1901 Pennsylvania Ave. N.W., Washington, D.C. 20006. Publishes: *The Living Wilderness* (quarterly), *Wilderness Report* (bimonthly).

Wildlife Management Institute

709 Wire Building, 1000 Vermont Avenue, N.W., Washington, D.C. 20005. Publishes: *National Wildlife Magazine* (monthly).

Wildlife Society

1701 Wisconsin Avenue #611, Washington, D.C. 20014. Publishes: *Wildlife Society Bulletin* (quarterly), *The Journal of Wildlife Management* (quarterly), plus numerous books and pamphlets.

Young Men's Christian Association of the United States of America

National Council, 291 Broadway, New York, New York 10022.

Young Women's Christian Associaton of the United States of America

600 Lexington Avenue, New York, New York 10022.

16

Today's Dreams– Tomorrow's Reality

Only recently we celebrated the 200th birthday of our nation. Think back to the time of the Declaration of Independence, when horseback was the fastest mode of travel available to such great men as George Washington and Thomas Jefferson. As recently as 100 years ago horseback or carriage was still the primary mode of travel, aside from walking, although a few people of that era did ride on crudely built trains and steamboats. Fifty years ago most Americans did not own or have ready access to a motor driven vehicle, yet today there are nearly 100 million automobiles in the United States—one car for less than every 2.5 Americans. Large numbers of people travel by jet from Los Angeles to New York in four hours, and it is now possible to go to any civilized region of the earth within a day.

This miraculous progress in travel represents one of the most dramatic changes that has ever occurred in the history of man, but many other dramatic changes have also been taking place. For example, electricity with all of its ramifications, computerization and television are phenomena of recent origin.

Let us expand somewhat on the theme of television. Only recently has it been possible to watch the televised proceedings of a national political convention, or the live competition of the world Olympics wherever they may be held, or, almost better than in the stadium, a baseball, football or tennis game of national significance, or archeological exploration in progress in Peru, or a renowned pianist in concert halfway across the nation. During the last three decades television has revolutionized the communication process and made possible the spreading of information almost immediately to people all over the nation, and even a large portion of the world. Further, television has revolutionized the kinds of information that people have at their fingertips. In terms of education it has had a positive effect on "general information" unequalled by any medium in the past. It has made us aware of conditions and circumstances in a variety of settings and it keeps us current on regional, national, and international events. Even though a detriment to those who abuse themselves by watching it too much or failing to be selective, television has been a significant influence toward a better informed and more aware public, as well as a major source of spectator recreation.

In two or three decades from now another author will be able to write about changes that are equally as dramatic as the changes that we are experiencing. He may talk about sightseeing tours in outer space or excursions deep under the ocean in capsules or glass submarines. He may lament the plight of the wilderness hiker before the development of individualized flying devices that silently carry individuals to mountain tops and to once-remote fishing, hunting and scenic areas. He will refer to new forms of computerized golf, baseball and basketball designed especially for less space, less expense and less travel time. He will talk of the school's leisure time counselor, and of the more affluent individuals who have personal counselors to help them select and arrange leisure time pursuits to best fit their needs and interests. He may even talk of the reservation that he has made for himself on Moon Flight 732.

Certainly some of these ideas seem farfetched, but not many years ago it would have seemed just as farfetched to talk seriously about making 25 ski runs from the top of Beaver Mountain in a single day of skiing and returning home refreshed, or circling the earth in a space craft several times in a 24-hour day, or landing men on the moon while the rest of us watched via television.

Is it possible that these projections are not really farfetched, or in fact may be not even far away? Is it possible that the fast rate of change in our living conditions will continue? Where and when will it all stop, or will it stop, or will it even slow down? How will the various changes of the future affect our life-styles and how well will we adjust to them? More particularly, what can be expected relative to work and leisure, and what will be the social and psychological implications? How successful will we be in preparing ourselves and other members of the population for the conditions that will prevail?

Making predictions about the future is a hazardous practice, even in relatively static times, and making predictions about trends and events in rapidly changing times might seem the height of folly. Yet we must justifiably project our thoughts and estimates into the future, because unless we do we have little basis for planning and little direction for our efforts.

TECHNOLOGICAL ADVANCES WILL CONTINUE

We stand at the threshold of a new world in terms of scientific and technological advances. This should not be frightening because during the past several decades we have constantly stood at the threshold of rapid change, and we have stepped over it time and time again.

The world that we presently face is one which will be powered largely by atomic and solar energy, guided largely by electronics, and geared toward automated systems which will perform with precision and rapidity unmatched by humans. *Cybernation*, a recently invented term which covers technology, automation and computerization, is going to cause changes in our life-styles and our social systems unlike anything we have experienced in the past. Push-button living as we know it today is only a beginning. The amount of mechanical energy available to each of us will be vastly increased in the near future, to the point that we will be able to produce significantly more goods and services in less time then we do at the present.

Many results of all of this are presently unknown or at least unapparent, but two results important to the topic of this text are obvious and highly significant—less time on the job, and more time, energy and resources for off-the-job living.

Ten years ago Americans owned only two-thirds as many automobiles as we own today. Computerization at that time was in the embryo stage. Atomic energy for nonmilitary uses was still highly questionable, and our ability to capture solar energy and put it to practical use seemed doubtful. With respect to these problems, and many others that could be mentioned, great changes have taken place in just one decade.

A decade from now most school children will have their own computers, and a computer will be no more novel to them than ball-point pens were to some of us. Heating fuel will be replaced by solar energy, successfully captured. Gasoline driven automobiles will become obsolete as cars powered by electricity and hydrogen become popular. High-speed trains will travel smoothly over a cushion of air. Air travel will continue its revolutionary trend, but with the use of nonpetrol fuel and much quieter engines. There will be many disposable containers, some of which will be eatable. Large amounts of nonanimal foods will be harvested and processed from the sea, and a host of other imaginative changes will occur, many of which will affect recreation and leisure. Associated with these material changes will be equally important and complex changes in our social structure and other aspects of our lives. Fortunately humans are highly adaptable, because in the future, as in the recent past, *change* will be the most prominent characteristic of our society.

WORK AND LEISURE PATERNS
WILL CONTINUE TO CHANGE

Today Americans pursue both work and leisure with vigor. On the one hand we crave the satisfaction that a job can provide—a sense of self-worth and belonging and means to fulfillment. On the other hand we demand time away from work—time to relax, to refresh our outlook and to enjoy life's pleasures. Both of these aspects of life are important to development and ultimate satisfaction.

Unfortunately many Americans fail to reach these goals. Some leave school unprepared to participate in the world of work, let alone find satisfaction there. Others are just as unready to handle the increasing amounts of free time that have become part of our life-style. They relate leisure more often with boredom than with constructive and creative pleasure.

All available evidence leads to the inevitable conclusion that leisure will continue to increase, although this gift of free time probably, at least for many years, will not be distributed evenly among our people. Many managerial and technical workers, as well as members of the professions, may have to work longer hours in the immediate future, rather than fewer, while the increase in leisure will fall upon less capable workers. Eventually, following a period of transition to a way of life based on the widespread use of atomic energy and other technological developments, it may reasonably be expected that everybody will have more leisure and the security to enjoy it.

We can be fairly sure that work in the future will be increasingly intellectual in nature, more highly specialized, more automated, necessitating more education, and probably even less satisfying than in the past. The more highly specialized a job becomes, the less it challenges the whole man. This decreases the satisfactions to be found in work and spurs man on to find compensatory gratifications in his leisure.

The average *work week* will gradually become shorter, moving toward 36 hours and then 32 hours per week. There will be more three-day *weekends,* with some occupational groups moving toward a four-day work week with the work day ranging between 8 and 10 hours. The average length of annual *vacation* will continue to increase from the present three weeks to three and a half and then four weeks per year. The average *retirement age* will gradually work its way toward age 60, whereas now it is about age 64.

Americans do a multitude of different jobs, but most of them are not very demanding physically and most of them require technical knowledge and specific skills. Most people's jobs are piecemeal in the sense that the worker performs a piece of a larger project. Assembly line work where a particular person puts in bolt #67 is a meaningful example, but many people in the white collar and executive fields also play piecemeal roles. As our production systems continue to become more complex, the trend toward piecemeal occupations will continue. This kind of employment lacks satisfaction because the worker has no opportunity to produce a finished product, and he must seek exciting and ego-building experiences during the off-the-job hours.

Most people need and seek a clear-cut well-defined position which has permanence and will lead them through lifelong satisfying employment. In our present dynamic society people change occupations on the average of three times during their employable life. This is a significantly greater rate of change than in the past, and the trend probably will not be reversed in the foreseeable future. This is a frustrating circumstance for many people because it leaves them feeling unable to get hold of an employment opportunity which has the desired elements of significance, permanency and security.

FINANCIAL AFFLUENCE WILL INCREASE

The gross national product in the U.S. now exceeds 1,100 billion dollars per year, more than twice what it was 20 years ago. Further, annual personal income per capita in the United States now exceeds

Figure 43. Tourism goes hand-in-hand with long weekends, paid vacations and early retirement. (Bureau of Reclamation photo.)

$5,500 per year, twice as much as it was only 10 years ago. Of course, inflation has partially destroyed the purchasing power of people's increased gross income, but it is a fact that on the average Americans have more purchasing power today than at any time in history, and the trend is still upward. What do people do with this extra money? In many cases they build larger homes or remodel their present ones. They buy a more expensive or an additional car, or they buy jewelry, or better clothes, or other such material goods. Among the leading uses of the additional money is the purchase of boats, off-road recreational vehicles, snowmobiles, ski equipment, summer cottages, or vacation condominiums. People hunt and fish in far-away places, go sightseeing to the four corners of the earth, and do a multitude of other things for off-the-job enjoyment.

The trends relative to increased affluence and the way that people spend their additional money have been quite consistent over the past few years, and these same trends will probably continue during the foreseeable future. The exact kinds of things that people purchase will change as the supply of purchasable items changes, but the general nature of the expenditures will remain essentially the same.

THE POPULATION WILL BECOME LARGER AND MORE URBANIZED

A hundred years ago 90% of the American population lived in rural areas and were associated with the agricultural industry. Most of them were farmers. Today the situation is almost reversed. About 10% of the population are associated with the agricultural industry, and only about 8% are actually farmers. As early as 1950 America became predominately urban, and the strong trend toward urbanization has remained intact.

The population of the United States was about 219 million people at the end of 1976. At the anticipated rate of increase (about 1.5% annually), it will reach about 226 million by 1980, and by the turn of the century another 70 million people will have been added to our population, bringing the total to 296 million. The rate of increase has been significantly less in terms of percent during the last five years than at any time previously. However, even with a relatively low percentage increase, the number increase will continue to be large.

In addition to the overall population growth, the trend toward urbanization will continue. At the end of 1976 about 74% of the population (162 million people) lived in urban areas. By 1980 75% (170 million people) will live in urban areas, and by the turn of the century 78% of the estimated 296 million people (230 million) will be classified as urbanites. This significant increase in urban living will cause a large increase in the need for community facilities, programs, and leadership, and the overall population increase will place much additional demand on all forms of recreational resources regardless of where they are located.

As the life expectancy increases and the birth rate percentage remains relatively low, the average age of the population will gradually increase and the proportion of older people will become greater.

PHILOSOPHICAL CHANGES WILL OCCUR

There is an increasing awareness that people who have a strong sense of values and who are ethically sound can find worthy uses for off-the-job time, and that through the proper selection of involvement many people can actually contribute more to society and to their own fulfillment than if they worked longer hours. However, dedication to the idea that increased off-the-job hours provide greater opportunity for enrichment of one's self and society has reached only a small minority of the population. At the present time too many have yet to catch the vision of what increased leisure can and should contribute.

Unfortunately, some of those who have not caught the vision are recreation and park professionals. As a result many of these people manage their professional affairs on the premise that anything entertaining that will attract a clientele is justifiable, even time-filler and time-waster activities that make no contribution to the community or the individual. There is real danger in the application and perpetuation of this kind of philosophy through public-sponsored, tax-supported programs.

If we are unsuccessful over a period of time in our efforts to foster and perpetuate a sound sense of values relative to leisure, the eventual result will be catastrophic. This is true because each person's individual sense of values forms the basis for his aspirations and the decisions he makes relative to uses of time and resources. If people's choices lead them into nondevelopmental, low-quality and demeaning activities, then the accumulation of individual choices will have a weakening effect on our society. Over a period of time this can create a strong destructive force, and lead us along a course similar to that of other great societies that experienced some of the same problems that we face, such as Thebes, Athens and Rome.

The responsibility to perpetuate positive change in people's philosophy toward leisure lies primarily with professional recreation personnel and educators. Leaders in these occupational fields must set the tone through example and sponsorship, prepare people with an adequate number of desirable alternatives from which to choose, and then evaluate and monitor the results on a continuing basis.

BETTER LEADERSHIP WILL BE NEEDED

There is no substitute for adequate leadership. Regardless of what else is done by way of support, a program will not exceed its level of leadership, because the leadership sets the tone and defines the limits within which the program operates. There is little justification for poor leadership, because vast potential for expertise is all about us, and, with the correct emphasis and adequate dedication, leadership can be either acquired or developed. In connection with this is the good advice that "The best way to get rid of a poor leader (teacher, recreation leader, or whatever) is to develop him into a good one." Certainly this is idealistic to some degree, but still it has much practical meaning and application.

Some people take the limited view that leadership preparation is the responsibility of the colleges and universities. This is only partially true. In any occupational field the primary role of colleges and universities is to supply the profession with new people who have adequate basic education to enter the field and function effectively. The growth and development of professionals must, however, be continuous. This can come about with valuable on-the-job experience, some of which must come in the form of in-service training, conferences, institutes, clinics, regular reading of professional literature, and tutoring from those who are professionally more mature and better informed.

Some of the most important leaders in the future will need to be well-educated and highly sensitive connoisseurs who have broad perspectives as to the development of cultural change and individual tastes and preferences. These leaders, who will stand at the pinnacle of the profession, will have to demonstrate tremendous insight into the needs of individuals and groups, and be able to define and perpetuate the characteristics of the good life and a strong society.

ADDITIONAL FUTURE PROJECTIONS

This section consists of brief statements of pertinent facts, or what appear will be facts, that relate closely to leisure time and other aspects of the recreation and park movement.

1. There will be increased need and increased pressure for the educational system to do a better job of preparing people of all ages to use their increased leisure beneficially. However, at the same time there will be a need for additional emphasis on other aspects of education, because we will become more advanced in technology and automation, and this will require more specialization. Educators will face a difficult challenge in trying to keep the educational emphasis in proper balance under changing needs and circumstances.

2. The trend in recent times toward increased continuing education among adults will escalate. People will need to be better educated in order to compete effectively in a highly specialized job market, and they will want to broaden their interests and skills for more effective use of leisure time. Probably the greatest increase in continuing education will be among older citizens who are approaching retirement or who have retired.

3. In the recent past almost all categories of recreation have grown faster than population. This has been especially true with those involving the use of outdoor recreation resources. It appears that this trend will continue during the foreseeable future.

4. The economic impact of recreational activities will continue to occupy a

prominent position in the total economic scene. In fact, the economic significance will steadily increase as leisure time and per capita income increase.

5. It appears that sometime in the near future leisure time counselling will become a branch of the profession. Whether most of it will take place through the schools or outside the schools remains to be seen. Probably some of it will occur in the schools, some through organized recreation programs, and some by private counselors. Counselling will be primarily in the form of helping people review the leisure time alternatives open to them in view of each one's particular skills, interest, and finances, and in the light of the activities available in the vicinity. The counselor will help people crystallize their thinking about what they would like to do and what they want to become in terms of leisure time participants, and how they can go about achieving these objectives. Another aspect will be the counselling of people who have particular physical, social and psychological problems of the kind that leisure time activities can help to solve.

6. There is a recognition of the need to broaden the recreation program content in the area of the cultural arts, and to utilize more fully the personnel in organizations within the community to expand and improve cultural arts programs. The emphasis on creativity as a desirable use of leisure time will have an increasingly positive effect on cultural activities for the masses.

7. With the expected increases in leisure time and financial affluence there will be a marked increase in commercialized recreation. Those with good business minds will find many opportunities to convert people's leisure time into financial profit. Hopefully the commercializers will demonstrate good judgment about what is good for society, and keep exploitation to a minimum. The recreation professionals are going to have to aid in this by enforcing checks and balances along the way. This can be done by bringing community pressure against undesirable commercialism, and by sponsoring appealing programs through community agencies that will combat the popularizing of undesirable commercial activities. Caution will need to be exercised against unfair competition of public agencies with commercial enterprise.

8. With people's increased awareness about the need to maintain an acceptable level of physical fitness and health, leisure time will become increasingly occupied by activities that promote fitness. There will be more joggers, more cyclists, more golfers, more tennis players and more participants in practically every popular form of fitness activity. Hopefully there will also be more emphasis on other aspects of life that contribute to health, such as weight control and discretion in the use of tobacco, alcohol, drugs and other harmful substances.

9. The emphasis on research will increase steadily. As leisure and recreation becomes more prominent in people's lives, and as additional resources are devoted to leisure, there will be an increased need for more exact information and better methods in all phases of the recreation field.

10. Voluntary organizations, most of which are youth serving, will continue to make their unique contributions to recreation, in addition to their other objectives. There are no indications that these agencies will change their approaches or their emphases, except through normal adjustments to meet the changing needs and interests of their members.

11. Fortunately there seems to be a decline in destructive action by youth in general. In particular there has been a decline in vandalism and other forms of misbehavior on public parks and playfields. There seems to be a mild reawakening of respect for public property. However, this is still a serious problem, especially in heavily populated areas, and there is no clear indication that the problem will lessen much beyond its present level. Young people must be better educated toward respect for public property and pride in their surroundings.

12. People in the future will be considerably more recreationally literate than the people of the present; on the whole they will be better informed about the

values that can accrue from proper use of leisure time, and they will develop for themselves more leisure time alternatives from which to choose.

13. Fortunately there is some indication of a reemphasis on the family as the basic structure of society. The pendulum has swung a long way from this concept, and it appears that it is now swinging back. Traditionally recreation has been a molder of family unity, with the stress on the idea that "the family that plays together, stays together." Hopefully the recreation professionals of the present and future will see more clearly the need and the opportunities to mold family unity through wholesome recreation participation.

14. Employee recreation (often called industrial recreation) will increase faster than the recreation movement in general, because the trend toward further urbanization will be accompanied by increased employment by large companies and industrial plants. At the same time there will be continued emphasis on improved fringe benefits, of which one is employee recreation. Some large companies and even universities have found that the provision of attractive recreation opportunities often means more to employees than a higher salary, particularly if these benefits are available to members of the whole family.

15. The therapeutic approach to recreation for the ill and handicapped will continue to gain momentum, because it is now well accepted that carefully planned and well-directed recreational activities can benefit the handicapped and long-term hospital patients. Particular emphasis can be foreseen for camps for the handicapped, physical rehabilitation centers and mental hospitals.

16. The move toward conservation and environmental protection in connection with the hordes of recreation users of the out-of-doors has already been firmly established. It will be absolutely necessary for this trend to remain intact. In fact, the emphasis will need to be intensified as increased numbers of people make even more extensive use of our diminishing supply of natural resources.

17. Because of the steady increase expected in all forms of recreation participation it will be necessary for communities to increase their involvement in the sponsorship of recreation. Specifically, communities will need to:

    A. Do more advanced planning relative to open space acquisition.

    B. Show greater concern for the everyday living environment of people, and employ whatever methods are feasible in the particular locality to maintain a respectable and pleasant surrounding.

    C. Employ more expertly qualified and a greater number of leaders as the increased needs of the community justify doing so.

    D. Provide better coordination of the different commercial, voluntary and government agencies which contribute to the overall recreation opportunities in the community.

    E. Provide a broader offering and better balance in order to adequately satisfy the diversified interests of the public, who in the future will be better informed and more recreationally literate.

18. State government agencies will play a more significant role in the future, and they will need to:

    A. Take a more responsible and long-range approach to the planning and development of state-owned areas used for recreation—state parks, water areas, state forests, wildlife resources, etc. The needs and demands of the public will require that states give more attention to the recreational use of these resources.

    B. Review periodically the adequacy of state enabling legislation to be sure that it truly fits the needs of the political subdivisions.

    C. Establish and enforce more exact regulations concerning the recreational use of state-owned properties, which the increased use of the properties will necessitate. This problem can be partly alleviated by planning the areas so they will accommodate heavier use without sacrificing too much in terms of the quality of experiences.

D. Improve and expand fish and wildlife conservation methods, if hunting, fishing, and other wildlife activities are to continue as forms of recreation. These resources are already near exhaustion in some states.

E. Give special attention to the multiple use of water areas within their jurisdiction. Boating, sailing, fishing, water skiing, and swimming are increasing unusually fast, and these diverse uses of water resources will require truly expert planning and improved regulation.

F. Respond to increased needs for state highways and access roads into areas of recreational potential.

G. Encourage desirable commercial recreation developments to supplement the efforts of public agencies.

H. More clearly identify and define the recreational responsibilities of the different state agencies, to reduce duplication and to prevent voids in necessary state services.

I. Give more leadership to master planning on both state and local levels.

19. The federal government will also need to do more toward improving its effectiveness in the following ways:

A. Resource management agencies of the federal government will need to do a better job of identifying, developing and managing the more desirable recreation attractions on federal lands.

B. More clearly stated definitions of the recreation responsibilities of certain federal agencies will be needed.

C. Federal agencies will need to continue to motivate and assist state and local government and nongovernment agencies to better meet their responsibilities for the provision of recreation opportunities.

D. Federal government agencies should be cautious about becoming too directly involved in the affairs of states and communities. Unfortunately, there is no clear indication that this will be avoided, because the trend is toward federal domination. It will be a challenge to recreation and park leaders to keep the influence of the different levels of government in proper perspective.

20. In connection with the field of outdoor recreation, nongovernment organizations and private enterprise will have to become more involved. Government agencies and government resources will simply not be able to meet the rapidly increasing demands. The majority of land in the United States (60%) is in private ownership, and the highest proportion of privately owned land is near the heavily populated areas of the nation. Much of this land has potential for outdoor recreation not yet developed. For example, there is unusual potential on private lands for small game and bird hunting, fishing, picnicking, camping, horseback riding and numerous other such activities. This potential has been utilized slowly because the demand has not been great enough to motivate private landowners to become involved in outdoor recreation either for service or profit. Noticeable progress in this direction has been made in recent years, but the trend has only begun.

21. There must be renewed emphasis on the idea that the best recreation is that found in everyday life—the beauty of the immediate surroundings and pleasing everyday experiences. Recreationists call this a "recreation environment," an environment that contributes to the pleasantness of each day. In order for most future Americans to be able to live in such environment, increased and continuous efforts will need to be given to ways to depollute our lakes, bays and streams, and to clean up our air and our landscape. People on a broad scale will become more conscious of the fact that we do not destroy matter, we only change its form. Once we make millions of cars, billions of cans and bottles, and thousands, millions and billions of other objects which eventually become useless, we must have in

mind some viable method of converting them into other forms. People will be more aware of the fact that they cannot mar the landscape with all sorts of unattractive litter and still have a pleasing environment. In the future even greater strides must be taken toward all aspects of pollution control. Such controls, in many instances, will carry large price tags, a fact that people will have to accept. The costs of pollution control will simply have to be built into the system.

PROBLEMS FOR STUDY AND DISCUSSION

The problems stated here are not confined to specific localities or situations; they have some application to almost all localities. Even though some of these problems are not completely solvable, we must recognize, define, and deal with them and work toward their solutions. Sometimes the nature of a problem will change, and we need to cope with it in its revised form. By studying these problems we will recognize and have insight into the kinds of broad problems that must be dealt with by present and future recreation and park professionals.

1. What steps should be taken with respect to this field to cause it to more nearly fit the description of a profession and to more fully gain professional status?
2. With the large number of colleges and universities that have developed curricula in the recreation and park field during recent years, what can be done to ensure that the students graduating from these curricula are truly well prepared to enter the field? What steps can be taken to guarantee that many students are not being expediently processed through watered-down programs which are under the direction of poorly prepared administrators and teachers?
3. Some attention has been given to stating and perpetuating the goals of the recreation and park profession, but to date these goals have not been well communicated or widely accepted. How could universally acceptable goals for the recreation and park profession be established and applied for adequate direction?
4. If we are to strengthen the family structure as the basic unit in society we must do it largely through off-the-job activities. What steps can be taken and which changes in emphasis should be made for the recreation profession to do its part toward the achievement of this desirable outcome?
5. If we are to perpetuate democratic living, attention must be given to democratic ideals in the various aspects of life, one of which is the use of leisure time. How can recreation programs and activities be designed to teach and perpetuate democratic ideals and a democratic life-style?
6. What is the responsibility of the recreation profession in solving such social problems as delinquency, crime, vandalism, and environmental pollution? How can the recreation profession contribute better toward the solution of these important problems?
7. In the face of a steady long-term increase in population and a corresponding increase in urbanization, how can a highly livable environment be developed and maintained in large urban areas? What roles should park and recreation professionals play in connection with this immense problem? What kind of leadership will be needed by recreation and park professionals in order for them to effectively contribute to the solution?
8. In view of the tremendous encroachment and damage that have occurred with outdoor recreation resources, and in the face of continued increase in the use of those resources, what can be done to conserve and preserve a sufficient quantity and quality of outdoor recreation resources for the future? How can recreation and park professionals effectively cope with this pressing problem?

Who will furnish the insight and foresight that will be needed to protect the long-term outdoor recreation interests of the public?

9. To what degree are community recreation leaders obligated and responsible to cooperate with other agencies in the community? Who will coordinate the overall community effort toward providing recreational opportunities, including sponsorship by private, voluntary, commercial and public agencies?

10. What will be the alternative methods of adequately financing public recreation, which methods will be the most frequently used, and which will prove the most effective?

11. How will recreation and park planners be able to secure and retain the land resources necessary for adequate facilities and areas in the face of financial squeeze, land price escalation, and an increasing population? What steps must be taken, what alternatives for financing will be available, and where will help be obtainable both within and outside the immediate locality?

12. As the recreation movement becomes more prominent to both individuals and society, many questions will need to be answered and many problems will need to be thoroughly studied. How can the profession build a sound program of basic and applied research which will both contribute to the status of the profession and help in the solution of present and oncoming problems?

13. The need for people to be properly educated for the use of leisure time is apparent. What is not apparent is where this education should take place, and which agencies should be involved. In this regard, what will be the role of the schools, recreation and park departments, the family and voluntary agencies? What can be done to ensure a more effective approach toward education for the worthy use of leisure?

SOME EXPRESSIONS OF HOPE

We must avoid perpetuation of the idea that increased leisure time is a license to cheap entertainment, simple abuse and time wasting. Especially we must combat the idea that leisure affords people the right to participate in pursuits that are demeaning and self-destructive. Even more important, we must provide opportunities that will prevent increased leisure time from contributing to socially unacceptable acts, crime and delinquency. All of this indicates that leisure time activities must, for the most part, have substance and be meaningful. Leisure should be viewed as time to ''put the frosting on the cake of life,'' time to do good for others and to benefit one's self in terms of enrichment, enjoyment and personal fulfillment.

It is hoped that through appropriate education and the perpetuation of the wise use of leisure, the great majority of people will overcome the negative practices of overeating, underexercising, and other bodily misuses and abuses.

It is hoped that an environment can be created based upon ideals of good health, tranquility and sincere concern for individuals.

It is hoped that an ethical code and ethical practices relative to human values and human relationships can be perpetuated, both through the use of leisure time and in connection with it.

It is hoped that we can become more free of competitive status buying, that we will escape perpetual victimization by the heavy persuaders and the waste makers, and that we really will emerge as a nation that shows a high level of leisure time sophistication.

Appendix

THEORIES OF PLAY

Contained here are fifteen theories of play which are categorized into three tables. This interesting and careful analysis of play theories was made by M. Jay Ellis in 1971.*

* Ellis, M. Jay: Play and its theories re-examined. *Park and Recreation Magazine,* August 1971, pp. 51-55. Reprinted with permission.

Table 1: CLASSICAL THEORIES OF PLAY

Name	Play is caused:	This explanation assumes:	It can be criticized because:	Verdict
Surplus Energy I	by the existence of energy surplus to the needs of survival.	1. energy is stored. 2. storage is limited. 3. excess energy must be expended. 4. expenditure is made on play, by definition.	1. children play when fatigued or to the point of fatigue so a surplus is not necessary for play. 2. the process of evolution should have tailored the energy available to the energy required.	Inadequate
Surplus Energy II	by increased tendency to respond after a period of response deprivation.	1. response systems of the body all have a tendency to respond. 2. response threshold is lowered by a period of leisure.	after periods of disuse, eventually all available responses should reach a low enough threshold to be discharged. Some responses available to the person are never used.	Inadequate as written but has been incorporated in learning theory.
Instinct	by the inheritance of unlearned capacities to emit playful acts.	1. the determinants of our behavior are inherited in the same way that we inherit the genetic code that determines our structure. 2. that some of those determinants cause play.	1. it ignores the obvious capacity of the person to learn new responses that we classify as play. 2. the facile naming of an instinct for each class of observed behavior is to do no more than to say "Because there is play, there must be a cause which we will call an instinct."	Inadequate

Theory			
Preparation	by the efforts of the player to prepare for later life.	1. play is emitted only by persons preparing for new ways of responding, and in general is the preserve of the young. 2. the player can predict what kinds of responses will be critical later. 3. instincts governing this are inherited imperfectly and are practiced during youth.	1. it requires that the player inherit the capacity to predict which responses will be critical. This requires the inheritance of information about the future. 2. play occurs most frequently in animals that live in rapidly changing circumstances. 3. when acceptably prepared the person should stop playing.	Inadequate. However play may have by-products that are advantageous later.
Recapitulation	by the player recapitulating the history of the development of the species during its development.	1. critical behaviors occurring during evolution of man are encoded for inheritance. 2. person emits some approximation to all these behaviors during his development. 3. since they are currently irrelevant they are play. 4. the stages in our evolution will be followed in the individual's development.	1. no linear progression in our play development that seems to mirror the development of a species. At one point, late boyhood and adolescence, there may be similarity between sports and games and the components of hunting, chasing, fighting, etc., but before and after there seems little relation. 2. does not explain play activities dependent on our advanced technology.	Inadequate
Relaxation	the need for an individual to emit responses other than those used in work to allow recuperation.	1. players work. 2. play involves the emission of responses different to those of work.	1. it does not explain the play of children—unless they are clearly working some part of their day. 2. does not explain the use in play of activities also used in work.	Inadequate

Table 2: RECENT THEORIES OF PLAY

Name	Play is caused:	This explanation assumes:	It can be criticized because:	Verdict
Generalization	by the players using in their play, experiences that have been rewarding at work.	1. that there are at least two separable categories of behavior. 2. that the players transfer to play or leisure, behaviors that are rewarded in another setting. 3. that to be useful we understand what rewards an individual at work.	1. it seems to exclude play of preschool children. 2. it assumes that at least some aspects of work are rewarding.	1. Data tend to support this as a view of leisure behavior preferences in adults, providing a chronic or long-term view of their behavior is taken. 2. We must wait for more data.
Compensation	by players using their play to satisfy psychic needs not satisfied in or generated by the working behaviors.	1. that there are at least two separable categories of behavior. 2. the player avoids in play or leisure behaviors that are unsatisfying in the work setting. 3. the player selects leisure experiences that meet his psychic needs. 4. that to be useful we understand the mismatch of needs and satisfactions in the work setting (or vice versa).	1. it seems to exclude the play of preschool children. 2. it assumes that work is damaging, does not satisfy some needs.	1. Such data as exists gives support to the idea in the long term. 2. We must wait for data.
Catharsis	in part by the need to express disorganizing emotions in a harmless way by transferring them to socially sanctioned activity. This concept has almost entirely been limited to questions of aggression, and will be so here.	1. frustration of an intention engenders hostility towards the frustrator. 2. this hostility must be expressed to reduce psychic and physiological stress. 3. this frustration or hostility can be redirected to another activity.	1. it is a partial explanation for only the compensatory behavior engendered by hostility. 2. the data show conclusively that sanctioning aggression increases it. 3. the planning of activities to provide outlets for aggression constitutes its sanctioning.	As an explanation for some aspects of play and leisure pursuits (usually vigorous games), it has no support in the aggression literature.

Psycho-analytic I	in part by the players repeating in a playful form strongly unpleasant experiences, thereby reducing their seriousness and allowing their assimilation.	1. simulating unpleasant experiences in another setting reduces the unpleasantness of their residual effects.	Both ignore play that is not presumed to be motivated by the need to eliminate the products of strongly unpleasant experiences.	There are few data, or conceptual analyses of these tenets. The work is strongly clinical and concerned with individuals. We need clear formulation of what the psycho-analytic view of play is, so that it may be tested.
Psycho-analytic II	in part by the player during play reversing his role as the passive recipient of strongly unpleasant experience, and actively mastering another recipient in a similar way, thus purging the unpleasant effects.	1. achieving mastery, even in a simulated experience, allows the elimination of the products of an unpleasant experience by passing similar experiences on to other beings or objects.		
Developmentalism	the way in which a child's mind develops. Thus play is caused by the growth of the child's intellect and is conditioned by it. That play occurs when the child can impose on reality his own conceptions and constraints.	1. that play involves the intellect. 2. that as a result of play, the intellect increases in complexity. 3. that this process in the human can be separated into stages. 4. that children pass through these stages in order.	1. it doesn't account for play when and if the intellect ceases to develop.	The best known thinker in this school is Paiget who is concerned with the cause of play, but more importantly with its content. This concept must be integrated with a more precise theory of motivation and learning.
Learning	the normal processes that produce learning.	1. the child acts to increase the probability of pleasant events. 2. the child acts to decrease the probability of unpleasant events. 3. the environment is a complex of pleasant and unpleasant effects. 4. the environment selects and energizes the play behaviors of its tenants.	1. it doesn't account for behavior in situations where there are no apparent consequences. (However this theory would maintain that there are no such settings.) 2. it doesn't account for the original contributions to behaviors made by an individual's genetic inheritance.	Cultural, sub-cultural and familial differences support the view that quantity and content of play behavior is learned. The theory can account for the content of an individual's play if not his inherited tendencies to play.

Table 3: MODERN THEORIES

Name	Play is caused:	This explanation assumes:	It can be criticized because:	Verdict
Play as Arousal-Seeking	by the need to generate interactions with the environment or self that elevates arousal (level of interest or stimulation) towards the optimal for the individual.	1. stimuli vary in their capacity to arouse. 2. there is a need for optimal arousal. 3. change in arousal towards optimal is pleasant 4. the organism learns the behaviors that result in that feeling and vice versa.	1. it is very general and handles equally well questions of work and play. In fact it questions the validity of separating work from play.	Together with learning and developmentalism as a package is a very powerful theoretical base for our professional operations.
Competence/Effectance	by a need to produce effects in the environment. Such effects demonstrate competence and result in feelings of effectance.	1. demonstration of competence leads to feelings of effectance. 2. effectance is pleasant. 3. effectance increases the probability of tests of competence.	1. for the organism to constantly test whether it can still competently produce an effect seems to require an effect seems to require uncertainty as to the outcome. Uncertainty or information seem to be the very attributes of stimuli that are arousing. 2. thus it can be argued that competence/effectance behavior is a kind of arousal-seeking.	Is best subsumed as an explanation that developed as theorists moved towards the arousal seeking model.

SELECTED RECENT TEXTBOOKS ON
LEISURE AND RECREATION

AAHPER: *Professional Preparation in Dance, Physical Education, Recreation Education, Safety Education, and School Health Education.* AAHPER, Washington, 1974.

Artz, R. M.: *Guide to New Approaches to Financing Parks and Recreation.* National Recreation and Park Association, Washington, 1971.

Bannon, J. J.: *Leisure Resources—Its Comprehensive Planning.* Prentice-Hall, Englewood Cliffs, 1976.

Bannon, J. J.: *Problem Solving in Recreation and Parks.* Prentice-Hall, Englewood Cliffs, 1972.

Beal, G. M., Bohlen, J. J., and Raudabaugh, J. N.: *Leadership and Dynamic Group Action.* Iowa State University Press, Ames, 1967.

Brantley, H. and Sessoms, H. D.: *Recreation, Issues and Perspectives.* Wing Publications, Columbia (S.C.), 1969.

Brightbill, C. K.: *Educating for Leisure-Centered Living.* The Stackpole Company, Harglewood Cliffs, 1961.

Brockman, C. F.: *Recreational Use of Wild Lands,* 2nd ed. McGraw-Hill, New York, 1973.

Bucher, C. A. and Bucher, R. D.: *Recreation for Today's Society.* Prentice-Hall, Englewood Cliffs, 1974.

Butler, G. D.: *Introduction to Community Recreation,* 5th ed. McGraw-Hill, New York, 1976.

Butler, G. D.: *Pioneers in Public Recreation.* Burgess, Minneapolis, 1965.

Carlson, R. E., Deppe, T. R., and McLean, J. R.: *Recreation in American Life,* 2nd ed. Wadsworth, Belmont, 1972.

Case, M.: *Recreation for Blind Adults.* Charles C Thomas, Springfield, 1966.

Clawson, M. and Knetsch, J.: *Economics of Outdoor Recreation.* Johns Hopkins Press, Baltimore, 1966.

Corbin, H. D.: *Recreation Leadership.* Prentice-Hall, Englewood Cliffs, 1970.

Corbin, H. D. and Tait, W. J.: *Education for Leisure.* Prentice-Hall, Englewood Cliffs, 1973.

Danford, H. G., revised by M. Shirley: *Creative Leadership in Recreation,* 2nd ed. Allyn and Bacon, Boston, 1970.

Dattner, R.: *Design for Play.* Van Nostrand Reinhold, New York, 1969.

deGrazia, S.: *Of Time, Work and Leisure.* Twentieth-Century Fund, New York, 1962.

Doell, C. E. and Twandzik, L. F.: *Elements of Park and Recreation Administration,* 3rd ed. Burgess, Minneapolis, 1973.

Douglas, R. W.: *Forest Recreation.* Pergamon Press, New York, 1969.

Dulles, F. R.: *A History of Recreation: America Learns to Play.* Appleton-Century-Crofts, New York, 1965.

Dumazedier, J.: *Toward a Society of Leisure.* Free Press, Collier-Macmillan, New York, 1967.

Duran, D. B. and Clement, A.: *The New Encyclopedia of Successful Program Ideas.* Association Press, New York, 1967.

Edwards, M.: *Recreation Leader's Guide.* National Press, Palo Alto, 1967.

Eisenberg, H. and Eisenberg, L.: *Omnibus of Fun.* Association Press, New York, 1969.

Everhart, W. C.: *The National Park Service.* Praeger, New York, 1972.

Fischer, D. W., Lewis, J. E., and Priddle, G. B.: *Land and Leisure.* Maaroufa, Chicago, 1974.

285

Fish, H. V.: *Activities Program for Senior Citizens.* Parker Publishing, West Nyack, 1971.

Frye, M. V. and Peters, M.: *Therapeutic Recreation: Its Theory, Philosophy, and Practice.* Stackpole Books, Harrisburg, 1972.

Gabrielsen, M. A.: *Sports and Recreation Facilities for School and Community.* Prentice-Hall, Englewood Cliffs, 1958.

Gold, S. M.: *Urban Recreation Planning.* Lea & Febiger, Philadelphia, 1973.

Guggenheimer, E. C.: *Planning for Parks and Recreation Needs in Urban Areas.* Twayne Publishers, New York, 1969.

Hanson, R. F. and Carlson, R. E.: *Organizations for Children and Youth.* Prentice-Hall, Englewood Cliffs, 1972.

Harris, J. A.: *File O'Fun* (Card File for Social Recreation). Burgess, Minneapolis, 1970.

Hawkins, D. E. and Vinton, D. A.: *The Environmental Classroom.* Prentice-Hall, Englewood Cliffs, 1973.

Hjelte, G. and Shivers, J. S.: *Public Administration of Recreational Services.* Lea & Febiger, Philadelphia, 1972.

Hormachea, M. N. and Carroll, R.: *Recreation in Modern Society.* Holbrook Press, Boston, 1972.

Jacks, L. P.: *Education through Recreation.* McGrath Publishing Company and the National Recreation and Park Association, Washington, 1972.

Jensen, C. R.: *Issues in Outdoor Recreation,* 2nd ed. Burgess, Minneapolis, 1977.

Jensen, C. R.: *Outdoor Recreation in America,* 3rd ed. Burgess, Minneapolis, 1977.

Jensen, C. R.: *Recreation and Leisure Time Careers.* Vocational Guidance Manuals, Louisville, 1976.

Johnson, E. R.: *Park Resources for Recreation.* Charles E. Merrill, Columbus, 1972.

Jubenville, A.: *Outdoor Recreation Planning.* W. B. Saunders, Philadelphia, 1976.

Kaplan, M.: *Leisure in America—A Social Inquiry.* John Wiley, New York, 1960.

Kraus, R. G.: *Recreation and Leisure in Modern Society.* Appleton-Century-Crofts, New York, 1972.

Kraus, R. G.: *Recreation and the Schools.* Macmillan, New York, 1964.

Kraus, R. G.: *Recreation Today: Program Planning and Leadership.* Appleton-Century-Crofts, New York, 1966.

Kraus, R. G.: *Therapeutic Recreation Service.* W. B. Saunders, Philadelphia, 1973.

Kraus, R. G. and Curtis, J. E.: *Creative Administration in Recreation and Parks.* C. V. Mosby, St. Louis, 1973.

LaGrasse, A. and Cook, W.: *History of Parks and Recreation.* American Institute of Park Executives, Washington, 1965.

Lee, J.: *Play in Education, 1905.* Reprint, National Recreation and Park Association, Washington, 1972.

Lucas, C: *Recreational Activity Development for the Aging in Homes, Hospitals, and Nursing Homes.* Charles C Thomas, Springfield, 1962.

Merrill, T.: *Activities for the Aged and Infirm.* Charles C Thomas, Springfield, 1967.

Millar, S.: *The Psychology of Play.* Penguin Books, Baltimore, 1968.

Miller, N. P. and Robinson, D. M.: *The Leisure Age: Its Challenge to Recreation.* Wadsworth, Belmont, 1963.

Miller, P. L.: *Creative Outdoor Play Areas.* Prentice-Hall, Englewood Cliffs, 1972.

Mitchell, V., Crawford, I. B., and Robberson, J. D.: *Camp Counselling,* 4th ed. W. B. Saunders, Philadelphia, 1970.

Murphy, J., Williams, J. G., Niepoth, E. W., and Brown, P.: *Leisure Service Delivery System.* Lea & Febiger, Philadelphia, 1973.

Musselman, V.: *Making Family Get-Togethers Click.* Stackpole Books, Harrisburg, 1968.

Nash, J. B.: *Philosophy of Recreation and Leisure*. W. C. Brown, Dubuque, 1960.

Nash, J. B.: *Recreation: Pertinent Readings, Guide Posts to the Future*. W. C. Brown, Dubuque, 1965.

Nathans, A. A.: *Maintenance for Camps, and Other Outdoor Recreation Facilities*. Association Press, New York, 1968.

National Workshop on Recreation: *The Recreation Program*. Athletic Institute, Chicago, 1963.

Nelms, C: *Developing Leadership in Recreation*. Pacific Coast Publishers, Menlo Park, 1968.

Nesbitt, J. S., Brown, P. D., and Murphy, J. F.: *Recreation and Leisure Service for the Disadvantaged*. Lea & Febiger, Philadelphia, 1970.

Owen, O. S.: *Natural Resource Conservation*. Macmillan, New York, 1971.

Parker, S. R.: *The Future of Work and Leisure*. Praeger, New York, 1971.

Pomeroy, J.: *Recreation for the Physically Handicapped*. Macmillan, New York, 1964.

Poor, R.: *4 Days, 40 Hours, Reporting a Revolution in Work and Leisure*. Bursk and Poor Publishing, Cambridge (Mass.), 1970.

Reader's Digest: *Book of 1,000 Family Games*. The Reader's Digest Association, Inc., Pleasantville, 1972.

Rodney, L. S.: *Administration of Public Recreation*. Ronald Press, New York, 1964.

Sessoms, H. D., Meyer, H. D., and Brightbill, C. K.: *Leisure Services*, 5th ed. Prentice-Hall, Englewood Cliffs, 1975.

Shivers, J. S.: *Leadership in Recreational Service, Principles, Process, Personnel, Methods*. Macmillan, New York, 1963.

Shivers, J. S.: *Principles and Practices of Recreational Service*. Macmillan, New York, 1967.

Stein, T. A. and Sessoms, H. D.: *Recreation and Special Populations*. Holbrook Press, Inc., Boston, 1973.

The Athletic Institute: *College and University Facilities Guide*. The Athletic Institute and American Association for Health, Physical Education and Recreation, Chicago, 1968.

Tillman, A.: *The Program Book for Recreation Professionals*. National Press Books, Palo Alto, 1973.

Totten, W. F. and Manley, F. J.: *The Community School, Basic Concepts, Function and Organization*. Allied Education Council, Galien (Mich.), 1969.

U.S. Bureau of Outdoor Recreation: *Federal Outdoor Recreation Programs, the Nationwide Plan for Outdoor Recreation*. U.S. Government Printing Office, Washington, 1972.

Van der Smissen, M. E.: *Bibliography of Theses and Dissertations in Recreation, Parks, Camping and Outdoor Education*. National Recreation and Park Association, Arlington (Va.), 1970.

Van der Smissen, M. E. and Knierim, H.: *Fitness and Fun through Recreational Sports and Games*. Burgess, Minneapolis, 1964.

Yukic, T. S.: *Fundamentals of Recreation*. Harper & Row, New York, 1963.

Index

ACCREDITATION OF PROFESSIONAL PREP-
ARATION CURRICULA, 238-240
Activity, calorie expenditure of, 118-120
importance of, 109-121
need for, 82
Agricultural Stabilization and Conserva-
tion Service, 133
Allsen, P. E., 109
Amateur Athletic Union of the United
States, Inc., 256
Amateur Fencers League of America, 256
Amateur Hockey Association of the
United States, 256
Amateur Softball Association of America,
256
Amateur Trapshooting Association of
America, 257
American Alliance for Health, Physical
Education and Recreation
(AAHPER), 40, 49, 50, 51, 57,
201, 205, 254-255
American Alpine Club, 257
American Association for the Advance-
ment of Physical Education, 53
American Association of Botanical Gar-
dens and Arboreta, Inc., 257
American Association of Museums, 257
American Association of Park Superinten-
dents, 54
American Association of Zoological Parks
and Aquariums, 49, 257
American Automobile Association, 231
American Badminton Association, Inc.,
257
American Bowling Congress, 257
American Camping Association, 257
American Casting Association, 257
American Federation of Arts, 257
American Folklore Society, 257
American Forest Institute, 258
American Forestry Association, 29, 53,
258
American Game Protective and Propaga-
tion Association, 31, 48

American Hockey Association of the
United States, 256
American Horse Shows Association, 258
American Institute of Park Executives, 38,
51, 54, 56
American Lawn Bowling Association, 258
American Motorcycle Association, 258
American Nature Association, 258
American Platform Tennis Association,
258
American Psychiatric Association, 7
American Recreation Society, 40, 50, 56
American School of Wildlife Protection,
31
American Snowmobile Association, 258
American Society of Landscape Ar-
chitects, 258
American Water Ski Association, 258
American Wildlife Institute, 32
American Wildlife Society, 32
American Youth Foundation, 258
American Youth Hostels, Inc., 258
Anderson, William Gilbert, 53
Antique Automobile Club of America,
Inc., 258
Appalachian Regional Commission, 135
Argentina, recreation in, 187
Aristotle, 6
Armed Forces recreation, 202-203
Assessment, special, 159
Association of College Unions, 259
Association of Interpretive Naturalists,
Inc., 259
Athletic Institute, 259
Attitudes, changes in, 77-78
Australia, recreation in, 186
Automation, 65-66

BABE RUTH BASEBALL, INC., 259
Banks, William, 99
Barney, V., 109
Bicycle Institute of America, 259
Bond election, 159

289